THE GOOD BOOK

THE GOOD BOOK

An Introduction to the Bible

Brian Redhead
&
Frances Gumley

Duckworth

Second impression January 1988
First published in November 1987 by
Gerald Duckworth & Co. Ltd.
The Old Piano Factory
43 Gloucester Crescent, London NW1

Illustrations from *The Sacred Histories of the
Old and New Testament represented by very
artificial figures:* Nicolaus Visscher,
Amsterdam n.d. (?c. 1700).

ISBN 0 7156 2153 X

British Library Cataloguing in Publication Data

Redhead, Brian
  The good book: an introduction to the Bible
  1. Bible—Commentaries
  I. Title   II. Gumley, Frances
  220.6   BS491.2

ISBN 0-7156-2153-X

Photoset in North Wales by
Derek Doyle & Associates, Mold, Clwyd
and printed in Great Britain by
Redwood Burn Limited, Trowbridge

Contents

Preface

The Bible is, and always has been, the best selling book in the world. It is also the most abused, the most misquoted, and the most misconstrued book in the world. Queen Victoria maintained that it was the greatest jewel in her Imperial Crown. Napoleon said it was more powerful than any army, even his. Kubla Khan thought the world of it.

It is a book of wisdom, which has been used to launch a thousand crack-pot theories. It is a book of peace, which has been used as an excuse for war. It is an ancient book, which is still waiting to be understood. Most of us at one time or another have promised ourselves that one day we shall set out to try to understand it. That promise was the inspiration of a series of radio programmes on which this book is based.

The programmes, which followed a wandering path from Eden to Armageddon, sought the opinions of people of widely differing beliefs – exiles and academics, Islamic scholars and Zionists, psychologists and archaeologists, rabbis, priests, monks, nuns and missionaries. All had one thing in common – the belief that the Bible is the most important collection of documents in the world.

The Bible is unique. People live by it, and die for it. It charts failure as well as success. It points to a vision always one step ahead of those who describe it. It chronicles the activities of saints and scoundrels, of moral degenerates and hopeless optimists, of misfits and dreamers, of bad-tempered prophets and talking donkeys.

But it still moulds the lives of more people on this planet than any other ideology has ever done. It belongs to 192,000,000 Jews and Christians and Moslems too, who share Abraham the wanderer as their father in faith.

And that is not all. It bites deep into the lives of those who will never read it, or ever believe a word it contains. It is part of our language and central to our ideas of life and death. Without it there can be no understanding of power or of justice. But it can also be used as an excuse not to think.

The Bible plays tricks with time and makes nonsense of conventional wisdom. In it paradise is a home of sin, slaves are the symbol of freedom, a failed and broken kingdom provides an ideal kingship, and a sordid death turns man's cruelty into proof of God's love.

The Bible has a sense of direction all its own. It is not a map of the journey from Eden to Armageddon, it is the journey. This little book, on the other hand, is a sketch map of that journey.

B.R. & F.G.

Illustrations

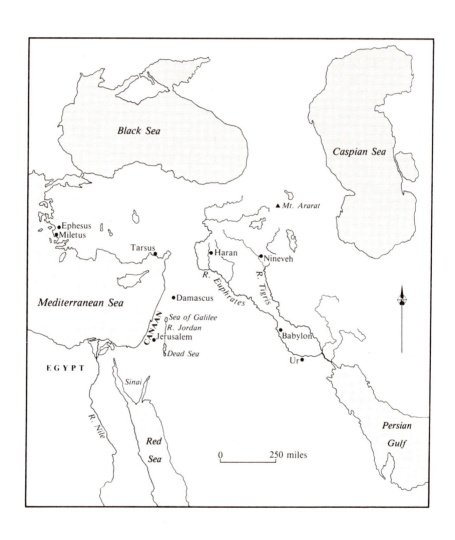

Black Sea

Caspian Sea

▲ Mt. Ararat

•Ephesus
•Miletus

•Haran

•Nineveh

Tarsus

R. Euphrates

R. Tigris

Mediterranean Sea

•Damascus

Sea of Galilee
R. Jordan
Jerusalem•

CANAAN

Babylon•

Dead Sea

Ur•

EGYPT

Sinai

R. Nile

Persian
Gulf

Red
Sea

0   250 miles

A First Word

Take a scroll and on it write all the words I have spoken to you about
Israel, Judah and all the nations, from the day I first spoke to you
until today.

Jeremiah 36:2

The prophet Jeremiah, who although a shy man was not
afraid of kings, heard these words when King Jehoiakim, a
weak man who loved comfort, sat uneasily on the throne of
Judah 2,500 years ago. Jeremiah knew who had spoken to
him. The voice, he said, was the voice of the Lord, the voice of
the God of Jacob and of Isaac and of Abraham, the voice of the
God of Noah's Flood and of Eve's Garden. Jeremiah took his
God at his word. He began at once dictating to the scribe
Baruch ben Meriah words of prophecy and of poetry and of
power. When he had finished, the scrolls were read to
Jehoiakim, and as the King listened to these indictments of
old sins and promises of a new order he became enraged. With
his penknife he sliced up the scrolls and fed them piece by
piece into the flames of the brazier which warmed his winter
court. Jeremiah's warnings of present dangers and his
promises of everlasting blessings quickly turned to ash.

But Jeremiah did not give up. We know this story because
Jehoiakim was about to become an early victim of that
strange phenomenon – the ability of the Bible to survive. One
set of scrolls was destroyed, so Jeremiah promptly began
dictating another, and this time he added a verse or two. Is
that a story of human obstinacy or of divine persistence?

What makes the Bible unique? Is it the work of God or the
wistful testimony of man? What truth is there in this, the
world's most misquoted book? Much biblical debate concen-
trates on details and leaves out essentials. The simple
questions are also the important ones and they will be asked
at every stage of this journey. Is the Bible fact or falsehood,
history or fantasy? Is it an account of divine creation or a
creation of human ingenuity? Must the Bible be swallowed

whole or can it be used piecemeal?

Before gatecrashing the garden of Eden, it is important to recognise the consistent efficiency with which the Bible has been preserved, even after the battle of Jeremiah and Jehoiakim. This has never been made more obvious than in this century. In 1947 the discovery of the Dead Sea Scrolls rolled back the credentials of the Bible in a quite extraordinary way. Before the discovery in the Qumran Caves, the earliest surviving text of the Hebrew Bible of any significant size dated back only to the 9th century AD. The Dead Sea Scrolls transformed that picture. We now have fragments of every single book of the Bible, except for the book of Esther, dating back to the time of Christ and perhaps before. The Scrolls, assiduously corrected and annotated as they are, form a solid testimony to the remarkable fidelity with which the ancient Biblical scribes worked. And those standards did not fall away with the passing of the scribes.

In the University Library in Cambridge Alan Jesson looks after the largest collection of Bibles in the world. It is owned by the Bible Society and consists of 30,000 different volumes in 2,000 languages from Aboriginal Pitjatjangarra to High German. The work of translation is still continuing and Alan Jesson points out that, even in print, the Bible has led a charmed life. Not only was it the subject of unique scribal care and reverence before the invention of printing, but in many languages it was one of the first books to be printed. The combination of sacredness and wary respect for new technology has meant that it often receives a degree of care and attention denied to other texts. Alan Jesson is certain that the Bible's tenacity is not a matter of historical fluke. He sees it more as an example of the survival of the fittest. He argues that people had only bothered translating and preserving the Bible because they found that it spoke to the human condition in a way which had a meaning for them in their time and place.

For more than one and a half billion Jews and Christians, the Bible still is the good book that nourishes their faith – and it is more than that. It forms the minds of millions who have never read it. Birth-rights are sold for messes of pottage, the animals go in two by two and some stories are as old as Methuselah. The Bible is entangled in our language whether we know it or not – and, whether they believe in it or not, it influences the attitudes of more people on questions of law and morality, mercy and justice, life's purpose and death's meaning, than any other single document. But it is important to remember that the Bible has never been merely a single document.

Robert Davidson, a minister in the Church of Scotland and Professor of Old Testament Language and Literature at Glasgow, says we should see it not as a book but as a whole library of books which each age must re-evaluate and question. The Bible, he says, has grown gradually into its present shape and form. Even the books of the Hebrew Bible, the Christian Old Testament, were not in their present shape until the end of the 1st century AD. This was partly in response to the shock of the fall of Jerusalem in 70 AD and partly a reaction to the growth of the Christian Church. A climate of loss and confusion had contributed to a feeling of insecurity. This in turn was allayed by a new emphasis on the authority of scripture.

The formative decisions about what should be included in and what left out of a Hebrew Bible were taken in Palestine at a place called Jamnia in about 90 AD. Those making the decisions were the leading scholarly and rabbinical minds of the age. They had gathered at the school of Johanan ben Zakkai, a rabbi who had personally experienced and escaped the violence and sacrilege of the siege of Jerusalem.

For the Jew, the Hebrew Bible consolidated at Jamnia falls into three parts: the Law (the first five books of the Bible, sometimes referred to as the Torah or the Pentateuch), the Prophets and the Writings. For the Christian, the Bible is made up of two Testaments: one Old, based on the Hebrew Bible, and one New, based on the writings about Jesus, who remains the bridge and the barrier between Judaism and Christianity.

Christians may not read the Bible from back to front, but they favour the New Testament and often seem to look upon the Old as little more than an introduction. Even the scriptures shared by both communities are divided up differently, and what is at stake is more important than niceties over textual order. Both communities agree on the position and order of the Pentateuch – that is, Genesis, Exodus, Leviticus, Numbers and Deuteronomy – but after that there are differences. For the Jew, the books of Joshua,

Judges, Samuel and Kings are treated as prophetic books; for the Christian they are classified as historical.

Does that matter? Rabbi Jonathan Magonet, Principal of Leo Baeck College, London, is emphatic that it does. He maintains that the Christian approach has missed a whole seam of Biblical treasure by an overdependence on history and a lack of openness to prophecy. To illustrate his point he tells a story from the book of Judges, about an unlovable character called Abimelech, a man with ambition and no scruples who lived and murdered in the 12th century BC in a place called Shechem near the modern town of Nablus. Abimelech, like many after him, knew what he wanted. He wanted to rule his world, and to this end he killed off all his seventy brothers save one. Abimelech may have been a thug, but he was a persuasive thug. His determination could appear in the attractive guise of authority. The elders of Shechem helped and supported him with funds. He even received silver from the temple of the local deity, and he quickly put that money to bad use, by paying others to do his killing for him.

Abimelech's rise to power can be seen simply as a particularly bloody page in the history of the people of Shechem, but Rabbi Magonet thinks it should not be limited by early history – it is, he maintains, a story of more than antiquarian historical interest. Jews read the story in a prophetic way, facing up to the unpalatable fact that Abimelech belongs to many centuries, particularly our own. Abimelech's career is a step-by-step paradigm of what happened when Hitler came to power with the backing of local people and with money from the state and even from local religious sources. Just like Abimelech's supporters, the Germans of the 1930s mistook fanaticism for authority and learned blindness as their countrymen were turned into accomplices in evil. In this way Rabbi Magonet argues that it is possible to read Abimelech's story as prophecy for the present and the future as well as history of the past. The story of Shechem is not prophecy in the sense of prediction which will be fulfilled at some unspecified date. It is prophecy because it talks about human nature and the dangers faced by every age. There is a frequent complaint that the Bible is too savage a book to teach holiness. True, it *is* full of unsavoury characters – human beings – and they are important precisely because their pettiness and venal banality anchor the story of the Israelites in the real, non-ideal world.

1. The Flight from Mystery

Genesis 1 – 11:9

In the beginning God created the heavens and the earth. The earth was without form and void, and darkness was upon the face of the deep, and the spirit of God was moving over the face of the waters. And God said, 'Let there be light'; and there was light. And God saw that the light was good; and God separated the light from the darkness. God called the light Day, and the darkness he called Night. And there was evening and there was morning, one day.

The Jewish approach to the historical books of the Bible with its constant emphasis on interpretation and re-interpretation is needed not only because it brings the Bible alive – and it is noticeable that in re-telling Bible stories Jews favour the present tense while Christians slip into the past rather too easily – but also because it gives the pages of the Bible a dimension which its original writers had fully intended. Even when the Bible is history, it is history with a purpose.

But who wrote it? Who started the whole process off? When did the first scribes begin their work? Professor John Rogerson of Sheffield believes that parts of the scripture now in our Bible began to be written down in about 1100 BC. At first the work was fragmentary – a few laws were written, later some poems. The real work of the scribes did not start until the reigns of David and his horse-dealing son Solomon in the 10th century BC, but, once begun, the process went on unabated until the 2nd century BC. This means that the Bible was about 800 years in the making. Now those dates bring in their wake another problem: the Bible claims to deal with stories as old as time, stories which would certainly pre-date the office of scribe in the court of David or Solomon, so what did the first scribes use as their sources?

Professor Rogerson believes that it is important not to underestimate the role of story-telling. Among the Israelites there was a lively oral tradition. When people gathered together in sanctuaries or holy places, much of the teaching was done by story-telling, which represented the shared memory of the chosen people. But if the oral tradition was alive and well, why did anyone bother to write anything down in the first place?

Dr John Goldingay of St John's College, Nottingham believes the answer lies in human nature. He thinks that many of the prophecies, in particular, were written down at a very early stage in the Bible's history because the prophets found that few people listened to them and fewer remembered their words. The act of writing their warnings down and sealing them against the day when they might be fulfilled served both as an act of faith in the future and as one way of prolonging the life of their teaching. There was also a practical legal motive for the first scribes. To be referred to and observed, laws had to be written down. So it was in the interest both of prophets and of law-makers to commit their words to something less changeable and selective than human memory.

*

But that still does not explain who wrote the words at the head of this chapter, the opening words of the Bible. They have assurance, beauty and simplicity, and even Darwin could not quarrel with the order of creation – plants, trees, fish, birds, animals, man; and yet there can have been no eye witnesses, no first memory into which an oral tradition could be instilled. So it is valid to ask when this account of creation was written, by whom and for what purpose. What reason is there for assuming that ancient man without the benefit of our scientific knowledge could speak with any degree of authority about the world before time, aeons before *Homo habilis* began talking, making fire and fashioning flint? Historically, the stories of Adam, the first man, and Eve, the first woman, leap through time. With their sons Cain, the tiller of the soil, and Abel, the first shepherd, and their descendants Jabal, the first nomad, Jubal, the first musician, and Tubal, the first metal worker, they cover in the space of a few generations a period stretching from 2,000,000 BC to 3,500 BC. Any attempt to take this part of the Bible as literal history is an insult to all those who have played a part in passing its wisdom down to us. Genesis is not an exercise in forensic dating. If you wish to avoid absurdity, avoid Biblical mathematics. Otherwise you will fall into the trap which swallowed Archbishop Ussher, the 17th-century Church of Ireland divine who began counting on his fingers and concluded that the world was created in 4004 BC at 9 o'clock on the first morning.

The writers of Genesis were further removed from the world of pre-history than we are from them, so why should we listen to what they have to say? Professor Davidson believes that the insights in Genesis are more than documentary. In common with many other books of the Hebrew bible, Genesis most probably came into its present shape and form during the time of exile in Babylon in the 6th century BC. This was a time when the Jews had lost everything they had hitherto regarded as central to their faith. They no longer had their country or their city. They no longer had the Temple, and above all they were cut off from the land in which they had lived and for which their fathers had fought. Everything that was important or familiar to them had been destroyed. Their world had collapsed, and they reacted by making a massive statement of faith. They made defeat into victory by looking back over the long-remembered traditions and putting those ancient stories and folk memories into writing. By giving them a shape which could speak to them and speak to the crisis of faith which they were facing during their period of exile, they were perfecting a treasure which could never be carried off and melted down – a treasure which would survive any exile or invasion.

Whenever Genesis was first committed to animal skin, it was without a doubt many thousands of years in the making. It is possible to trace widely different sources in it. This increases, rather than diminishes, its value. Professor Davidson compares Genesis to one of the great medieval cathedrals, the products of generations of craftsmen and builders, enriched with different styles of architecture which yet, for all their variety, merge to make a building of striking unity.

All this seems a long way from the traditional picture of Moses single-handedly writing down the first five books of the Bible – and indeed it seems strange that if Moses wrote it all there should be particular passages beginning 'Moses wrote'.

Undeniably, the first five books of the Bible are a 'mosaic' reflecting the faith of the children of Israel and the teaching of their greatest prophet, but as Rabbi Albert Friedlander puts it, 'this does not mean that everything came straight from Moses' typewriter'.

*

The generally accepted breakdown of the sources for the first five books of the Bible is that there were at first four different versions written over a period of five or six hundred years. Scholars have given these the labels J, E, D and P: J for the earliest narrative, finally written in about the 10th centry BC, which refers to God by the sacred name 'Yahweh'; E for the slightly later narrative which uses the noun 'Elohim' for God; D for the Deuteronomic work finalised in King Josiah's reign in the 7th century BC; and P for the Priestly code, mainly consisting of a law which was not put together until approximately a century later after the Babylonian exile. These four books, so the theory goes, were combined at various stages, so the present Pentateuch represents what Professor Norman Whybray of Hull calls 'a dove-tailing' of the four different traditions. But this, it must be emphasised, is only a theory, much disagreed about in detail. Some have even called upon computers to prove that there are secret kabbalistic messages woven into the text by a single hand. There seems no doubt that this will always remain a lively fringe of Biblical scholarship.

Less extremely, Professor Whybray is one of a number of scholars who find the JEDP argument rather too complicated. He thinks it not impossible that there was one major hand, though not Moses', behind the writing of the first five books of the Bible. When asked who this unseen sub-editor might be, he posits a nameless and unknown man probably living in the 6th century BC just after the exile. This man, he maintains, was not writing fiction, but he was writing about a world of which he had no direct knowledge. He was using many sources and many traditions. Professor Whybray believes that the hand behind the first five books of the Old Testament was someone who was living in Israel, because the writer plainly saw that there was a future for the people of Israel in their own land and therefore he must have been writing 'at home'.

But that is an unfashionably old – and an unfashionably new – view. Multiple authorship is generally thought to be more likely, but whether or not the first five books of the Bible were collated by a single dominant hand, what matters is the singularity of vision and purpose – the conviction that man belongs to a world greater than his own and the belief that the children of Abraham were chosen to represent that truth to the world: a privilege which would bring as much suffering as glory.

One of Professor Whybray's main objections to the JEDP theory, which has been generally accepted for so long, is that it makes the Bible an unnecessarily complicated literary puzzle. On the other hand it has to be admitted that the Bible is a complicated book. After the first description of the creation in seven days, we come across this familiar story:

> In the day that the Lord God made the earth and heavens, when no plant of the field was yet in the earth and no herb of the field had yet sprung up – for the Lord God had not caused it to rain upon the earth, and there was no man to till the ground; but a mist went up from the earth and watered the whole face of the ground – then the Lord God formed man of dust from the ground, and breathed into his nostrils the breath of life, and man became a living being. And the Lord God planted a garden in Eden, in the east; ...The Lord God took the man and put him in the Garden of Eden to till it and keep it. And the Lord God commanded the man, saying, 'You may freely eat of every tree of the garden; but of the tree of the knowledge of good and evil you shall not eat, for in the day that you eat it you shall die.'
>
> Genesis 2:4-9 and 15-17

That story is plainly different from, though not necessarily contradictory to, the first account of creation. Why were two versions left in? Is that an example of Biblical schizophrenia, or simple scribal inefficiency?

Professor Davidson says these questions are questions of a modern mind. In the ancient world the tendency was to preserve. If there were two different accounts of a story, they kept both and put them side by side. In Genesis there are two different accounts of how a place called Beersheba got its name. One story links it with Abraham and one with his son Isaac. Obviously there were two different traditions about the one place, but what gain could there be in recording them both? How is the reader supposed to handle apparently contradictory traditions? Do you believe one more than the other? Why record both – why not suppress one? Time and

1. God breathes the breath of life into man

again Genesis comes down on the side of retaining all current traditions. There are no cosmetic excisions. There are two accounts of creation, two genealogies of the sons of Cain, or Kenan, and two strands of Flood stories. But having decided on this approach, what did the writers expect the future readers to make of doublets and inconsistencies? Were they to believe both equally? And if you believe two contradictory things equally, can they both be true?

Professor Davidson claims that, in Genesis, it is possible to believe the two accounts and believe them equally, even if on a superficial documentary level they do not seem to be true. The ancient mind was less pedantic than its modern counterpart. It saw the richness of complementary stories where we see the problem of contradiction. He insists that it is important to be clear about what lies behind the apparently simple question 'Is that story true?' Are we, for instance, limiting our understanding of the Bible merely to forensic historical truth? Any understanding of the Bible is dependent on the recognition that it sets out to provide us with more than historical facts. The different versions prepare us for a spectrum wider than history. The Bible reveals an attitude towards life and an attitude towards faith where it is possible for an identical message about basic beliefs to come through stories which on the surface seem almost contradictory. If we treat Genesis like a 20th-century European scientific handbook it will appear ridiculous.

*

It is important to remember that we are talking about a remarkable document which, although current in the modern world, comes out of the world of the ancient Near East. In the creation stories, it must be borne in mind that the Israelites were not the first to wonder how the world began. There are a large number of stories, rich in insight, which can be traced both to ancient Babylonian and to ancient Egyptian sources about how the world began. Often, according to Professor Davidson, they are more than stories told simply to explain how everything began; they are also stories told to reassure people of something more important – they contain the message that the cosmos makes sense, that the ordinary world in which man lives will not simply collapse into chaos. Many of the stories share a common element – a description of how order comes out of chaos, often through a struggle between the gods of chaos and the gods of order. Genesis is written against this background but, argues Professor Davidson, it differs from most similar stories from the ancient Near East in one essential respect: it refuses to base creation on conflict. It refuses to talk about any kind of struggle between gods or between conflicting forces. It simply says that the world was created by the one God. Professor Davidson points out that it does not say 'out of nothing'. In fact, in Genesis chapter 1 there seems to be a belief that there is some kind of chaos lurking in the background, but it is purely a passive backcloth to the actions of the God who can bring order out of chaos and who alone can bring light into darkness.

But in spite of that essential difference, Genesis remains part of a picture of world faith. In the ancient world, even among those people whom the Hebrews regarded as pagan, religion was everywhere. As far as we know, atheists did not exist. The Hebrews were not the only people dominated by curiosity about the divine, and many myths of their near neighbours have a familiar ring to them. From Nineveh, for instance, there are cuneiform tablets telling the story of Adapa, the first man, who lost his chance of immortality because he was tricked by the god Ea into refusing the food of life and death, and the Babylonians had their own flood story in the epic of Gilgamesh.

Wilfred Lambert, Professor of Assyriology at Birmingham, maintains that the beliefs of the ancient Hebrews nevertheless stood out from the beliefs of their near neighbours. The Hebrews were unique because of their consistent emphasis on monotheism and their adherence to a God who was at once outside the physical universe and also completely in control of it. This was in marked contrast to other fashionable religious ideas. The Babylonians, for example, thought of earth itself as a deity, a kind of original intellect in the universe, as well as being more obviously a block of soil. For the Babylonians and many other nations, the earth deity was present in the earth, but for the Israelites earth was just one of the elements which God was manipulating. God was more than the physical world, and above and beyond it. Throughout their history, the Israelites were certainly aware of the differences between their own system of belief and that of peoples around them. In fact, far from trying to share in neighbouring beliefs, they were always anxious to distance themselves from the lure of the other religions.

Dr Goldingay believes that there is even a hint of this in the creation story itself. He points out that the religion of the Babylonians was in part astrological. This is why the role of the sun and the moon and the stars in the order of creation is played down. The sun and the moon are not even spoken of by name. The writer does not mention them until day four in the creation because he wants to score a deliberate polemical point. Such combative motives are not confined to the ancient world. Even now the book of Genesis, more than any book in the Bible, can be used to score points. It has not been well served by those down the ages who have used it to stultify scientific enquiry. There are many people now, particularly in the United States, who take the Biblical account of creation literally, and, as a rule, the newer the church the stronger the literalism. Asked about the Jewish view of creationism, Rabbi Magonet merely quotes an old rabbinic teaching to the effect that anyone who reads the Bible literally needs his head examined. But for many people the literal interpretation is compelling. Dr R. T. Kendall, Minister of Westminster Chapel, London is one of those who believes that a literal interpretation of creation is essential. He is sure that this century will be remembered as a time when the ultimate religious stigma was to have taken the Bible at its word. He is convinced that Genesis chapter 1 should be taken literally, no matter how historically awkward that may be.

Dr Anthony Phillips, former chaplain of St. John's College, Oxford and now Headmaster of the King's School, Canterbury, holds that the whole creationist argument is misplaced. He believes that the seven-day creation is hinting at a truth greater than any literalism. He maintains that it is ridiculous to make the first chapter of Genesis a matter of scientific debate – that, he says, belittles the entire point of the book. Genesis chapter 1 is a work of complex crafted theology. He believes that in its origin Genesis 1 is most probably drawn from an eight-day account of creation which was then squashed into six days. The six days work up to a climax on day seven, which sees the creation of the sabbath. Dr Phillips thinks that this contains one of the most crucial messages in the creation account. Why is the sabbath given such a position of importance? He believes that the sabbath was included at the end of the account because the only people in the ancient world who kept the sabbath were the Jews. Therefore the author is reassuring his readers, saying, 'Look, with the very creation of the world, God had the Jews in mind.' It is almost as if the world cannot exist without the Jews. The writer of Genesis tells us that they are as necessary to the world as the sun and the moon, as vegetation, animals, sea and man. So it is as if the sabbath, by being fixed in the very fabric of creation, assures the Jews that they are the elect. Even in the appalling situation of exile in Babylon, this distinctive mark at the moment of their defeat was a sign that God had chosen them from the beginning of time.

*

But what about the other versions of the creation story: the story of temptation and gullibility which lies behind the mystery plays and carols – about the Garden of Eden, Adam and Eve and the forbidden fruit, and a snake who was too plausible? The snake who persuaded Eve to eat the forbidden fruit of the tree of the knowledge of good and evil has a close cousin in the epic of Gilgamesh. Gilgamesh, the hero, manages to find the secret herb of immortality which the gods keep for themselves, but man's hope of earthly immortality is shattered by the wily serpent who steals it. The serpent also has more benign overtones. In both Canaan and ancient Greece it was associated with healing. Its ability to shed old skins and live suggested to the ancient mind that snakes had acquired the godlike or magic gift of reincarnation. In Eden, the snake's ability to escape death is reversed into a demonic curse which deprives the first man and woman of the gift of eternal life which was theirs.

Dr Goldingay believes that there is greater significance in the choice of the serpent as the villain of the piece in the Garden of Eden. He believes that we have here another piece of religious propaganda. The serpent was a widespread fertility symbol in Canaan and elsewhere. So the tempter of Eden has a double function. He leads Eve astray, but he also stands for the timeless threat of the lure of magic and false religion which would threaten the Israelites long after the dream of Eden was shattered. Just as, in the seven-day account of creation, the sun and moon and stars are demoted for being part of the false Babylonian religion, so in the Garden of Eden the serpent points to the shortcomings of the local Canaanite pagan religion.

But are there other hidden messages in the Garden of Eden story? Mickey Yudkin, an orthodox Jew who has researched into Biblical attitudes to women, believes there are. Woman, she says, was blamed for the fall from grace, not because she was considered too weak but because she was considered dangerously strong. She believes that the Eden story is shadowed by the fear of the ancient Mother Goddess who is seen as both the giver of life and the harbinger of the tomb and who ties mankind to a cycle of fertility and death. Eve was cast in the role of seductress by men who wanted to ensure that a dangerous power was kept in its place.

The story of Eve's creation has long been a matter of dispute. Was she condemned to inferiority from the moment of her birth?

> Then the Lord God said, 'It is not good that the man should be alone; I will make him a helper fit for him.' So out of the ground the Lord God formed every beast of the field and every bird of the air, and brought

them to the man to see what he would call them; and whatever the man called every living creature, that was its name. The man gave names to all cattle, and to the birds of the air, and to every beast of the field; but for the man there was not found a helper fit for him. So the Lord God caused a deep sleep to fall upon the man, and while he slept took one of his ribs and closed up its place with flesh; and the rib which the Lord God had taken from the man he made into a woman and brought her to the man. Then the man said, 'This at last is bone of my bones and flesh of my flesh; she shall be called Woman, because she was taken out of Man.'

Genesis 2:18-23

Many women feel that this downgrades them to a secondary order of creation. Dr Goldingay believes there is another interpretation: that the story of Adam and Eve is an admission that man cannot cope on his own. So God has to provide him with a helper. Now 'helpmate' is the word used in the authorised version, and it has been quoted as proof that woman is continually put down in the Bible, but Dr Goldingay believes that there is a deeper message behind the Adam and Eve story. If you look at the word 'helper' where it is used at other points in the Bible, you find the person most often described as such is God. If you can help somebody you are not likely to be their inferior. You are more likely to be at least their equal and probably their superior.

Eve and her daughters received a bad press in the Middle Ages, portrayed as a victim, not as the guilty party. She is persuaded by the serpent and in turn persuades a spinelessly compliant Adam. The real villain of the piece is male. Indeed throughout Hebrew tradition the serpent has been seen as male. Mickey Yudkin says there is an old midrash – that is, a legend of the rabbis – which poses the question 'Why does the serpent always creep along on its belly?' The answer is that he was castrated by God who wanted to protect Eve from his advances. The maleness of the serpent will be immediately obvious to any Hebrew reader, but not so obvious to a reader without Hebrew.

*

From its very beginning Genesis prepares us for the idea of language as an obstacle. When the men of the plain of Shinar build the Tower of Babel, their vertical dead end, God punishes their arrogance by multiplying their languages, and the harmony of creation is fractured by human ambition. In the Babylonian epic of Gilgamesh, the gods send a flood because they cannot endure the clamour of different languages.

Rabbi Magonet believes that language can still be an irritant in understanding the Bible. He maintains that most of us who read the Bible in translation are much the poorer for our ignorance. We miss the innuendo and the inter-connection between parts, verses and phrases. The story of Jezebel is all the more shocking when you realise that her name means chastity. The prophets Jeremiah and Isaiah proclaim their allegiance to God in the 'iah' part of their name. Emmanuel, 'God with us', is a promise and a hope as well as a name. But, particularly in Genesis, the proper names of the main characters fill in word-pictures in Hebrew which non-Hebrew readers have to struggle to understand. Rabbi Magonet cites the name Adam, which comes from the word 'Adamah' meaning ground; so in the very name of the first man we are given the idea of someone who comes from, and belongs to, the earth and will be returned there. Inevitably, the origins of Adam are continually recalled for the Hebrew reader whenever the word is used. The name Eve, or 'Hawwah', was related to the root 'Hayah' meaning 'life', and so there is something about the essence of generation and creativity in her name itself.

In the next generation, Abel, the shepherd brother killed by Cain, has a name, 'Havel', which means 'the breathing out' – a word used in Ecclesiastes' 'vanity of vanities'. Abel's name is something which almost has no existence, no substance, no staying power, and that, Rabbi Magonet points out, is echoed by Abel, who disappears almost as soon as his name and has no long life or continuity. Cain, the fratricide, and the elder of the two brothers, is more of a problem. When he is conceived, Eve says, 'I have acquired a man with the help of God' – the word 'Quanah', the root for gain and acquisition, is linked to Cain's name. Cain is doomed from the moment of birth. Only Adam and Eve's third son, Seth, neither murderer nor murdered, restores the balance. His name means 'He has granted', echoing Eve's first words of thanks for her third child, 'God has granted me other offspring.'

Cain's name contains within it other ideas – connotations of metal work and civilisation, a man-made world which will

2. The tower of Babel

destroy Abel's pastoral idyll. The story of that conflict is a fascinating one. Cain murders Abel because he cannot accept that Abel is more pleasing to God. This lays bare a theme which will recur – in God's eyes the rights of the first-born are meaningless. Status is a hindrance, not a passport to divine favour. Human laws are not necessarily God's – Cain's mark of guilt is also a mark of protection. And there is yet another layer of interpretation. Cain spills his brother's blood 'in a field' – the story condemns the fertility rituals which demanded blood for the renewal of fallow ground.

Throughout the Bible there are clues to the development of religious ideas even in the several names for the one God. The Hebrew Bible contains several names for the one God. He is Elohim, the deity, El Shaddai, the God of the mountains, El Elohe Israel, the God of Israel, Adonai Sabaoth, the lord of hosts, as well as the name revealed to Moses which was too holy to be pronounced. Rabbi Magonet believes that these names do not cloak a lurking polytheism but do document the gradual acceptance of monotheism by a people surrounded by polytheism. It is almost as if there was a stage at which the different names of local gods were absorbed into the Israelite people and they found one God in the middle of them all, but still used all the names which had become sacred because they were secure in the belief that there was only one God, and deity was indivisible. They felt free to refer to the one godhead by different names, much as we can use different titles to emphasise different aspects of the same person.

*

The Israelites learned from, as well as reacted against, the theologies of the surrounding people – and they adopted some of their conventions of belief. In common with the Sumerians they credited their ancestors with a great old age. Methuselah's 969 years pale into callow youth beside the multi-millennial reigns in the early Sumerian king-lists.

Genesis draws from the whole pool of ancient religious knowledge and insight. Before embarking on the story of the Flood it uses the widespread tradition of an age of super-heroes – the mysterious Nephilim, the offspring of the sons of God and the daughters of man, who for all their prowess and lifespan found no place in Noah's ark of faith.

The Nephilim are close relations of the Titans of Greek mythology and their kind – a shared response to the mystery of huge dinosaur fossils and gigantic megalithic remains: a conundrum all over the world, including the ancient Near East. But however much Hebrew monotheism borrowed from the other traditions around it, Professor Lambert maintains that it alone produced a superior morality which in the end stood the test of time. He argues that this was because the Bible's message of one God who controls the physical universe presented a world picture in which it was possible for there to be one ideal and one aim to which human beings should strive. This ultimately made more sense than a polytheistic framework where different gods represented every aspect of the universe.

Inevitably, polytheism brings with it the problem of conflicting divine wills. This is why the mythologies of many surrounding cultures spoke about the gods fighting and killing each other. Canaanite Baal fought with Mat; Babylonian Marduk conquered Tiamat. Many religious codes saw nothing contradictory in having gods of evil as well as of goodness. Professor Lambert believes that the Israelites made the great leap forward by seeing their God as a being more complete than the poor mixture which was man. This, he believes, is the answer to the enigma of why the religion of the Hebrews has survived as a living faith when so many of its religious contemporaries from more developed cultures have died. Equally, it is wrong to suppose that the Israelites were alone in their religious quest. All ancient peoples were seriously trying to understand the world in which they found themselves. But as religious ideas developed, many of the religiously-minded scaled their gods down to human size and lost their keen interest in explaining the physical universe. They became more concerned with the concepts of anthropomorphic gods – beings with power, but not with moral superiority.

Professor Lambert believes that when the philosophical debates of Miletus and Athens began to have a wide currency in the classical world, the idea of the gods as super-human beings became no longer acceptable. In fact the whole system of polytheistic religion became at best intellectually untenable and at worst ridiculous. But then the rough-hewn Israelite view of one deity outside a physical universe was something that could stand up to the test of time and philosophy. In the ancient world the Jews alone could preach a faith which was in some ways more grandiose and intellectually more defensible even than the new insights of the Greek philosophers. This is why children the world over know the name of Noah but not of Utnapishtim, the only survivor of the flood story contained in the epic of Gilgamesh, or of Deucalion, the boat-building hero of the Greek deluge myth.

*

Much energy has been expended trying to pinpoint Noah's flood in history. Excavations at Ur and neghbouring sites have confirmed that there were periodic disastrous floods in the Tigris/Euphrates valley, and the Sumerian chronologies use one particularly bad flood as a dating marker. There have been many expeditions to Mount Ararat to find traces of Noah's ark at its final resting-place, now inconveniently straddling the Turkish/Soviet frontier.

Both the historical and the geographical quests miss the

point of Noah's adventures. The Hebrew flood story, a chronicle of disaster vanquished by obedience, ends with a covenant between God and man – partly based on Noah's reverence for God and partly on God's promise of protective love. Other flood heroes have had more tangible rewards: the Greek Deucalion had the glory of being the father of rulers, the Sumerian Zuisudra received immortality, and the Babylonian Utnapishtim became a god. Utnapishtim also received a necklace of lapis lazuli from the goddess Ishtar, but Noah merely received the rainbow, an ephemeral sign of an eternal covenant. The story of Noah is an ideal example of how using the Bible simply as a historical checking-service is a path of poverty, missing out the richness and maturity of its understanding of God's relationship with man.

This is precisely why Rabbi Magonet believes that even the very early stories of Genesis deserve more than relegation to ancient history or nursery tales. He tells the story of a man he met who had been a holocaust survivor in Holland. Reprieved from the shadow of the death camps, he had become an alcoholic, until one day he began to read the story of Noah – the slightly odd second part of the story which deals with the return to normality and describes how Noah planted a vineyard after the trauma of the flood and became very drunk. The incongruous passage made sense to him and made sense of his life. He understood Noah because he himself had come back into a world in which his entire family had gone and everything he had taken for granted had been destroyed. He had no bearings any more. Noah had become drunk, just as *he* had become an alcoholic. Rabbi Magonet says that, as he spoke to this man who, like Noah, had seen a world destroyed, he realised how important it was not to confine the Bible to history but to let it live.

There are those who disagree, who say that Genesis is too difficult and too primitive. They try to dispense with Genesis chapters 1 to 11, with stories of the creation and Eden and the flood and Babel. They maintain that we should start, not in the Bible story's infancy, but later with Abraham, or even with Moses. But Dr Phillips argues that the early Genesis stories are the prologue to the entire Bible story. They also offer clues about the way the whole Bible journey will develop. Hebrew story-writing is not a surprise. It tells you what is going to happen right at the beginning. Dr Phillips compares

3. Noah's ark

it to the writing of a detective story, where the writer lets you know not only the identity of the corpse but the identity of the murderer. Once these essential facts are established, the fuller story can be unravelled. The essential facts of Genesis with its two creation stories, its heroes and its long-lived patriarchs, are simply this: it prepares us for what is to come and assures us that all will be well because God is not going to desert man. God has chosen man and desires a relationship with him – the only uncertain factor is man. Once we have absorbed that, we have absorbed a large part of the message of the entire Old Testament.

But if so need we read on? If the essential truth is so easily encapsulated in the first eleven chapters of Genesis, why battle through the other books? Professor Davidson believes that the best reason for reading the whole Bible is that in some sense we are ready to walk with the faith to which it points. Reading the Bible is a pilgrimage. That does not mean that we have to give it a documentary status it never claimed – without question the Bible journey is pointless – but the important part of the journey from Eden to Armageddon is not only to question Adam, Eve and Noah and all the nameless scribes, but to accept them as our travelling companions and allow them to question us.

2. Pride and Patriarchs

Genesis 11:27 – 35:29

In Jerusalem, a year or two after an unemployed carpenter turned preacher had died a criminal's death on a hill shaped like a skull, a Hellenised Jew named Stephen was arraigned before the high priest's council, the Sanhedrin, charged with blasphemy. He defended himself with a speech rich in the devices of classical rhetoric, but he began by appealing to the memory of an illiterate nomad chief:

> Brethren and fathers, hear me. The God of glory appeared to our father Abraham, when he lived in Mesopotamia, before he lived in Haran, and said to him, 'Depart from your land and from your kindred and go to the land which I will show you.' Then he departed from the land of the Chaldeans and lived in Haran. And after his father died, God removed him from there into this land in which you are now living; yet he gave him no inheritance in it, not even a foot's length, but promised to give it to him in possession and to his posterity after him, even though he had no child.
>
> Acts 7:2-5

It is not surprising that Stephen chose to invoke the name of Abraham, the descendant of Noah. Even today the story of Abraham remains one of the most enduring the world had known. It is a mixture of bizarre instructions and implausible promises – a wild paradox of the divine and the mundane. The landless will inherit the land. The childless will have descendants more numerous than the stars. Abraham bargains successfully with God and tells lies inefficiently. He entertains angels and is henpecked by his wife. Of his free will he enters into a covenant unbound by time. In return he receives a promise which is still a matter of sharp contemporary political controversy.

Even if we take the Biblical account of Abraham literally, the only monuments he could have left behind are no more substantial than footprints in the sand somewhere on the ancient trade routes between modern Iraq and Egypt. Yet those footprints overshadow the more tangible remains of the temples whose gods, we are told, he rejected, and the city states whose walls he dared not enter.

However elusive Abraham may seem, it is with him that the Biblical journey begins in earnest. We leave behind the cosmology of Eden and the epic of the Flood and start walking at a more human pace, resting by night in something not unlike the black goat-hair tents still used by Bedouin all over the Near East. With Abraham we are in the historical world of between 3,500 and 4,000 years ago – but whether we are in the company of a single historical figure is another matter.

*

The Bible presents Abraham the traveller, rich in cattle, goats and camels, not as a hero but as the first in the line of patriarchs – that strange succession of flawed and often misguided men through whose domestic squabbles, interminable wanderings and occasional brushes with the divine it is claimed that God first chose to reveal his purpose to men.

But are the stories of Abraham, Isaac and Jacob anything more than folk tales, tribal memories speaking directly only to the Israelites of the 10th century BC – when the stories were first written down – and answering a need for an ancestor and a history? For the Russian Orthodox Archbishop, Metropolitan Anthony of Sourozh, the voices of the patriarchs carry clearly across the millennia with a message which is not yet old. He believes that they can speak to us now. The land and the time may be distant, but the situation is very familiar to millions of people nowadays: people who have had to abandon their country, to find a new one, and who, being uprooted, discover that they have roots elsewhere, not in the earth that gave them birth, but in eternity or in the kingdom of God.

Abraham and his sons and his grandsons may fit into the framework of eternity but are their stories valueless unless viewed with the eyes of faith? Is there any objective truth in the Abraham story? Is it historical fact or pious fiction? Ronald Clements, Professor of Old Testament Studies at King's College, London, thinks it is historical, because he senses that, rooted there, is a firm, positive tradition of

4. Abraham leaves for Canaan with his family and livestock

Abraham as an individual human being. However, the stories about him were recorded not at the time, but by his descendants long afterwards. In that way they remembered the features of Abraham that had a continuing significance for them and perhaps for us.

Yet even among those descendants opinion is divided. For both Christians and Jews, Abraham is the architect of the covenant and the first monotheist. And for Jews, Abraham is more: he is inextricably bound up with their sense of identity as a believing community. Any convert to Judaism is referred to as a 'child of Abraham': Abraham remains literally his father in faith. But even this does not necessarily imply a belief in Abraham's historical existence.

Rabbi Julia Neuberger does not believe that there was a historical Abraham, although she admits that it is a difficult judgment to make. She thinks you can tell that there was a series of peoples who had a life style rather like Abraham's. Different stories about Abraham abound. There seem to be two traditions in the book of Genesis: one that he came from

Ur of the Chaldeans and another that he came from Haran up in the north of Mesopotamia. It is much more likely from the account of his life style that he came from Haran, which was a nomadic centre, a market town for cattle and sheep, than that he came from Ur, which was one of the most civilised of the Mesopotamian cities. Rabbi Neuberger believes that it is highly implausible that Abraham came from that kind of background, because it was an urban, sophisticated, musical, cultured civilisation, very different from what we know of him, with his goats and tents. Whatever the doubts about Abraham's historicity, we know that people who had the life style described in the book of Genesis existed.

The Bible claims that Abraham travelled from Ur to Haran, from Haran to Canaan, from Canaan to Egypt, and from Egypt back to Canaan: in all some 1,300 miles. But would one man have travelled so far at that time? Dr Kay Prag, a researcher into Near Eastern archaeology, thinks that Abraham may easily have been a real person but that many ancestral stories accrued in the course of time. She doubts if a man from the urban society of Ur would settle happily for the life of a pastoralist in Canaan – it is a journey more likely to have been made over several generations.

Both Christians and Jews are reluctant to limit Abraham to history. He belongs to it but also exceeds it. For Metropolitan Anthony there is no doubt about Abraham's existence and the reality of his wanderings, but the historical question marks are less important than the theological exclamation marks. According to him what we know from the Bible is a message so full of meaning that even if we miss a great deal, because we belong to another culture, or because we do not know as much, the few things that are there are extremely precious. There is Abraham – pious, honest, devout, and living among his own people – and one day he hears God addressing him directly, saying, 'Abraham, stand up, and leave your country, leave your kindred and go wherever I will tell you and take you.' This, Metropolitan Anthony believes, is something we must learn from, because we all belong to natural surroundings, both human and spatial. We belong to a country, we belong to a society, we belong to a family, and at times we can perceive clearly that, unless we let go of everything, we will not be able to come to the place where – in total freedom – we can meet and obey God.

The stories of Abraham may fit comfortably into the historical framework of 2,000 – 1,500 BC, and the religious lessons of obedience may speak loudly to believers today, but this still does not prove that there was an individual called Abraham. Professor Davidson, however, believes that if we search only for Abraham the man we may fall into the trap of underestimating the Bible. He thinks that Abraham is not simply an individual. The people who came from Abraham are the sons of Abraham and, in a sense, what you see happening in the case of Abraham is something that goes on happening in the experience of these people. Genesis is not interested in whether there was simply a man called Abraham who moved west from Mesopotamia towards the Mediterranean at some time in that period. The stories about Abraham are told because they reflect the faith of the community. They are remembered only because they are important for the community that sprang – or believed it sprang – from Abraham. There is no reason to doubt that Abraham may have been a historical person, but to ask whether the details in Genesis can be taken as cold, accurate historical facts is another question.

On the other hand, if the historical facts are side issues, what is left? What is the element in the story of Abraham the singular man, or Abraham the composite tribal leader, that has won him an unrivalled place in Judaism and Christianity? Professor Clements thinks that it is the directness of a personal relationship to God which makes the fullest impression, that Abraham senses that his own life and the life of the whole clan are under a providential purpose and are working towards a providential goal.

*

The idea of providence, of God choosing a people and using it to fulfil his purpose, is not confined to professional theologians. Dr Dan Bahat, an Israeli archaeologist, is anxious to keep the science of archaeology and the stories of Genesis separate. He will not talk about the 'patriarchal' period of ancient history, preferring the less appealing label 'Middle Bronze Age II'. But to the question 'What made a Middle Bronze Age II man travel from Mesopotamia to Canaan?' his reply is surprising. 'God's providence,' he says, and, backing up the divine by the mundane, observes that there are still movements of people through the Middle East to this very day. You can see it when you go to the desert or the fringe area around the country. It is a permanent movement of people. Wanderers come to the desert, and from the desert to the fertile country come people who are pushed by the wanderers or the shepherds. They are forced to the coast, or the mountains or the fortified city. The cities grow. It is an endless process. Dr Bahat believes his excavations can make sense of the Genesis accounts of the patriarchs arriving at towns but stopping short of going inside them.

Some years ago he and his colleagues excavated a village a mile outside the Biblical town of Beth Shemesh. It was a fine site, with a handsome network of streets and houses and a temple at the top of a hill. It appeared to confirm the Biblical stories about the patriarchs arriving at towns but settling outside them. But what would be the point of skulking on the outskirts and deliberately avoiding the safety of the city walls? Dr Bahat's explanation is that in the Caananite cities life was very similar to the feudal system in medieval Europe. You had to belong to someone in order to be well ranked in the system. The patriarchs were probably outsiders, and that is why they could not get into the system, or into the cities.

Abraham the outsider may have left no monuments behind him, but we do have his name and the whole cluster of names belonging to his family. What clues do they offer? Dr Prag says that the names used in the patriarchal stories turn up in related, understandable forms in early Semitic languages over a considerable period. Some of the texts found in the last few years at Ebla in north Syria go back to about the 24th century BC. So, as far back as the third millennium there is a pattern of early Semitic names into which the patriarchal names can be fitted.

But what about patriarchal behaviour? Does the Sunday School image of Abraham with his tents and his herds fit in with the historical picture? Dr Prag says we know that pastoralist nomads used tents, if from nothing else from an Egyptian story which was probably composed at the very beginning of the second millennium. It tells of an Egyptian called Sinouhi who fled from Egypt and dwelt among pastoralists in part of Palestine or southern Syria. It describes these people as living in tented encampments, and as having cattle and growing grain. They had a considerable range of weapons: bows and arrows, javelins and spears, which would fit the archaeological evidence for the early part of the second millennium. Such pastoralists would have lived in the region at almost any time, and the image of Abraham as a pastoralist in his tent is quite reasonably drawn.

But are the other elements in the story of Abraham as reasonably drawn? We talk about the patriarchs, but what about the matriarchs? Had they been pushed aside? Rabbi Neuberger thinks they had. Some scholars say that Abraham had supplanted a matriarchy, and she finds this theory tempting because, from the stories of what happened to the matriarchs – Abraham's wife Sarah and Isaac's wife Rebecca and Jacob's wives Leah and Rachel – it does look as if there was a background matriarchy in the shape of a formidable, powerful collection of women.

Certainly Rebecca outmanoeuvres Isaac and manages to secure his blessing on her favourite son Jacob, rather than Esau, and later Rachel steals her father's household goods to ensure that the leadership of the family goes to her husband Jacob. These stories imply ingenuity and lack of scruple, but hardly power. Is there any evidence in the patriarchal stories of female authority? Was Abraham henpecked? Julia Neuberger thinks he was, and cites a medieval commentary as evidence. When Abraham and Sarah are unable to have a child, Sarah naturally becomes distressed. She hands over her handmaiden, Hagar – the first historical account of surrogacy – to Abraham, and he has a child by Hagar, Ishmael, later taken as the father of the Islamic people. Later Sarah has a child, Isaac. Sarah believes Ishmael is mocking Isaac, the later born, saying, 'Who is this child Isaac?' Sarah reacts fiercely and defensively and says to Abraham, 'You must send Ishmael and Hagar away, out into the wilderness.' Abraham prevaricates rather feebly, but Sarah's determination wins the day and Hagar is sent out, with Ishmael, into the wilderness with nothing but a leather bottle full of water. Abraham is obviously dubious about this, and asks God, 'Should I really do this?' The reply comes, 'All that Sarah tells you, hearken to her voice.' In other words, 'You obey her.' The commentary in Rashi, one of the medieval commentators, says this should teach us that Sarah was superior to Abraham in prophecy – a lesson Rabbi Neuberger enjoys repeating to her women students.

So Abraham rose early in the morning, and took bread and a skin of water, and gave it to Hagar, putting it on her shoulder, along with the child, and sent her away. And she departed, and wandered in the wilderness of Beer-sheba. When the water in the skin was gone she cast the child under one of the bushes. Then she went, and sat down over against him a good way off, about the distance of a bowshot; for she said, 'Let me not look upon the death of the child.' And as she sat over against him, the child lifted up his voice and wept. And God heard the voice of the lad; and the angel of God called to Hagar from heaven, and said to her, 'What troubles you, Hagar? Fear not; for God has heard the voice of the lad where he is. Arise, lift up the lad, and hold him fast with your hand; for I will make him a great nation.'

Genesis 21: 14-18

*

That great nation lives and thrives today. Abraham belongs not only to the Hebrew Bible and the Christian Old Testament. His roots are just as deep in the Qur'an. He and Ishmael are the ancestors in faith of Muslims the world over. Every year in Mecca, in Saudi Arabia, the story of Abraham's dismissal of Hagar is commemorated by Muslims obeying the fifth pillar of Islam – the call to Haj, the great annual pilgrimage.

Dr Hasan Askari, Lecturer in Islamic Studies at Selly Oak College, Birmingham, explains that Hagar's tears are embedded in Islam's sense of the tragic. Just as she leaves with the child Ishmael, and goes to look for water, so every Muslim pilgrim has to walk seven times between two mountains, imitating the search for water by Hagar. For Dr Askari, Hagar is important because of her faith in God and her sense of posterity – despite her search for water, her thirst, her tears, her crying to God when, according to Islamic tradition, the angel appears and says, 'Where to, you go?' and she says, 'I go unto God.'

But Abraham's treatment of Hagar is scarcely inspiring. Why is he held in such esteem by Muslims? Because, says Dr Askari, he is not just a patriarch, as he is in the Bible, but the model for mankind: the faithful one who turned to God, with all his mind and heart. And the Qur'anic words refer to him not as a Jew, nor yet as a Christian, but as one who turned to God with all his heart, and joined not gods with God. Abraham became a point of departure for transcending divisions. For that reason, in Muslim Haj, it is not Mohammed who is central, but Abraham.

Muslims refer to Abraham as the model, the basic paradigm, of faith – a man who symbolises for all of us, whether we are Jews, Christians or Moslems, a total turning to God, the commitment beyond all name and symbol. As in the Bible, so in the Qur'an, Abraham is more than a single individual. He is the community himself, the means whereby an individual becomes a collectivity. The expression in the Qur'an that he is 'a nation by himself', in terms not only of the past but of the crucial moment of convergence of faith – in that sense, all of us, wherever we are – all theistic people in the world – are walking on the path of Ibrahim, the Arabic name for Abraham.

Abraham's importance to Muslims is not confined to times of pilgrimage. He is woven into the daily round of prayer, taking precedence even over Mohammed. Every Muslim has to invoke a blessing after he finishes his obligatory prayer, five times daily. This involves calling a blessing on the house of Abraham, and *then* on Mohammed and his family. The traditions of Islam add to Abraham's travels and accomplishments. Muslims believe that Abraham went to Mecca and there constructed the q'aba, the first temple to a god whose image could not be carved.

Abraham and Ishmael are referred to in the Qur'an as putting brick over brick, and offering prayer unto God. 'O God make this house the house of peace.' For this reason, Dr Askari explains, around the q'aba in the sacred city of Mecca, no birds, no animal can be slaughtered. It is the perfect shrine, where there is total peace, where humanity enters in all humility, dressed in a shroud – two pieces of white unseamed cloth. The entire congregation foreshadows the rising from the dead, on the last day, and the single cry, 'O God, here we are.'

Christians are inclined to gloss over the story of Hagar and Ishmael. It shows Abraham in a weak, if not a culpable, light. Why then did the writer of Genesis leave the story in – through oversight or deliberately? David Clines, Reader in Biblical Studies at Sheffield, thinks the story is there for a definite purpose. We are meant to be shocked and stunned. We recognise Abraham as a man of flesh and blood, and are meant to judge him and not admire him in such an episode.

*

But how can we explain away the story of Isaac?

> After these things God tested Abraham, and said to him, 'Abraham!'
> And he said, 'Here am I.' He said, 'Take your son, your only son Isaac,
> whom you love, and go to the land of Moriah, and offer him there as a
> burnt offering upon one of the mountains of which I shall tell you.' So
> Abraham rose early in the morning, saddled his ass, and took two of
> his young men with him, and his son Isaac; and he cut the wood for
> the burnt offering, and arose and went to the place of which God had
> told him. On the third day Abraham lifted up his eyes and saw the
> place afar off. Then Abraham said unto his young men, 'Stay here
> with the ass; and I and the lad will go yonder and worship, and come
> again to you.' And Abraham took the wood of the burnt offering, and
> laid it on Isaac his son, and he took in his hand the fire and the knife.
> So they went both of them together. And Isaac said to his father
> Abraham, 'My father!' And he said, 'Here am I, my son.' He said,
> 'Behold, the fire and the wood; but where is the lamb for a burnt
> offering?' Abraham said, 'God will provide himself the lamb for a
> burnt offering, my son.' So they went both of them together.
>   When they came to the place of which God had told him, Abraham
> built an altar there, and laid the wood in order, and bound Isaac his
> son, and laid him on the altar, upon the wood. Then Abraham put
> forth his hand, and took the knife to slay his son. But the angel of the
> Lord called to him from heaven, and said, 'Abraham, Abraham!' And
> he said, 'Here am I.' He said, 'Do not lay your hand on the lad or do
> anything to him; for now I know that you fear God, seeing you have
> not withheld your son, your only son, from me.'
>
>   Genesis 22:1-12

Over the centuries the savagery of Mount Moriah has been
tamed. The Fathers of the early Church saw Isaac as an
inside-out echo of Christ, another willing victim who would
walk up a hill carrying the wood by which he was to die. But
clearly that was not in the mind of the writer of the story. Nor
was there at that time a prevalent tradition of child sacrifice
against which to react. So is the Isaac story too gruelling and
too primitive to speak to anyone now? Would a believer today
obey such a barbaric instruction?

Metropolitan Anthony thinks the answer to such a question
must be yes – not perhaps in the very terms of Abraham, in
the sense that one does not take a child, use a knife and
murder it: but one would certainly send one's own child to
death for a cause that was worthy of the sacrifice. One would
trust God to look after the problem, and say 'You must go, and
if necessary, you must die.'

But what does the Isaac story tell us about Abraham?

5. Abraham about to sacrifice Isaac

David Clines thinks that Abraham was in a sense being limbered up for obedience. He thinks the story of Abraham and Isaac is the story almost of an automaton who, when God says 'Jump', jumps. And it is not just at the beginning of the story, when he says 'Take your son, your only son, the son you love and sacrifice him', but at the end, where the command to sacrifice is countermanded and he has to hold the knife back, that there is a test of obedience. The Israelite mind rather liked that notion of a man's attitude to his God.

For Metropolitan Anthony the lesson behind the story is deeper. In it, he says, we nowadays see first the bloody side of the story of Abraham and Isaac, but there is another side. It is a moment when Abraham proved capable of believing God more than he believed what he had understood of his promise. We tend to cling to the words: Abraham clung to the person. He obeyed, and God looked after everything.

Above all, Abraham stands out as the man who came to a business arrangement with God:

[The Lord] said to him, 'Bring me a heifer three years old, a she-goat three years old, a ram three years old, a turtledove, and a young pigeon.' And he brought him all these, cut them in two and laid each half over against the other; but he did not cut the birds in two. And when the birds of prey came down upon the carcasses, Abram drove them away...

When the sun had gone down and it was dark, behold, a smoking fire pot and a flaming torch passed between these pieces. On that day the Lord made a covenant with Abram, saying, 'To your descendants I give this land, from the river of Egypt to the great river, the river Euphrates, the land of the Kenites, the Kenizzites, the Kadmonites, the Hittites, the Perizzites, the Rephaim, the Amorites, the Caananites, the Girgashites and the Jebusites.

Genesis 15:9-11 and 17-21

That account of halved carcasses may seem strange and bloodthirsty. It has nothing to do with the idea of sacrifice to a god. It is a reflection of the normal procedure in the ancient world for ratifying a solemn agreement between men. Usually both parties would walk between the severed carcasses, thus accepting that a similar fate would befall whoever defaulted in the agreement. In the Abrahamic covenant only God, seen in smoke and fire, accepts the penalty, while Abraham sleeps. But does not this reduce God to the status of a political or commercial ally? Is there not something sacrilegious, or even ridiculous, in the idea of a treaty with God? Professor Clements thinks that pacts were very important for society as a whole, at a stage of human development where the extended family, the kin group, was the natural, protected environment in which people lived. If you were going to have any dealings with people who did not fall within a kin-group category, you had to have some understanding of where you were and where they were, and a pact, a covenant, a treaty of some kind was the natural way of doing that. To extend that to God was perhaps not too difficult a jump to make. What is important in the covenant is that it allows for that degree of human responsiveness. God does not take over in a human sense. He wants co-operation. He does not want to suppress the individual in his own existence.

But why the preoccupation with land? What is religious about a piece of real estate? It meant more than real estate, Professor Clements points out. It was the way by which people earned a living. It was a condition for survival. It was a framework for a national existence. It was also a promise of economic advancement and prosperity. For people in ancient times, it held a great mystery, because why the land makes things grow was always divine activity, not just a purely physical or biological fact. It was understood in that sense to be the work of God. It was also tied in with a big transition from a way of life in which people were continually moving about with flocks of sheep, which was their basic economic good, to a way of life in which they wished to till the land, grow cereals and become richer. One of the great features of stories of this kind is that they do not make a distinction between material and spiritual things.

But does the Bible lose sight of the distinction between material and spiritual things? In Genesis, smooth-skinned Jacob cheats his elder and hairier brother Esau out of the inheritance which should have been his by wrapping animal skins round his hands to fool the blind Isaac into giving his blessing to his younger son. How can the Bible be seen as a moral book when it seems to sanction and reward such cunning? Professor Davidson believes that that is the most exciting thing about the Bible. It is a human book. It deals with people as they are, not with plaster saints. Many of the people who according to the Old Testament are used by God are some of the biggest twisters who ever walked this earth. There is no bigger twister than Jacob. But this is encouraging, because if God is to use any of us he has to face the fact that we are not going to live up to everything he wants.

With patriarchs the Bible journey has moved into history and politics, with new ideas of national identity, and pride in a land and a covenant. But are there any other lessons that Abraham the wanderer can teach a world in which 192,000,000 Jews and Christians and Muslims revere his name? Dr Askari, as a Muslim, believes that Abraham is asking all his children to say, simply 'Our God and your God are one. Unto Him we surrender, and unto Him return.'

3. The Bridge between Dreams

Genesis 37 – Exodus 19:20
Exodus 24:12-18
Numbers 10:33 – 14:38
Deuteronomy 29:2 – 30:20

Why is this night different from all other nights? That question was old when Solomon the Wise built his temple of gold and cedar to the unseen God on Mount Moriah in Jerusalem. It has survived the jagged edge of history for more than 3,000 years. It has known prosperity and despair, the pain of exile and the obscenity of death camps.

It is part of the Seder, an annual family celebration of wine and merriment in which Jews the world over commemorate the Passover, a night of blood and fear when, they claim, an angel of death took the lives of the Egyptian first-born so that the Israelite slaves could escape into freedom.

That implausible story has bitten deep into the imagination of people throughout history. It contains all the elements of classic folk tale – a foundling hero, competition of magic, an artillery of signs and wonders, a sky which turns black, a river which turns red, and a sea which splits in half. Moses is the tongue-tied leader of the weak and Pharaoh the evil king. The Passover is the last stage in an unequal contest in which the wilful stupidity of the powerful is routed by the winning persistence of the powerless. It is a good story that deserves to be remembered – but is it more than that?

Down the centuries the persecuted in the Old World and the enslaved in the New have claimed that it is. They have taken the stammering Moses as their own leader. Today, in the shanty towns of Brazil and the gulags of the Soviet Union, the book of Exodus belongs to the present as well as the past.

*

There can be no doubt about the strength of the ideological credentials of the exodus from Egypt, with the salt tears of

36

slavery in a land of plenty replaced by the honey-sweetness of manna in the wilderness – heaven-sent food in a barren land. But what about the historical roots? The simple living colours of the exodus dominate the arcane hieroglyphs of the dead. That imbalance itself is part of the mystery. We even remember the Pe Ro, literally the 'Great House', the ruler of Upper and Lower Egypt, the incarnation of the sun god Ra, through the lips of those who knew him by the Hebrew word 'pharaoh'.

The dream of freedom contained in the drama of the exodus tempts credulity. But however good the story line, some basic questions remain. Is there any evidence to show that the Israelites went down into Egypt, and if they did, why did they go?

The writer of Genesis tells us that, just after Jacob had taken the name Israel, the exodus dream of freedom grew from an earlier, more primitive dream of dominion told by a favoured son with a coat of many colours to his disgruntled brothers.

> Joseph, being seventeen years old, was shepherding the flock with his brothers; he was a lad with the sons of Bilhah and Zilpah, his father's wives; and Joseph brought an ill-report of them to their father. Now Israel [Jacob] loved Joseph more than any other of his children, because he was the son of his old age; and he made him a long robe with sleeves. But when his brothers saw that their father loved him more than all his brothers, they hated him, and could not speak peaceably to him. Now Joseph had a dream, and when he told it to his brothers they only hated him the more. He said to them, 'Hear this dream which I have dreamed; behold, we were binding sheaves in the field, and lo, my sheaf arose and stood upright; and behold, your sheaves gathered round it, and bowed down to my sheaf.' His brothers said to him, 'Are you indeed to reign over us? Or are you indeed to have dominion over us?' So they hated him yet more for his dreams and for his words.
>
> Genesis 37:2-8

As Joseph dreamed again, seeing the sun, the moon and the stars bowing down before him, even his father was exasperated and his brothers sold him to some Midianite traders, who in turn sold him as a slave in Egypt. With Joseph the dreamer the Bible changes gear. The grandeur and mystery of the creation story have been left far behind. The domesticity of Abraham's tent and Esau's pottage gives way to a larger story. Joseph the master of dreams is the link between the family history of the patriarchs and the national history of the people called Israel.

Joseph is also the uneasy bridge between two cultures. He resists the amorous advances of his owner's wife in a style which is more Egyptian than patriarchal. He uses his old skills in interpreting dreams to rise high in Pharaoh's service. He is put in charge of famine relief in his new home and is finally able to gain land and protection for his father and brothers when they are forced by hunger to seek refuge in Egypt. As an individual Joseph seems one-dimensional – the ideal son, the perfect civil servant and an efficient social climber.

Rabbi Julia Neuberger thinks he is not a very attractive character – although a powerful individual, who becomes totally Egyptianised. She points out that an extraordinary feature of the book of Genesis is that the titles Joseph is given match up completely with titles we know from Egyptian history. There is virtually no evidence within Egypt that the Israelites were ever there. Some scholars have said that the Hyksos people's invasion of Egypt was the invasion of the Israelites, but that is very difficult to argue, historically speaking. But whether they went or not, there is an enormous amount of knowledge of Egyptian society in the book of Genesis. Egyptian titles, the Egyptian way of life displayed in the chapters of Genesis that deal with the Joseph story are all convincingly accurate. In the early chapters Joseph is not a pleasant character. He is vile to his brothers, and is continually saying that they will bow down to him, as is proved right. There is an arrogance and unpleasantness about him. In later chapters he is dressed in the fine linens which we know were worn by Egyptian court officials. He is the bearer of the seal, the bearer of the ring – he has all the titles that are known to us from Egyptian records – and he becomes a typical Egyptian character. Then his own character almost disappears.

There is evidence that foreigners could rise high in Pharaoh's service, and it was common practice for Egypt to accept shepherds and nomads from the east driven towards the unfailing richness of the Nile in times of famine. But after that the historical problems get knottier. According to the ancient Egyptian historian Manetho (3rd century BC) the Hyksos were foreign invaders who infiltrated the Nile delta

6. Joseph sold by his brothers into captivity

and ruled Egypt from 1730 BC to 1580 BC. It would certainly be fanciful to identify Joseph's starving family with conquering princes, but it is not far-fetched to pin-point the time of the Hyksos as a time when Israelites could have prospered. The fact remains, however, that for all Joseph's courtly titles no inscription bearing his name has been dug up from the sands of Egypt. Is the Bible story therefore enough evidence by itself that Israel was in Egypt?

Rabbi Neuberger cannot believe that you find that kind of memory, that kind of historical recollection, in a people expressed so strongly without some basis in fact. All we can say is that the historical evidence we might expect within Egypt of a mass group of Israelites coming down does not appear to exist. On the other hand, we could argue that the Egyptians had such a hatred of foreigners that they quickly Egyptianized them. The evidence of wall paintings and tomb paintings is of Asiatics. They are always referred to as Asiatics, and they look different from the Egyptians, but perhaps one generation later they were as Egyptian as anyone else.

The Egyptians were vague about racial definitions. If we accept that Israel prospered in Egypt under the Hyksos, that would explain why their fortunes suddenly changed and they found themselves persecuted and enslaved. In 1580 BC an Egyptian once again wore the double crown of Egypt. The Pharaoh Amosis drove the Hyksos out of the country and inaugurated the New Empire. To have prospered under the Hyksos would ensure the disfavour of any pharaoh of the new dynasty.

*

But a problem remains. The book of Exodus says specifically that 600,000 Israelite slaves escaped with Moses, not including women and children. Can we believe that a community of more than two million left so few archaeological traces?

Dr Ben Isserlin, an expert in Semitic archaeology, admits that modern scholars have questioned the Biblical head count. Biblical figures certainly seem rather excessive. But he believes that it is extremely likely that the Hebrews were in Egypt fitting in with the many other non-Egyptians there. Recently a settlement of Asiatics who may have been there at about the same time as, or perhaps before, the Hebrews has been uncovered at a place called Tel el Dabar. Scholars have sometimes wondered whether all the Israelites, or only some, were there, while others stayed in Palestine and then rejoined them.

If the numerical accuracy is so shaky, is the rest of the story devalued? Professor Jurgen Moltmann of Tübingen thinks not. There is more behind the book of Exodus, he says, than on-the-spot reporting. There is historical evidence behind it, but it has become more than history, it has become the story of a people repeated again and again. It becomes an existence-bearing story, which is more than just news from history. We should develop a new concept of story. We all have a name, we are all persons, but we have no definition. As human beings we have a story to tell and we understand each other if we tell our life story. It is the same with the collective biography of a people, of the people of Israel or of the Church.

It is more likely that only a small number of Israelites were in Egypt – after all we are told that all Israelite births were supervised by only two midwives – and that later the experience of the exodus became part of the heritage of the whole Hebrew nation. There may be other clues. The word 'Hebrew', or something like it, turns up in several Egyptian inscriptions, as Dr Isserlin explains.

The *ha'baru*, or *ha'beru* or *uberu*, in Egyptian inscriptions are a population of nomads, mercenary soldiers and robbers who are attested all over the fertile crescent from Babylonia to Egypt from early in the second millennium down to the time when the Israelites were supposed to have left Egypt – say, the 12th century or thereabouts. The word may or may not be linked with the word *Hebrew*. Many people think it is, but it is probably a wider grouping. The Hebrews may have been linked with the *ha'baru* group, but not every *ha'baru* was a Hebrew in the Israelite sense.

The events of ancient history are usually viewed from the position of the powerful. The exodus breaks that rule – we have a worm's eye view. We travel with the escaping slaves, not with their owners. The exodus may have been on a smaller scale, but that does not diminish its importance.

*

But if the numbers are fictitious what else has been made up? Was a child called Moses ever found in the bulrushes? Is it a coincidence that the ancient Mesopotamian king Sargon I was found in suspiciously similar circumstances?

Rabbi Neuberger thinks the story of Moses in the bulrushes has been given more importance than is due to it. There are many stories in different cultures about babies found in mysterious places, or born in mysterious places, who become saviours. You could draw a parallel with Jesus born in a manger or Romulus and Remus suckled by a wolf. It seems a significant attribute of the human psyche that the great redeemers, the great saviours, the great founders of cities are often described as people who had odd beginnings. That is the significance of the finding of Moses in the bulrushes. It is an exemplar of the mysterious beginnings of adults who are to grow up to do great things.

For Professor Davidson, whatever elements of legend now cushion the story of the infant Moses they do not detract from the reality of the man Moses or the importance of his

7. Moses found in the bulrushes

achievement. Professor Davidson sees no reason to doubt that Moses was a real person, and Moses is associated forever in Hebrew tradition with the story of the exodus from Egypt and the giving of the law on Mount Sinai. That is the event that is as central to the faith of the Old Testament as the cross and the resurrection are to the New. If you asked a Hebrew to define God, he would probably say, 'Simple – he is the God who brought us out of Egypt, out of enslavement.' The exodus is the crucial event to which people look back, and in a sense they believe that in every generation they live through the exodus in their own experience.

The name Moses is usually connected with the Hebrew verb to 'draw out' – a suitable name for a Hebrew child drawn out of the water – but if you make that connection you fall again into the trap of looking at the story through Israelite eyes. The word Moses is also the most common ending of Egyptian names, meaning 'is born'. Usually it is added to the name of a god. Thus we have Thuthmosis, 'Thut is born', or Rameses, 'Ra is born'. Now why should anyone have half an Egyptian name? It is an oddity that would fit in with the story of a Hebrew child adopted and brought up as an Egyptian who, as an adult, rejects the Egyptian gods and chooses to follow a god beyond name.

For Rabbi Neuberger the adoption story identifies Moses as a marked man. What is particularly significant, she says, is the way Moses is adopted by Pharaoh's daughter. Strictly speaking Moses should not have survived. According to Pharaoh's edict, all male Hebrew babies were to be thrown into the Nile. Moses is found by Pharaoh's daughter going down to the river with her maidservants. It would have been an open place. It would not have been easy to hide a baby in the bulrushes. The Princess goes down and finds the baby and says, 'Ah, what a lovely baby.' Now two minutes' thought would have suggested to her, 'This must be a Hebrew child. I ought to throw it in the river.' But instead the child is adopted. That is very much a case of somebody being set up for some particular task.

But after such a flying start the Moses stories take a curious turn. The stock hero of the infancy legends is replaced by an uncertain and human leader. Moses kills an Egyptian he sees mistreating a Hebrew and then flees in terror for fear of Pharaoh's anger. In the wilderness he hears the voice of God speaking to him from a burning bush, urging him to return to Egypt to lead the Israelites to freedom. It is an offer he tries to refuse.

For Professor Davidson this reluctance is important. In the book of Exodus the interesting thing about Moses is that he trots out excuse after excuse for not doing what God wants him to do. 'I can't go to the people. I don't know how to speak. Are they going to believe me if I go? What's going to happen?' One by one God counters the excuses and says, 'I understand, but you've still got to go.'

There are those who would make Moses the world's first political idealist, fighting for the material welfare of his people. For Archbishop Desmond Tutu he was more. He was a man who put the spiritual in the centre of his life, and yet he did not make this an excuse for turning away from involvement in life's harsh realities. The Archbishop is particularly attracted to him because of his commitment to justice. Two stories are told of Moses which are important indicators: first his defence of the mistreated Hebrew, and secondly at the well when he takes the part of the daughters of his future father-in-law who are pushed aside by the other shepherds. That is a very attractive attribute.

But Moses did more than react to human injustice. He tried to form a framework by which the justice of God could be proclaimed. In terms of religious ideas he came up with an understanding of God which is sophisticated even today.

Professor John Sawyer of Newcastle says that we can really talk about Moses as a historical figure and a religious pioneer. In the book of Exodus there is a convincing and astonishing story which presents a new dimension in the history of religion. The ban on images, for example, is a quite remarkable new idea. The sabbath is another – with no parallel outside the Mosaic tradition.

However important Moses' insights into God, they are not what he is remembered for. Moses may have devised a unique religious calendar and a tortuous code of laws, but these cannot compete with the drama of the escape from Egypt, with its catalogue of disasters. The Nile is turned to blood, the land is overrun by frogs, gnats, sand-flies and locusts, the cattle sicken and men are covered with Nile scab, the sky rains hail and fire and then turns black. Are we in the realm of fact or fantasy? If of fact, surely some Egyptian historian must have noticed the troubles which preceded the loss of some Israelite slaves.

Dr John Bimson says this is not the sort of event that we would expect the Egyptians to commemorate. Egyptian inscriptions traditionally record events that will glorify the king in the eyes of posterity, and losing his slave labour force is not going to do that. So we should not expect an Egyptian account of the the flight from Egypt.

By any reckoning, the plagues must have been remarkable. They read, says Dr Bimson, like a severe version of what does happen occasionally in Egypt, or at least did happen before the construction of the modern dams which have completely altered the environment. But they must have been a very severe version if they brought Egypt to its knees in the way we read.

As for what caused the plagues, a whole range of possibilities has been suggested, from very heavy rainfall in Africa having all manner of side-effects in Egypt to more drastic events such as a disintegrating comet passing by at the right time, or even the volcanic eruption on the island of Thera (Santorini) in the Aegean, which supposedly spread a great pall of ash over the whole eastern Mediterranean basin.

*

All these are controversial theories, but there does seem to be good evidence that Israel escaped from Egypt in the midst of a widespread natural upheaval, whatever its cause. At the crossing of the Red Sea something remarkable clearly happened to allow the Israelites across and to prevent the Egyptians following them. Various scholars have pointed to parallels in modern volcanic and seismic activity, where the sea has been drawn back drastically and suddenly returned with catastrophic effect. Some earthquake activity may well have been involved in that incident.

Several periods of volcanic and seismic activity are recorded in the ancient Near East. The eruption of Thera which cloaked the Cretan palace of Knossos with dust indicates that there was a period of considerable instability in the first half of the 15th century BC – and this fits in with the Bible's own dating, as Dr Ben Isserlin explains.

In the first book of Kings it is stated that the dedication of Solomon's Temple happened 480 years after the exodus. That would mean a date somewhere near 1440. There is similar testimony in Judges 11, where we are perhaps in the 12th century and are told that the Israelites had been in Trans-Jordan some 300 years.

In the last two decades or so more research has been done at Thera. The explosion in 1500 BC or thereabouts would account for the cloud and darkness – volcanic clouds of this dimension would spread very far – and such phenomena as insect plagues are known to have occurred in connection with other volcanic eruptions.

But there is a fly – or rather there are two flies – in the historical ointment. A 15th-century date for the exodus is rejected by many scholars because of two cities, Pithom and Ra-amses, built according to the Bible by Israelite slave labour. As Dr Bimson explains, the name of the second city, Ra-amses, obviously echoes the name Rameses, the name of the Pharaoh. Rameses II did have a city built in the eastern delta of Egypt, and so the usual view is to link the building work done by the Israelites with the building of that city for Rameses II, who reigned from 1290 to 1224 BC. So if the Israelites really did work on the city of Piramases, the name of the city in Egyptian texts, the exodus cannot have occurred before the 13th century, or they would not have been there to do it.

So part of Exodus suggests the 15th century and part the 13th century. Is there any way of making sense of the confusion? Dr Bimson believes there is. He thinks the simple solution is that the writer is using that name retrospectively. He is talking about the city and giving it the name it had in his own day, not the name it had when the Israelites built there. It would be as if a modern historian said that the Romans built York. He would be using the modern name instead of the name Eboracum which it bore when the Romans actually built it. There is evidence that the writer would work in this way at Genesis 47:11, where the name Rameses is used to describe the area in which the Israelites first settled. No one would seriously suggest that they settled in Egypt as late as the reign of Rameses II, or even Rameses I, who preceded him by only a decade or so. We can be quite certain that he is using the name retrospectively there – so why not also Exodus 1:11?

Recently it has been suggested that the parting of the seas was caused by a tsunami, or tidal wave – an idea that Dr Isserlin discounts. The exodus story is quite clear as to what happened. At Exodus 14 it says that there was a strong east wind which dried out the waters. The Israelites could walk across on dry land, and the waters were like walls for them to the right and to the left. This does not sound like a great wave coming along at speed and engulfing anybody who happens to be in its way. The Israelites would have been perfectly capable of describing that, but they describe a scene which is very different.

Dr Isserlin believes that the sea the Israelites crossed was not the Red Sea but a sea of papyrus reeds – possibly an area of shallows north of the gulf of Suez, now, in post-canal days, filled in with water. That would explain the Israelites' safe passage – but what about the drowning of the Pharaoh's troops? Dr Isserlin thinks there may be a clue in the writing of ancient geographer Strabo.

Strabo talks about the Lebanese coast and coasts south of

8. Moses drowns the Egyptians in the Red Sea

it, and he notices that once at the time of a battle the sea submerged some fugitives. Some bodies were carried off into the sea, while others were left for dead on the strand. Then the wave covered the shore again and disclosed yet more bodies of the men lying among dead fish. Now, Strabo goes on, similar occurrences take place in the neighbourhood of Mount Cassius, situated to the west of a coast lagoon betwcen Gaza and the Nile mouth, and many have thought that this is the place of the miraculous rescue at sea.

The spate of natural phenomena did not stop with the crossing of the sea. The Israelites' wandering through the wilderness towards Sinai, sustained by low-flying quail and the sticky secretion of plant lice, was punctuated by outbreaks of fire, by the ground swallowing up people, and by landslides. Some believe that the pillar of cloud and flame leading the Israelites is further proof of volcanic activity, and others say it is a memory of the custom of Bedouin travellers of carrying lighted braziers in front of the column. The volcanic theory would place the wandering in northern Arabia, as opposed to the more traditionally espoused Sinai peninsula. The most important fixed point is Mount Sinai, where Moses fell into conversation with God and received the law. But where was Mount Sinai? In Sinai? Not necessarily.

According to Dr Isserlin, the tradition that Mount Sinai is in the Sinai peninsula is only attested early in the Christian era, though it may be older. If you link the Sinai story with a volcano, it does not fit, because Sinai is a non-volcanic neighbourhood. If you wish to take a volcanic neighbourhood, that is to say northern Hejaz, the region of ancient Midian, you do have other evidence.

In 1908 an Austrian scholar, Alois Mussel, one of the explorers of Northern Midian, was shown by his local guide a volcano, Mount Badrah, which according to the guide was linked with the story of Moses. There were twelve standing pillars there and an altar, and also some caves, but he was not allowed to go there because it was holy ground. It is still unexplored.

Whatever the map reference and the meteorological and geological commentaries, Professor Sawyer of Newcastle thinks they can distract us from the main purpose of the writer of Exodus. His intention is to say not simply that the Israelites escaped out of Egypt, but that God took them out of Egypt. There were miracles involved. He wants to say that it was divine intervention that led to the escape, to the liberation of the Hebrew slaves from Egypt. The events are all accompanied by miracles, and all the stories are an integral part of the account of the beginnings of this new religion. One of the problems in Biblical scholarship is that we have have been so preoccupied with working out what actually happened and discounting the miracles that we have ignored 95 per cent of the story as told in the text. In recent years scholars have come back to looking at the text again and they see now that this is an amazing story of how a new religion evolves.

*

But does it matter if the story never happened? Professor Moltmann thinks it does, because the Judaeo-Christian faith is one that is firmly historical. That is to say, we believe that our God is one who does not deal nebulously but with hard, rude historical fact, and it would matter if the story never happened because this would be to deny an important truth that our God is one who has used human history as the arena of his revelation. Our God was underlining that human history is significant.

Above all Professor Moltmann believes that this God is a God who liberates oppressed people. He is not the idol of the powerful but the power of the powerless. This is important. It is the same God who reveals himself in and through the powerless and crucified Christ by his resurrection, and whoever becomes a Christian has the same impression that this God takes him up when he is down.

The exodus story of the Old Testament was later transferred into Christian history, the history of the death of Christ and of his resurrection and liberation from death into the glory of God, and then into the theory of the church as a church of the exodus of men and women out of their nations to form a new people of God. Finally it was translated into political terms. The Pilgrim Fathers, searching for the New World in America, used it as their own story.

The next bearers were the slaves in the United States of America who used it in the negro spirituals as their own story of liberation from slavery. The most recent development is the liberation theology of the Third World. The story is there as a model, a paradigm, for the liberation from oppression. God is on the side of the oppressed. This is how the story works. It is translated and transferred into the experiences and expectations of one people after another.

Dr Christopher Rowland, Dean of Jesus College, Cambridge, disagrees. He thinks it does not matter in the end whether or not the story is true. As far as the poor who are reading the Bible in Latin America are concerned, their primary question is not Did this actually happen? They simply take the story, listen to it, discuss it and relate it to their lives and their desire for social justice and liberation. It is the story itself which acts as the catalyst within the whole ferment for their struggle for social change. It is important to remember that when we look at the situation in many Third World countries we are talking about people who are oppressed and very poor indeed. They find that when they read certain parts of the Bible it speaks to them in a more direct way than it may speak to us. This is particularly true of the exodus.

For Archbishop Tutu the historicity of the book of Exodus and its message today are inextricable. The book demonstrates the fact that God's intentions cannot be frustrated ultimately. God was determined to deliver the Israelites, and that is what happened:

> Our God, the God of the exodus, is not a neutral God but one who takes sides. The story of the exodus is a story which says that we have a God who always takes the initiative. He took the side of a rabble of slaves long before they could have done anything to deserve it, and therefore it is one-in-the-eye for the achievement-ethic of modern society. It is a story that shows that dichotomies between the secular and the sacred, the holy and the profane, are unbiblical. Our God was concerned for the liberation of people politically, but he was also concerned for their wholeness.

4. The Path to Kingship

Exodus 25:8 – 27:8
Deuteronomy 31 – 34:12
Joshua 1 – 8:35; 10:40 – 43; 23 – 24:31
Judges
1 & 2 Samuel
1 Kings 1 – 1 Kings 2:12

There is a barren mountain range called Abarim in what is now Jordan. It lies north of the Dead Sea and east of the city of Jericho. From its modest summits it is possible to command a view over what was once the ancient land of Canaan. There, according to Biblical tradition, within sight of but not within the Promised Land, Moses the law-giver, the greatest of the Hebrew prophets, died and alone of all men was buried by the hand of God somewhere in the valley of Beth Peor in a place hidden from human eyes.

The story of the death and burial of Moses signals his unique position in the Jewish journey of faith. He had freed the Israelites from slavery by opening their eyes to the only kingship which mattered, the kingship of God. He had lead them from the certainty of oppression to the hazards of freedom in the desert. He had taught them to prefer the jealousy of the one God to the less predictable tyranny of one man.

But with the death of Moses, the Bible is about to make one of its most startling U-turns. Unlikely as it may seem, the unmarked grave of Moses the king-breaker is the beginning of the royal road to Jerusalem, a path to kingship winding through the books of Joshua, Judges, Samuel and the first book of Kings.

The idea of kingship was to be adopted by the Israelites and so taken for granted that a thousand years later Koheleth, a worldly-wise descendant of that dust-hardened rabble of freed slaves, could write the following observation on the value of monarchy from the comfort of a life softened by the gardens and the concubines of Jerusalem:

51

> If you see in a province the poor oppressed and justice and right
> violently taken away, do not be amazed at the matter; for the high
> official is watched by a higher, and there are yet higher ones over
> them. But in all, a king is an advantage to a land with cultivated
> fields.
>
> Ecclesiastes 5:8-9

What lies behind Koheleth's throw-away line, 'in all an advantage', apparently accepting and approving the concept of kingship with its foreign shadows, and its taint of pagan belief, is a very human story of conflict and compromise, a story of social evolution and of wanderers finding a home.

*

With the death of Moses, we are still in the ancient world, just approaching 1000 BC, but the problems being faced are not unfamiliar in the modern world. There is political squabbling. There are battles for good land. There is tension between town and country, between national loyalty and tribal duties, between north and south, even between rival technologies. There is the age-old clash between idealism and pragmatism.

The path to kingship is walked by people of all types. Saul, the first king who fails and falls with black despair, is not all bad, and David, the golden shepherd king, is not all good. We meet the mad and the bad, heroes and harlots, necromancers and prophets. But before any dreams of kingship could be conceived or achieved, the Israelites, now under the leadership of Joshua, the successor of Moses, had to face a practical difficulty in the promise of a land of milk and honey: the land was already inhabited.

How was it possible for a group of invaders with no lines of supply or fortifications to conquer the Canaanites?

Dr Andrew Mayes of Trinity College, Dublin, thinks the Israelites were probably in the right place at the right time. He says we should think of a Joshua-led group entering a land which consisted of a heterogeneous number of people, some of whom had come out of Egypt in the exodus. These people seem to have served as a catalyst for a movement that already existed in Palestine at the time. Power in Canaan was being transferred from the city-state system to a rural tribal element. Joshua and his group acted as a focus for this movement, and around him the Israel that we know of and that we read of in the Bible eventually crystallised.

In other words we should think of a process of gradual infiltration, fitting in with what was already happening anyway, rather than of a dramatic conquest. The walls of Jericho had crumbled long before Joshua entered the city aided and abetted by Rahab the harlot. The Israelites arrived at a time of weakness and pressed home their advantage. The reports of military success are exaggerated – a normal practice among the victorious even today.

But there was another factor in Joshua's success which is only hinted at in the account of the great tribal gathering at a place called Shechem, rich in patriarchal memories, near the grave of Joseph and Jacob's well.

> But Joshua said to the people, 'You cannot serve the Lord; for he is a holy God; he is a jealous God; he will not forgive your transgressions or your sins. If you forsake the Lord and serve foreign gods, then he will turn and do you harm, and consume you, after having done you good.' And the people said to Joshua, 'Nay, but we will serve the Lord.' Then Joshua said to the people. 'You are witnesses against yourselves that you have chosen the Lord, to serve him.' And they said, 'We are witnesses.' He said, 'Then put away the foreign gods which are among you, and incline your heart to the Lord, the God of Israel.' And the people said to Joshua, 'The Lord our God we will serve, and his voice we will obey.' So Joshua made a covenant with the people that day, and made statutes and ordinances for them at Shechem.
>
> Joshua 24:19-25

Those words are more than a renewal of the covenant vows of a wandering people. Remember, not all the Israelites went down into Egypt. The area round Shechem in central Canaan seems to have needed little conquest. The Israelites under Joshua may have met and merged with people with whom they shared common ancestors – people who accepted the exodus story as their own and were now required to set aside the Canaanite gods they had learned to live with.

The god Baal, his consorts the Ashtarts, and his sadistic sister Anat, worshipped by Canaanite city-dwellers, represented more than a simple fertility cult. They sanctioned a way of life that was anathema to the wandering tribes of Israel. It was as much a matter of social organisation as of religion.

According to Dr Mayes, Baal seems to have been associated primarily with the city-state society. Baal was chief god in a religious system which acted as a validation of a city-state system of rule – a system which was strongly class-divided, with a ruling class and a subject population: a system structured like a pyramid, with a king at the top and a lower-taxed class at the bottom. In this structure, the religion of Canaan functioned as a validating form, a validating system of beliefs, and here Baal was strongly rooted. In so far as Israelite society was antagonistic towards this sort of social structure, the form of worship practised by it would have been antagonistic to the form of worship practised by city-state society. There would have been considerable antagonism between the God of Israel and Baal.

As the Israelites began the slow work of securing the central hill country of Canaan they evolved a loosely-structured system of government based on local trouble-shooting and on a few strong characters, referred to as 'judges', a misleading title according to Rabbi Neuberger. According to her there is precious little evidence to suggest that the judges ever did any judging, or at least they did not do very much. They did some sorting out of disputes between one tribe and another, or between one part of a tribe and another, but they were not judges in the modern sense, or even in the later sense of judges who sat in a city gate and pronounced judgment when a case was brought. They were leaders in battle, and they were formidable. You would not have wanted to meet a judge on a dark night, Rabbi Neuberger believes.

According to the book of Judges, Israel fell into a cycle of crisis management. Periods of peace and security would give way to complacency about the covenant with God. Sin would be punished by defeat at the hands of foreign enemies, and only the intervention of a judge would restore stability.

Is it really feasible that any group of people would choose to survive by such an inept form of government? Dr Mayes thinks the system presupposes a tribal type of society – which has analogies outside Israel, particularly among African tribal groups. Typical of such societies is that there is no central system of government, no permanent system of rule. Power and rule are decentralised, and lie in the hands of tribal or clan leaders rather than individual leaders of the people as a whole. It is only in situations of emergency that a common form of leadership finds wide acceptance, and it is this temporary leadership that we refer to as charismatic leadership. It is to that system, to that framework, that

9. Jael greets the Israelites after killing Sisera

individuals like Deborah and Samson and Gideon and
Jephtha belong.

There is a famous song of Deborah, the judge and
prophetess, rejoicing in the bloody death of Sisera, whose
head was shattered by a tent peg driven home by Jael, the
Kenite woman (Judges 5:1-31). These were not gentle times.
Deborah overshadows the judges who preceded her – Othniel,
the left-handed Ehud and Shamgar who killed 600 Philistines
with an ox-goad. How did a woman come to be directing the
military forces of Israel? What was it that marked out
Deborah? Rabbi Neuberger thinks she was very different,
perhaps even freakish. Some argue that both the women
judges and the prophetesses were slightly touched, slightly
odd. There is a reflexive verb in Hebrew which comes from the
same root as the word prophet and means to 'work youself up
into a frenzy'. We may imagine that both the female judges
and the prophetesses had a technique of winding themselves
up into a kind of frenzy, shown in the magnificent Hebrew of
the song of Deborah. One thing is certain: Deborah must have

been extraordinary. None of her predecessors seems to have had quite that status.

To some extent Deborah overshadows her successors too. The judge Gideon is remembered less for training a crack troop of 300 soldiers than for the Bibles which bear his name today in hotels throughout the world. And Samson the Nazarite, notorious for an unwanted haircut and his weakness for Philistine women, is remembered as pathetic proof of the powerlessness of brute strength: he dies after breaking every part of his Nazarite vow, a blind slave providing comic relief for the Philistines celebrating the feast of Dagon, the god of grain.

So why is Samson included in the lists of judges? He has been described as a bawdy villain, and Dr Mayes thinks that that may be a good way to take him. He is a very earthy figure. The inclusion of a story such as that of Samson and the Philistines serves to remind us that in general the Old Testament is about the life of historical individuals who were no heroes, in any sense of the term, but men of whom God made use.

But for all their outward simplicity the failures and successes of Israel and the judges document a complex transition. Under the judges, the wandering people began to settle. They rejected the religion of their Canaanite neighbours but were influenced by Canaanite city culture. Their rudimentary political system existed only to defend their own faith and identity. The importance of their covenant with their uncompromising God meant that no more centralised form of government was necessary.

*

The days of the judges were numbered, however, regardless of their religious pedigree. History was about to catch up with them. Dom Henry Wansborough, a Benedictine monk and the revising editor of the New Jerusalem Bible, says that for 200 years it was they who kept Israel faithful. They were the successors of Moses in the sense that they received the spirit which Joshua himself received from Moses – the spirit of the Lord – and they guided the people in the way that Moses had guided them. But they were, as it turned out, insufficient, because of the Philistine threat.

This threat was part of a much larger change in life style that revolutionised the whole of the ancient world – Israel's journey of faith was being tested by the cold reality of metal. The bronze age was sliding into the iron age, and the Philistines, the enemies of the Israelites, were leading the way. The fact that we use the word Philistine to imply crass stupidity and bad taste shows the extent of Biblical bias in our language. The Philistines were a cultured, lettered people with a reputation for sharp-wittedness throughout the Mediterranean. They were traders and seafarers, skilled in pottery and glass work, with a monopoly of the prized murex purple dye. Above all they knew how to smelt iron, and the Israelites did not. The Israelites were powerless under the onslaught of the new Philistine weapons. Charisma would not cut through iron. Drastic action was needed.

Samuel, the last of the judges, gave in to the people's wishes to become like other nations and anointed Saul, a tall young man from a wealthy family, as Israel's first king. He warned the people about the ways of kings:

> He said, 'These will be the ways of the king who will reign over you: he will take your sons and appoint them to his chariots and to be his horsemen, and to run before his chariots; and he will appoint for himself commanders of thousands and commanders of fifties, and some to plough his ground and to reap his harvest, and to make his implements of war and the equipment of his chariots. He will take your daughters to be perfumers and cooks and bakers. He will take the best of your fields and vineyards and olive orchards and give them to his servants. He will take the tenth of your grain and of your vineyards and give it to his officers and to his servants. He will take your menservants and maidservants and the best of your cattle and your asses, and put them to his work. He will take the tenth of your flocks, and you shall be his slaves. And in that day you will cry out because of your king, whom you have chosen for yourselves; but the Lord will not answer you in that day.'
>
> 1 Samuel 8:11-18

Yet despite the warning the Israelites clamoured for a king. Why? Rabbi Neuberger says that what the king was supposed to do was to unite the tribes. But the king was to come into conflict not only with the judges, but with the early prophets – the Samuel characters, individuals who had immense power – as the seers, leaders and interpreters of God's will to the people. The nature of a king did not imply a close relationship with God. It must have been an enormous political intrigue, setting up kingship, killing off, effectively, the judges and the early prophets. The very nature of rule changed completely. Now there was a system with a single authority.

*

The transition to monarchy was not helped by the choice of the first king. Saul, of the tribe of Benjamin, seems unsure of his own status and his standing with God. When he was chosen he had some charismatic manifestations: he joined the prophets and danced with them in an ecstatic way. But then he sinned and had moods of black depression. Dom Henry Wansborough believes that his sense of failure, perhaps his sense of rejection by the Lord, was so great that he went mad in some way.

The relationship between Saul and Samuel was never happy. After his first victory over the Philistines, Saul began to tread on Samuel's priestly toes. He offered sacrifice at Gilgal without waiting for Samuel to turn up – an acceptable act for any other king, but not for an Israelite king. Worse was to follow. There was a breach between Saul and Samuel. Dr Gwillym Jones, Reader in Biblical Studies in the University of Wales, thinks this was because Saul assumed authority. He saved the Amalachite king, but he took the best of the cattle, when he was not supposed to under these Holy War regulations: they ought to have been destroyed. It was a sign that he was now gathering power into his own hands. From now on he seems to be under a curse and David appears to be coming up and taking attention from him.

In other words, in recognising the brotherhood of kings, Saul is behaving like a secular king. He is rejected by Samuel and goes completely off the rails, trying to kill David, the young court harpist from Bethlehem now favoured by Samuel. Finally, at Endor, broken and mystified, he resorts to the necromancy which he himself has outlawed. He consults the shade of Samuel, who offers no comfort. Next day, defeated by the Philistines, he kills himself – the Israelites' first king and the first recorded Biblical suicide.

In many ways Saul was not a full king. He did not create a hierarchy of officials nor shelter behind the privileges of a court. He did not levy taxes or enforce conscription. But he left behind him a legacy of kingship which we share in the modern world.

By preserving and wrestling with the idea of monarchy the Israelites were to transform it. The problem they had to face was religious. Wherever they looked the principal models of kingship trod dangerously close to blasphemy. To the south and west, Egyptian kings were divine from the moment of conception and, as rulers, were the living incarnation of Ra the sun god. To the north and east, Mesopotamian kings acquired divinity as they ascended the throne. How could the practice of kingship be squared with the jealousy of Israel's God? Dom Henry Wansborough thinks that to a certain extent it is a contradiction of everything the Israelites believed in, because the Lord God was the king of Israel and could have no rival. Samuel is clear that the institution of kingship is against this truth, and there is a stream of anti-monarchist tradition in the books of Samuel and Kings. Israel tried to keep hold of both ends of the rope, to retain some human kingship but also a divine kingship.

Rabbi Neuberger believes that the tensions caused by this rope trick explain the Israelites' constant preoccupation with royal weaknesses. Even Saul's idealised successor, David, lapses. Infatuated by the beauty of Bathsheba, he disposes of her husband Uriah by sending him to the front line, where his death is inevitable. Rabbi Neuberger thinks that kingship is sometimes seen, in early Israelite religion, as being a representation of the divine. The Babylonians saw their kings as incarnations, in a sense, of the divine – of the particular god concerned, of the city concerned. Pharaohs in Egypt were seen in that light, so it is not surprising. The Hebrew Bible, however, tends always to stress the humanity of kings. The only exceptions are David, though he is shown as having one particular human flaw, revealed in the story of Uriah and Bathsheba, and Solomon, who has the divine gift of wisdom. But in general the Hebrew Bible tries to play down the divine role in kingship.

*

Unlike Saul, David was not in search of a role. He had enough human gifts not to worry about a mask of divinity. He had been anointed by Samuel during Saul's lifetime and had survived Saul's attempts on his life. He had used the period of exile from Saul's court to build up contacts with the

Philistines and Judeans, his own tribe. He was anointed of God and a shrewd politician.

But does David seem remarkable merely because his predecessor was off his head and most of his successors were unremarkable? Where does he fit with the great figures of Israel's past? Is he as important as, say, Abraham or Moses? Rabbi Neuberger thinks that, in a sense, he is more important, because in Jewish tradition he is taken as being eventually the ancestor of the Messiah. The word Messiah, in Hebrew 'Meschiach', means the anointed one. It is out of the stock of David that the Messiah is supposed to come. He is a shoot from the stock of Jesse, and Jesse is David's father. David becomes a paradigm of kingship in the Hebrew Bible. Yet what is he? He is not the eldest son of Jesse, but the youngest. What is so special about him? He takes a sling and hurls a stone at Goliath and as a result is considered to be the greatest winner of all. He soothes Saul, who falls into terrible rages. Saul is the first king and, in most ways, a failure. David is held up as the great, the wonderful, the perfect king.

*

David's reputation is as golden as Jerusalem – the city he conquered. By making the old Jebusite city the focal point of the tribes of Israel, David made the dream of a unified nation a reality. Dr Mayes is in no doubt that David was Israel's most significant king. He is an ideal held up by the book of Kings against whom all subsequent kings are measured, and there is every reason for using him in this way. It was he who finally got rid of the Philistine menace for Israel, it was he who finally secured a place for Israel in Palestine. David also founded the first indigenous empire in Palestine – now, for the first time, an independent people and an independent kingdom existed in Palestine. To that extent, David was a most significant figure. He made Jerusalem the capital of Israel. From then on, it was the city of David.

Jerusalem was already neutral, being identified neither with the north nor with the south. David wished to make the city a sign of religious unity, and for that he needed one of the most powerful symbols of the wandering people – the ark of the covenant. What was that? Professor Davidson says it was a fairly small box that could be carried by the people during their wanderings in the wilderness, according to Old Testament traditions. We know that it was carried by the Hebrews into battle with them when they fought against the Philistines in the early days of the settlement in Canaan. There seem to be two theories about what it was in the Old Testament. One regards it simply as a kind of container in which were placed the tablets on which were inscribed the ten words or Ten Commandments, the other as a kind of throne on which God sat invisibly. Closely associated with the ark is God's title in the Old Testament as 'Lord of Hosts' – originally probably a title referring to God as the God of the battlelines of Israel, as the Israelites went into battle against their enemies. The interesting thing is that the ark was obviously regarded as a symbol of God's presence in the midst of his people.

David was overjoyed when the ark was brought into Jerusalem. The second book of Samuel describes him leaping and dancing before it, much to the disgust of his wife Michal. There was a hidden agenda behind his faith. Dr Mayes believes that David, the empire builder, was aiming at more than religious unity. While he made Jerusalem – an old city – the capital of the tribal people of Israel, he brought into that city the ark of God. The ark was an old tribal religious symbol. He had Abiathar as his priest in Jerusalem, and Abiathar was an old tribal priest of Israel. At the same time he had Zadok as priest in Jerusalem, and Zadok, from what we know, or suspect, was in fact a city-state priest rather than a tribal priest. So David seems to have effected a coming-together of cultures and social forms, and also indeed, to a certain extent, of religious forms, in Israel.

David consolidated his hold on the people by taking a census – something which could be used for enforcing taxes, labour and conscription: the black side of kingship, of which Samuel had warned. Israel now had a king like other nations who beautified his city and encourged trade. There remained one essential difference: the king was ruler under God and no more divine than his subjects. This makes the Bible unique in its time. Court historians recorded the humanity and weaknesses of their king in a way that is unprecedented in the ancient world.

In Dom Henry Wansborough's view the fascinating thing about David is that he is the first fully developed character we

10. The ark of the covenant on its way to Jerusalem

know in the whole world. The source we have, the second book of Samuel, chapters 9-20, and the first two chapters of Kings, was probably written at the court of Solomon, David's son. Obviously the writer knew all the characters well, and he writes with sympathy for them. David was completely human, and that is why he is the ideal of the king. When his own son, Absalom, rebels, David is extraordinarily weak. He retreats before Absalom, while retaining the most wonderful affection for him. When Absalom is killed, David mourns, saying, 'O my son Absalom, my son, my son, Absalom! Would I had died instead of you, O Absalom, my son, my son!' The army chiefs are appalled and grossly offended because David has given the impression that Absalom is all that matters and that the salvation of Israel, and their work as faithful followers of David, are unimportant.

So David's humanity is in no doubt. He is also a canny politician, and applies a double standard. If a murder suits his ends he merely wrings his hands and says 'How terrible', but if it doesn't he takes revenge. When Saul's son, the king in the north, is murdered, David takes a strong line because he wants to make it clear that kings are not to be murdered. On the other hand, when his own commander-in-chief murders the commander-in-chief of the northern kingdom, he merely says that it must never happen again.

David reaped all the success and failure of kingship. He died in weakness and old age with all the broken promises and domestic tragedy which surround human kingship. But even the unidealised memory of the ideal king would cast a long shadow. No one would ever live up to David's golden kingship. His descendants would break faith with their God and the kingdom would be split. But the story of kingship in the Bible is important, because its writers had a purpose which other royal chroniclers do not have. Dr Jones says that they wanted a tight correspondence between the life and behaviour of the king and their theory of retribution. If the king was really bad, he had to be punished; if he was good, he had to be rewarded. Sometimes it did not work out that way. In the case of Manasseh, for instance, who was really bad, and had a long reign, they could not fit the two together, so they devised an act of repentance. Again, Uzziah was a leper. But he was a good king, so they invented an act of sacrilege. This is presented as history. But it is history with an undeniable aim.

Even the feeble kings contributed to the aim of that history, which was destined to turn full-circle, pointing to another king who, like David, would be born in Bethlehem and who would die in Jerusalem. As Dr R. P. Gordon of Cambridge explains, they contributed to the ideal, despite themselves. In failing, a king caused people to think, 'Well, if God is at work with his people, if this ancient promise of an enduring dynasty has anything to it, there must be something beyond the present experience, there must be something better.' And so we find a decline in performance of the Judean kings, and at the same time an expectation that someone quite different will come. One prophet talks of someone coming from Bethlehem, as if to say, 'We shall have to go back to the beginning, back to the drawing-board.' Isaiah of Jerusalem talks in a similar vein of a shoot coming out of the stump of Jesse. That is really saying, 'What we know, what we have experienced, has not worked well, but we are not abandoning the hope. We're going back and starting again.' That is why

Jesus, whose kingdom was larger than political dreams, represents both discontinuity and continuity from the Hebrew ideal of kingship.

5. A Tent Made of Gold

1 Kings 6 – 9:9
Psalms 1 – 118; 120 – 136; 138 – 150

'Is there anybody there?' asks the satellite, beaming its coded message into the still darkness of space in the hope of making contact with an intelligence beyond our small world. This is not the stuff of science fiction – it is part of an American space programme undertaken by scientists with a background of stolid materialism. It is testimony to the lure of the infinite and to the impossibilty of believing that earthbound man is king of a universe he cannot understand.

So far the satellite message has not been answered – but it is only the last, and one of the more naive, of man's attempts to talk to a greatness which lies beyond him. The Bible story of the journey of the children of Israel would have faded long ago if it was only the account of how a group of nomad pastoralists wandered from Mesopotamia and finally settled in the country they believed was promised to them.

The reason the Bible story of fidelity and frailty, of disaster and hope, has lasted is that it claims to offer something that no philosophy or science has ever aspired to: proof of God's existence and of a belief stronger than reason that he wants to communicate with man. Running through the Bible is a further conviction that man can choose to talk to God. But is that an expression of man's ultimate duty, or evidence of his consummate arrogance? We have followed the Israelites on the bumpy road to kingship, and now in the first book of Kings we are on the threshold of Solomon's greatest glory – the tent made of gold, the temple of the unseen God which even David dared not build. The story of the Temple is one of the most extraordinary stories in the Bible, and it has lasted until today. The walls of the Temple may have crumbled, but its songs, found in the book of Psalms, are sung in every hour of every day in every continent.

In the ancient world there are many larger, older, more

beautiful temples, but only Solomon's Temple to the unseen God is remembered as *the* Temple. The children of Israel were scathing about other temples. Even Habakkuk, a little-known and permanently puzzled prophet who could not understand why God let the just suffer, was certain at least that, in their Temple, the Israelites were as right as everyone else was wrong. Three hundred years after the completion of Solomon's Temple, he wrote:

> What profit is an idol when its maker has shaped it, a metal image, a teacher of lies? For the workman trusts in his own creation when he makes dumb idols! Woe to him who says to a wooden thing, Awake; to a dumb stone, Arise! Can this give revelation? Behold, it is overlaid with gold and silver, and there is no breath at all in it. But the Lord is in his holy temple; let all the earth keep silence before him.
>
> Habakkuk 2:18-20

But that certainty had been hard won. The Temple grew out of a tradition of a God who had spoken to his people in time of crisis in a way that inspired fear as well as faith – through the thunder, lightning, smoke and noise of Mount Sinai, through the burning bush in the wilderness of Midian, through Joseph's dangerous dreams and a voice forbidding the sacrifice of Isaac on Mount Moriah. Only in the image of paradise, the garden of Eden before the Fall, does God walk in the cool of the evening to talk to men. The Temple could build on the tradition of the power of holy places and also on the belief that contact could be made with God by sacrifice.

*

But does not the idea of sacrifice belittle God? Professor Davidson says that it seems so to us because we are living in the twentieth century, in western culture: but it would not seem so to anyone living in the ancient world, especially in the ancient Near East. Sacrifice then was as much a part of ordinary religious life as prayer is today. It was simply a means whereby people approached and worshipped God in ancient Israel, whereby they expressed thanksgiving or confession or the desire for communion. It was simply a means to an end. We tend to talk about sacrifice as if it meant one thing, but there were many kinds of sacrifice. Just as when we refer to prayer we should ask whether we are talking

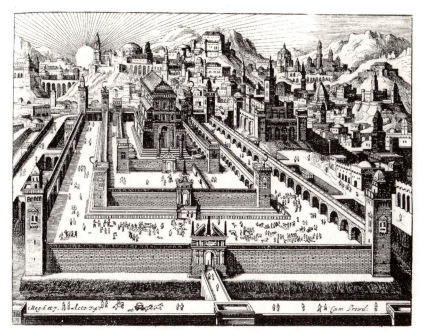

11. Solomon's Temple

about prayers of thanksgiving, or of adoration or of confession or of intercession, so there was a whole variety of different sacrifices, all designed to answer certain specific needs, and the rituals involved in them were very different.

The idea of sacrifice as a means of contacting the divine can still be found in many faiths and cultures. In the ancient world of the Near East, it was widespread. It could give believers a hold over otherwise capricious gods, and the unburnt offerings could feed priests and temple staff. Sacrifice combined elements of bribery, mysticism, magic and a comprehensive insurance policy for the renewal of favourable farming conditions.

But is sacrifice as described in meticulous detail in the Bible anything more than the adaptation of neighbouring religious practices? Was there anything distinctive about the sacrifices of the Israelites? Professor Lambert thinks there was. He says that if you look in other countries, although the word sacrifice may appear in texts, the idea itself is often absent. It is peculiarly Israelite. The word covers several quite different ideas. First of all: sacrifice as a gift. Nowadays, we pay it monthly, or weekly, in taxes. In the ancient world, they gave the ruler a gift. Most people were food producers, and since money in our sense of the word hardly existed they therefore gave in kind, in the food they produced, and since meat was a luxury and rulers expected luxuries, it was quite usual to offer fattened animals. But there was also sacrifice in a quite different sense, what we might call communion. People assembled in religious places and ate meals together. This was not just a matter of social life, though that was part of it. It was a means of joining together in a cultic performance. That is a second idea of sacrifice. Then there is the third idea, as providing expiation of sin, and although we find it in other nations it is not as conspicuous as in Israel. So, by emphasising the idea of sacrifice as a means of making amends for sin, the Israelites made the practice of sacrifice distinctively their own. But how could a temple be similarly distinctive? There were many temple models, all of them pagan. This provided Solomon with a dual problem – part challenge and part threat. His God was the true God, so his Temple would have to outshine all other temples, but the very existence of those others brought with it the risk of infection. The transition to temple worship was cautious. David's enthusiasm to build a house of cedar had been smothered by the prophet Nathan's word from God:

> Go and tell my servant David, 'Thus says the Lord: Would you build me a house to dwell in? I have not dwelt in a house since the day I brought up the people of Israel from Egypt to this day, but I have been moving about in a tent for my dwelling. In all places where I have moved with all the people of Israel, did I speak a word with any of the judges of Israel, whom I commanded to shepherd my people Israel, saying, "Why have you not built me a house of cedar?" ' Now therefore, thus shall you say to my servant David... 'When your days are fulfilled and you lie down with your fathers, I will raise up your offspring after you, who shall come forth from your body, and I will establish his kingdom. He shall build a house for my name, and I will establish the throne of his kingdom forever.'
>
> 2 Samuel 7:5-8, 12-13

Traditionally, it has been implied that the privilege of building the Temple was withheld from David because of his sin with Bathsheba, but Professor Davidson thinks that the real story is not so simple. There were other reasons behind it. There was real resistance within Israel to the whole concept of any kind of fixed building: there was a tension between the old

12. David on the roof sees Bathsheba bathing

nomadic ideal, when people were wandering in the wilderness and had no fixed abode, and the urbanisation and settlement in Canaan. And just as there were forces that were against the advent of kingship as a permanent institution in Israel, so there were forces against the concept of a permanent fixed abode for God.

Whatever the reservations about the appropriateness of the Temple for the God of Israel, Solomon began building operations in the month of Ziv – that is, late spring – in the year 961, using Phoenician expertise and a levy of forced labour. And however new his ideas, his choice of site shows that he was at least wise enough to embed his Temple in the rock of tradition. According to the Chief Rabbi, Sir Immanuel Jacobovits, the Temple was founded on one of the earliest dreams of the Bible. It goes back to Jewish tradition, to Jacob's dream of a ladder linking heaven and earth. When he awoke from that dream, he said, 'Surely this is nothing but the house of God.' That is the first time in recorded literature that the words 'house of God' are used. Jewish tradition has it that on that site, on which he had the dream, Mount Moriah, the Temple was eventually built in what was to become Jerusalem.

*

Solomon was an efficient but imperfect king. Though the third king of Israel, he was the first to be born into a royal family. He had a high idea of his own importance. While some workmen were concentrating on the Temple, others were working on a larger building, a palace for the king. Does not that cut God down to human, albeit royal, size? And how is it possible to make sense of God the creator needing to be housed by one of his creatures?

The idea, says Sir Immanuel, was not that God needed a residence, but that he was to be found only at a certain address in the capital of what became the first Jewish commonwealth. Solomon, in inaugurating the Temple, had already asked the question in the minds of all of us to this day: if the heaven of heavens cannot contain God, how can this house, which I have built him? Perhaps the best way in modern terms to understand the notion of Temple worship in Jewish thought is to compare it to a radio receiver. The waves of radio transmissions are present throughout the universe, only we do not hear them, because our ears are of flesh and blood and cannot register radio waves. We need instruments that translate radio waves into sound waves audible to the human ear: radio receivers. The Temple was a kind of receiver, translating the omnipresence of God, the universality of God, which is purely abstract and purely spiritual, into terms that could register on the worshipper.

Jews pray every day in the old city of Jerusalem at the western wall, the only part of the Temple left. But even those stones, with their crevices crammed with thin scraps of paper containing prayers of the faithful, are not Solomon's stones. Solomon's Temple was destined to be completely destroyed. It was rebuilt on a smaller scale and finally embellished by Herod the Great in 20 BC, before its final destruction in AD 70. But the books of Chronicles and Kings are so detailed in their description of the Temple that we know as much about it as about any other ancient religious building.

It was built on a Phoenician pattern with a huge courtyard

enclosing an altar for burnt offerings. The entrance to the temple was up a flight of ten steps. The huge doors of cypress were flanked by two bronze pillars, Joachim and Boaz. Another pair of doors enclosed the ornate sanctuary room with its sacred vessels and golden candelabra, its small altar decorated with gold leaf, and its table for the 'shew bread' – a symbol of the twelve tribes of Israel. Beyond this, another series of stairs led to the Holy of Holies, a windowless room lined with cedar. In Solomon's time this was where the ark of the covenant was kept, the old tribal symbol of God's presence. In later years the ark was lost.

The emptiness of the Temple would intrigue and mystify Gentiles, as Professor Davidson explains. The Roman general Pompey was totally astonished when he walked into the Temple in 63 BC to find an empty room in the Holy of Holies. That was one of the reasons why the story went round in the Greek world in early times that the Jews were simply atheists in disguise: because if you went down the street and asked a Greek to show you his gods he could take you to a statue of Athene, or Dionysus, and say, 'That's it.' But if you asked a Jew who his God was, where his God lived, he couldn't show you anything.

Historians recognise that the Temple grew into a unique focus of national unity. But for Sir Immanuel Jacobovitz that is only part of the story – it was an attempt to express the inexpressible: to bring home to man, remote from the perception of God and unable to feel him in the street or in the field, that there was one place where he could identify with his Creator. From there he could take God into his home, and into the rest of his experience on earth. But there was need for a concentrated form of godliness in order to make God into something more than a purely philosophical abstraction. That was the purpose the Temple served, and that is why it had such an immense impact on the religious as well as the national feelings of the people of Israel. The entire population of the country converged on Jerusalem three times a year for the three pilgrim festivals to participate in a single mighty act of worship. This must have made a tremendous impression on those who partook in such a mass demonstration of religion and spirituality.

*

As the people of Israel converged on Jerusalem they sang songs which survive today in the book of Psalms – the most frequently recited book in the Bible. The psalms are an extraordinary collection of 150 prayer-poems covering every human emotion from joy to mindless rage. In the psalms the whole world is alive – the hills clap their hands, and even the city gates lift up their doors in welcome. The language is simple and strong. For Cardinal Hume, Archbishop of Westminster and former Benedictine abbot, they are fixed in history and yet can move beyond history. They are Old Testament poetry expressing in a marvellous manner the relationship between God and Israel. Through the psalms the people of Israel were able to express their praise of God, especially for his intervention in their history.

> Praise him with trumpet sound; praise him with lute and harp! Praise him with timbrel and dance; praise him with strings and pipe! Praise him with sounding cymbals; praise him with loud clashing cymbals!
>
> Psalms 150:3-5

The liveliness of the words of the psalms contrasted with the more sombre religious music of other cultures. Though the psalms are often now recited, they were written to be sung. In the ancient world religion and music were inextricable. John Eaton, Reader in Old Testament Studies at Birmingham, says that we have to think of skilled musicians working in the service of the temples with skilled poets. They produced these poems together and they were sung to the accompaniment of the lyre and other instruments. This was the main medium of communication with the deity. They put their prayers in this form, and they received answers from him also in poetry. It was all sung together with praise and lament, a tradition going back to the most ancient time, long before Israel. We have psalms from the Babylonians, which are often similar in type but on the whole not as thrilling as those in our Psalter, though here and there there are some very fine pieces. There is a beautiful psalm from the wall of an Egyptian tomb, of the great Pharaoh Akhnaton, praising the deity he sees in the sun, which dates from before the time of Moses.

There was a strong musical tradition in Jerusalem even before the Temple was built, and much was inherited from the Canaanites who owned Jerusalem before it was captured by David. In David's time there was a great impetus, and

Solomon who followed him and built the Temple made it even more expressive of the place believed to be God's ruling presence in the world. The classical period of psalmody was the time of David and Solomon and that age probably produced some of the greatest pieces.

According to tradition Solomon wrote two of the psalms, and David is credited with 73. Is this true? Professor Davidson doubts it. David, he says, had a reputation as a musician. Witness some of the stories in the book of Samuel. It was therefore fairly natural that psalms should be attributed to David, just as all laws were attributed to Moses and the whole wisdom tradition to Solomon. But we do not really know how many psalms David composed, if any. Indeed the title 'to David', or 'concerning David', could simply be a way of indicating that it is a royal psalm, associated in some way with the monarchy.

Translating the psalms has not been easy. The writers are fond of repetition and not too bothered about tenses, and naturally the images are drawn from their world, not ours. The oil which flows down Aaron's beard in Psalm 133 is supposed to trigger images of fragrance and honour, not the messy black gold of Dallas or the North Sea. Peter Levi, Professor of Poetry at Oxford and a former Jesuit, who translated the psalms for Penguin, found that they contained many surprises. There was, he says, much more word play than he realised, most of which he found untranslatable, many puns, a great deal of alliteration, even a few jokes. He thought that the Psalms were probably much stronger if you took them literally. There are many places where they have been cleaned up by scholars, and even by their translators, usually wrongly. The most important thing is to aim for a clear, straightforward version.

Some translators have been more ambitious. One transatlantic version of Psalm 23 offers: 'The Lord is my probation officer, he helps me play it cool.' Why is that ridiculous, when the more literal version with the speaker playing the part of a sheep is not? Why does the ancient shepherd psalm still make sense? Peter Levi's answer is that it is very intense and has something about it in common with Shakespeare in his best poems. Every new verse, every new thought as it comes, is both quite unexpected and at the same time perfectly appropriate. The ideas in 'The Lord is my shepherd' are not dispersed, but are concentrated on divine protection, yet we see that it is a poem about life.

But the psalms are not all gentle. They speak of a world in which life is short and insecure, where pain is real and anger all-consuming. How can we cope with sentiments like the following:

> But God will shatter the heads of his enemies, the hairy crown of him who walks in his guilty ways. The Lord said, 'I will bring them back from Bashan, I will bring them back from the depths of the sea, that you may bathe your feet in blood, that the tongues of your dogs may have their portion from the foe.'
>
> Psalms 68:21-23

Cardinal Hume says that this has presented him with quite a difficulty. As a Christian he has had inculcated into his mind the importance of forgiveness and charity and here he finds himself cursing enemies. He has found that the only way he can pray such a psalm now is to interpret it, as it were, as cursing the forces of evil, whether of evil spirits or the evil genius in human nature, without personification. That is not an entirely satisfactory answer, he admits, but it is the only way he has found for coping with one or two passages which are particularly difficult, especially the verses which include the unedifying prospect of dashing the heads of children on stones. This is an appalling idea to have to utter, but if you can see it as expressing in a poetic kind of way the children that evil can breed you can make some sense of it. But there are problems.

Why have Christians held on to the psalms? On that question Cardinal Hume has no doubts. These were the prayers of Christ, he says, and of the Jews of his time, so when he prays the psalms he knows he is praying as Christ prayed. The early fathers, in the post-apostolic period, commented on the psalms, and wrote about them. The psalms were their prayer too. They praised the psalms in the light of the revelations in the New Testament – of all that Christ had given them and all he had done. So it was natural that the young church should take on the psalms as prayer, and the psalms became part of the prayer life of the early Christian community. When the first monks fled into the desert to live the life of hermits they took with them the psalms, and that was their prayer. Both St Benedict, the great legislator of monastic life in the western church, and St Basil, his counterpart in the east, centred the prayer life of their communities on the psalms.

*

So Christians as well as Jews have kept the worship of the Temple alive. But there are differences: the temple music was lost and new insights were gained. As John Eaton explains, when the Temple was finally destroyed by the Romans, the whole class of skilled psalmists seems to have disappeared and the texts were then preserved chiefly by the scribes and rabbinical scholars, while many of the details of the singing were lost. In the synagogues, they had no instruments, apart from the ram's horn used for signalling. The singing disappeared with the end of ·the Temple and its great functions. But then the Christians began to use the psalms, and the psalms had a remarkable way of chiming with the Christian point of view. The kingdom of God was again central, and the work through the anointed one, the Christ, all seems to be spoken of in the psalms, so that the whole Christian gospel seemed to be in a musical and poetic form already, prophetically, and ideal for worship. Thus we find the early fathers referring to their worship as full of psalms from beginning to end. 'The beginning, the middle, the end,' says John Chrysostom, 'it' is all David' – meaning the psalms. It became the practice to use the psalms in frequent rotation. Once a year, once a month, once a week, and even once a day they went through the whole psalter, and it became the great source and nourishment of Christian piety.

The worship of Solomon's Temple has survived and grown. Its psalms now belong to those who would never have been allowed to enter its doors. But that story of survival hides a greater mystery. If the Temple was so important, why was it never rebuilt after its final destruction in AD 70? The Chief Rabbi has the answer. The Temple was not rebuilt, he says, because Jewish tradition has it that only in the ultimate, messianic age of the Jews' final fulfilment will there be the restoration of the third temple, as forecast in the book of the prophet Ezekiel. The Jewish people are still dispersed to the four corners of the earth. Even with the restoration of a Jewish state in Zion, the majority of Jews still live outside.

Therefore they have to make do with synagogues, which are miniature temples, replica temples, in which prayer has replaced the sacrificial cult as the main form of worship.

Professor Sawyer believes that there may be another reason: part of the continuing and developing relationship between God and man. Throughout the book of Isaiah, he says, there is suspicion of the Temple. Chapter one contains an attack on sacrifice, and in the very last chapter the Prophet goes so far as to have God say, 'What is this temple you would build for me? Heaven is my temple. I don't need another.' Sacrifice, he says, is like murder.

This rejection of the Temple is a recurring theme in the Bible. Jesus takes it up, quoting Jeremiah. The Temple has become a den of thieves, and Jesus' first act when he goes into the Temple is almost to start a revolution by upsetting the tables. The crucifixion has an element of rending the veil of the Temple. And in AD 70, when the Second Temple was finally destroyed, the famous Rabbi Joachim is confronted with a scene of ruin in Jerusalem. His disciples say, 'What can we do now the Temple is destroyed?' And he says, 'Don't be afraid. There are other ways, better ways, such as doing deeds of kindness, of generosity, of love.'

For Cardinal Hume, the songs of the Temple are stronger than Solomon's pillars of bronze and panels of cedar. They are an invisible Temple whose doors are never shut, fixed in history and reaching beyond it. They express what goes on not only in the history of Israel but deep inside the subconscious of the human person. He quotes the opening words of Psalm 63:

> O God, thou art my God, I seek thee, my soul thirsts for thee; my flesh faints for thee, as in a dry and weary land where no water is. So I have looked upon thee in the sanctuary, beholding thy power and glory. Because thy steadfast love is better than life, my lips will praise thee.

He thinks that, as a prayer for somebody who may be going through a difficult period in life and has no clear ideas about God and yet feels he wants some relation with him, it can be a most marvellous prayer from a dark mind. When you pray that kind of psalm even from a dark mind, he says, you can find an extraordinary peace.

6. Prophets and the Sons of Prophets

2 Kings 1-13:23; 24:10-25
Isaiah
Jeremiah
Hosea
Amos

West of the baked and dusty caves of the Wadi Qumran, where the oldest texts of the Hebrew prophets lay hidden for nearly 1,900 years, and south of the town of Bethlehem, where an electronic star casts a this-wordly glow over the buses parked in Manger Square, there is an unprepossessing and largely unvisited site called the House of Zechariah nestling in the hills known as the mountains of Judea. In the early centuries of the Christian era, it was venerated as the crossroads of prophecy – the place where Jewish and Christian ideas about prophecy met, touched and parted. For according to local tradition it was the birthplace of John the Baptist, the wild man of the desert, who denounced present sin and pointed to a future hope – John, the political embarrassment, who proclaimed the kingdom of God only to be beheaded because of the guilty weakness of a king.

Luke, in his Gospel, describes an odd little domestic drama which took place in the house of Zechariah when John was born. Zechariah, a priest with a sceptical turn of mind, served in the Temple at Jerusalem. He was literally struck dumb at the news that his wife Elizabeth, who was surely too old, was to have a child. Only nine months later, at the circumcision ceremony, did his voice return, breaking through his relatives' well-meaning pantomime of sign language. To their surprise he spoke out in the language of the prophecies of Isaiah, and of Jeremiah and of Malachi, and he declaimed what amounts to a prophet's manifesto:

> Blessed be the Lord God of Israel, for he has visited and redeemed his people, and has raised up a horn of salvation for us in the house of his servant David, as he spoke by the mouth of his holy prophets from of

old, that we should be saved from our enemies, and from the hand of all who hate us; to perform the mercy promised to our fathers, and to remember his holy covenant, the oath which he swore to our father Abraham, to grant us that we, being delivered from the hand of our enemies, might serve him without fear, in holiness and righteousness before him all the days of our life. And you, child, will be called the prophet of the Most High; for you will go before the Lord to prepare his ways, to give knowledge of salvation to his people in the forgiveness of their sins.

Luke 1:68-77

That message of God's care for the people he had chosen, interwoven with a reminder of their duty to him and a promise of salvation, had been heard many times in the 950 years which separated the Temple which Solomon had built and the Second Temple in which Zechariah served. In those years the history of the Israelites, alone of any of their contemporaries in the ancient world, had been dominated not by kings and generals but by an odd collection of men – the slightly dotty and the stolidly practical, simple farmers and sophisticated courtiers. These men had one thing, and only one thing, in common – they believed they could hear the voice of God and, whether they wanted to or not, they had to pass the message on. It is their voices and their names that are remembered, not the two lines of kinglets, little men often with large names, who sat on the thrones of Judah and of Israel after Solomon had died and David's golden kingdom was broken in two.

*

The first great name to emerge in the divided kingdom was that of Elijah, the miracle worker who was fed by ravens, who could outrun a chariot and bring the dead to life. He and his successor Elisha, a humourless man who was sensitive about his baldness, are the two links between the sons of prophets – the wandering guilds of holy men with whom Saul, the first king, danced – and the new prophets of the Hebrew Bible: men who traced their descent from Moses the stammerer who outfaced the Pharaoh and spoke to God. The prophets were the leaders of the opposition by divine right. They were not the playthings of a court hungry for prediction. Even under King David they could speak out when everyone else had to keep silent. As Dr Henry McKeating of Nottingham says, a

13. Elijah fed by ravens

prophet, because he can appeal to religious authority, has a licence to criticise. Nathan, in the reign of David, can actually reprimand the king for commiting adultery. Probably nobody else around would have dared to do that. Nathan can do it and get away with it.

It is that combination of a licence to criticise and an authority independent of any court, king or institution which Lord Blanch, the former Archbishop of York, believes marked out the prophets from all other future foragers in the ancient world. There were no equivalents, he says. There were people who might have been confused with them. The ancient world was full of people who purported to tell the future: sooth-sayers, fortune-tellers, and astrologers. But while the prophets did predict the future in that way, that was not their primary interest. They were primarily concerned with establishing the law of God in society and thereby creating a harmonious and dynamic society. In that sense they stand quite alone. There was no one else in the ancient world who was prepared to stand against the powerful monarchs in whose state they may have served. Lord Blanch takes what they say seriously because they are called by God to give a particular message to a particular time. That in itself, he thinks, makes them unique in the ancient world.

The prophets were also revolutionaries who did not mind taking a risk. They acted out of compulsion in a way that often did not serve their personal interest. Fifty years or so after Elijah and Elisha had made life uncomfortable for the backsliding kings of Israel, two very different men took on the prophet's mantle. Isaiah of Judah turned on the court he belonged to and warned Jerusalem that she would pay for her ingratitude and infidelity. At the same time Amos of Tekoa left his flocks and his sycamore trees and went north and let fly at the corruption and idolatry of Israel. The women of Samaria were as mindless as the sleek cows of Bashan. There was only one solution – justice must flow down like a river and righteousness like a never-ending stream. The ivory beds and idle luxuries of Jeroboam's capital were repellent to God. Amos uses strong and violent language, Isaiah does not mince his words. Clearly the portrait of a prophet as a white-bearded bastion of propriety, a holy poet laureate, is misplaced.

What were the prophets really like? The Rev. Henry Mowvley, a Baptist Minister from Bristol, says they were not necessarily old men. Many of the prophets were quite young. Isaiah, for instance, who had his call in 740 or so and was still at work in 700, could not have been all that old when he first started. Jeremiah is said to have been a young man when he first began his prophetic work. For some it certainly seems to have been a great calling. People like Amos and Isaiah felt it to be something quite special when they were called to this particular task, though there are others who were simply prophets because it was their job, their role in life, and perhaps it was hereditary.

So prophecy was widespread. The spirit of prophecy was not limited to named prophets. Only the teachings of the most outstanding prophetic figures were preserved, but they were sustained by an openness to prophecy kept alive by more run-of-the-mill prophets and teachers now long forgotten. Lord Blanch says that they had schools of prophets, not unlike our modern theological colleges or seminaries, and presumably the traditions and oracles which they uttered were preserved in them, so that it passed from one generation on to another.

The Israelites were not the only people in the ancient Near East to listen to prophecy, but the status and purpose of their prophets was unlike all others. Elsewhere oracles and soothsayers could be bought or at least bribed, but the prophets of Judah and Israel were independent. They were God's messengers and they did not expect a pension. There is only one prophet who may be an exception to that rule – Nahum the consoler, a 7th-century prophet who predicted the fall of Nineveh. Henry Mowvley explains where he would have fitted into the Temple hierarchy. He says that there may well have been people within the temple staff who did it as a job and who were in fact paid for it. A book like Nahum might have been the work of such a person. There is some evidence. For instance in the book of Psalms, there are passages which have all the marks of prophecy. Within the cultic staff in the Temple there was therefore probably a group of people known to scholars as 'cultic prophets', and they may well have been supported by the institution. But on the whole the books that we have in the Old Testament come from people who did not get paid for it.

It may not be entirely coincidental that Nahum is the only Biblical prophet who neither condemns Israel nor calls the people to repentance. That shows a degree of diplomacy usually alien to the prophetic temperament, as Henry Mowvley explains. The prophets, he says, were always critical, and therefore were always rubbing people up the wrong way. That is why they ran into trouble. Amos comes to Bethel, the religious capital of the northern kingdom, as a southerner, and begins to complain about them and their behaviour. The priest says to him, 'Look, get back to Judah and do your prophesying there. You're a Judean. We don't want you here.' But Amos says, 'This is where I am to preach, because this is what God has told me to do and I must do it here.'

*

The urgency with which the prophets spoke was a reflection of the political dangers crowding in on the weakened, divided kingdoms of Israel and Judah. David and Solomon had been able to consolidate their power while the super-powers of the ancient Near East were going through a weak patch, but their descendants were not so lucky. By the time the prophet Micah, the countryman, was attacking the evils of city life, Assyria flexed its muscles and laid siege to Samaria, the capital of northern Israel. In 722 BC Samaria fell, and the fate of the northern kingdom's last king is not even recorded. But Micah survived and he turned his attention to Jerusalem and the city of Judah. His message to Ahaz and his successor Hezekiah was not encouraging. Jerusalem, he said, would fall as Samaria had fallen. It would become a heap of stones. But Micah also spoke of a city of Jerusalem in the future which would become a home for all nations:

> It shall come to pass in the latter days that the mountain of the house of the Lord shall be established as the highest of the mountains, and shall be raised up above the hills; and peoples shall flow to it, and many nations shall come, and say: 'Come, let us go up to the mountain of the Lord, to the house of the God of Jacob; that he may teach us his ways and we may walk in his paths.' For out of Zion shall go forth the law, and the word of the Lord from Jerusalem. He shall judge between many peoples, and shall decide for strong nations afar off; and they shall beat their swords into ploughshares, and their spears into pruning hooks; nation shall not lift up sword against nation, neither shall they learn war any more; but they shall sit every man under his vine and under his fig tree, and none shall make them afraid; for the mouth of the Lord of hosts has spoken.
>
> Micah 4:1-4

Fifty years after Micah had spoken of a new Jerusalem where swords would be beaten into ploughshares, Jeremiah, a young man of an old priestly family, echoed the prophecies of the fall of the old Jerusalem. Politically the situation was more dangerous. The kingdom of Judah was caught up in the larger power struggle between Assyria, now weakening, Egypt, now strengthening, and a newly vigorous Babylon. Jeremiah's prophecies of Jerusalem's capture would be fulfilled in his lifetime, but when first spoken they won him few friends. He was imprisoned by the Temple authorities and even threatened with death. He was also afflicted by self-doubt. For Dr McKeating, Jeremiah's chequered career is proof that the prophets were men working under orders. He says that one thing is clear from the texts. They felt they had no choice. That comes out strongly in Jeremiah, who actually says to God: 'Look, I prophesy all these things, you tell me to say them, they don't come true, I'm just going to shut up. This is a waste of time.' And then he says, 'I tried shutting up, but I

14. Jeremiah cast into prison

couldn't. The word was like a fire shut up in my bones!'

Jeremiah's prison experience was one of the occupational hazards of being a prophet. The disadvantage of the divine authority which the prophets claimed was that they could only lose. If their prophecies came true, they were merely repeating the word of God. If they were proved wrong, they were not only bad prophets but had also committed the blasphemy of putting lies into God's mouth. To look at it from the people's point of view, how did they know which prophets were inspired by God and which were fired by their own imagination? And what if two prophets, both claiming to speak for God, issued contradictory statements? For, as Dr McKeating says, they did not all agree with each other. In the book of Deuteronomy, an actual test proposes: 'Look, the way you know a true prophet from a false prophet is, if a true prophet prophesies, the things he says happen. If they don't, he was a false prophet.' This wait-and-see test is not very useful, because you often need to know now. But it shows that there was a real difficulty. Again, Jeremiah faced an acute problem because his prophecies did not come true, at least in the short term, and all the others contradicted him. He complained about it, and he began to doubt himself. He seriously suggested to himself that God might actually be giving him the wrong message for purposes of his own. But the reason why those who have their names in the book are named is that their prophecies were fulfilled, broadly speaking, in the longer term.

The main hazard about prophecies *outside* Israel and Judah was that they were immutable. Men who learned their fate only wrapped themselves more tightly in a web of necessity. The fact of their foreknowledge became itself one of the steps towards the fate they were trying to avoid. So Oedipus killed his father and married his mother *because* he attempted to avoid the fate pronounced for him by the Delphic oracle. Croesus, the last king of Lydia, sought the battle which would lose him his empire because he failed to read the fine print of the oracle. Compared with those prophecies, the prophets of Israel and Judah, however rough their tongues and dire their warnings, spoke of a future which was kinder and not predetermined. The Hebrew prophets describe a tomorrow shaped by, and dependent on, today. Man *could* change his fate. The solution lay not in magic but in practical action: repentance, faithfulness to God and justice for all. This gave humans a dignity which other nations reserved for the gods.

Professor Clements thinks that what is fascinating about the prophets is the way they manage to turn awareness of problems of malaise in what is happening in political or social events into a sense of responsibility on the part of the people themselves. The faults lie with them, and therefore in a measure the cure lies with them, if they can only re-focus themselves on God and recover the sense of their true identity as the people of God. The fascinating feature of the prophet's role in society is that he puts so much emphasis on the responsible people. Although he castigates them sharply, there is nevertheless a dignity even about his sharpness because he believes that they have the capacity for putting it right. It is not fatalism at all. The real prophet is pretty much the opposite of a fatalist. He is saying that you have the machinery in your own hands for responding to the situation you are facing.

*

The prophets were ignored time and again. But if the people had made up their minds not to pay attention to the prophets why did they bother writing down their warnings? Amos is the first prophet whose words were written down at any length. Dr McKeating thinks that the reason they were written down was that his prophecies were fulfilled relatively quickly. He prophesied some time in the 740s, and he talked about the destruction of the state. That happened in 722 or 721, and there would still be many people around who remembered what he had said. There may even have been a shorter-term fulfilment, since some of Amos' utterances could be interpreted as predictions of an earthquake. Perhaps Amos began to be taken seriously when the earthquake happened. People thought he had something after all, and it was confirmed twenty years later. Perhaps other prophets of doom were also taken more seriously, and people were prepared to wait just a bit longer to see whether they were right or not.

Yet even when the scribes had increased the shelf-life of the warnings of doom, the prophets were merely in a double dilemma – they wanted to be proved wrong. As Professor Clements says, Old Testament prophets are speaking about events which they profoundly hope will not happen. They want to impress their message so heavily on the minds of their hearers that they change their ways. Then the events will not need to happen. In that way prophets have an affinity to social reformers, but they are speaking about a society which they see to be on the wrong road and want to put back on the right road.

Men like Micah, Amos and Isaiah had prestige, but not personal prestige. In other cultures – even in our own horoscope-ridden generation – the idea lurking behind prophecy is the hope of stealing an advantage by virtue of privileged access to secret knowlege. The motives behind the Biblical prophets are much less primitive. They pointed out dangers and called people to *self*-assessment, which is no way to make friends. They saw themselves as the conscience, and sometimes as the scourge, of their society.

Not everything they predicted came to pass. Does that mean that they were failures? Dr Robert Carroll, Lecturer in Biblical Studies at Glasgow, says they were quite successful at what they actually did: namely, at disturbing people. But when it came to predicting the future, they were no better than anyone else. They were trying to analyse and even to shape the future – but to shape it, not predict it. Prediction is saying, 'Tomorrow it will be wet or dry.' Shaping is saying, 'If you people can sort yourselves out, we can deal with some of the problems.' It is not so much a prediction as an attempt to spur people on to a changed action. Whatever the Biblical prophets did, and they did it well, the language they used – the poetry – is impressive, and this was handed down. It could not be ignored, though it could not be handled in quite the same way as it had been originally given, because circumstances had changed. So, in new circumstances, their work was used in a slightly different way, and in that sense they were successful.

The prophets were the watchmen of their societies. Amos condemns the selling of the destitute into slavery, Isaiah gives dire warnings to property speculators and Jeremiah rails against sexual immorality and employers who exploit their labourers. Would the message of the prophets have had more impact if they had been more single-minded, perhaps concentrating on specifically religious matters? No, says Mary Evans of the London Bible College. Religion and behaviour cannot be separated. Some of the prophets are speaking firmly to people who believed that they were solid citizens, and saying, 'Rubbish! Your life style does not tie in with your religion, so although you carry out all the proper religious rituals, that is irrelevant, and God hates it.'

Excessive ritualism was not the only religious problem the prophets faced. It was not a question of there being too little religion, but of there being too much. The Baals were always getting toeholds in Jerusalem, and under the evil king Manasseh a form of Assyrian star-worship found a home on the roof of the Temple itself. The prophetic insistence on the worship of the one God was not a recipe for popularity. Professor Rogerson points out that the prophets denounce many practices that the ordinary people engaged in: their attraction to the fertility cults, their consulting of mediums, witches and necromancers, their interpretation of dreams. If you know where to look in the Old Testament, you can find that the prophetic view was often a minority view, pushing itself against the popular religion of the people, and often against the popular ideas of religion that the kings wished to uphold.

But the days of the kings were numbered. Jehoiakim backed the wrong imperial house by aligning with Egypt. His son Jehoiachim ruled for only fourteen weeks before he was deported with his entire court to Babylon by Nebuchadnezzar. Jehoiachim's uncle Zedekiah reigned in Jerusalem in his stead, deaf to Jeremiah's advice to co-operate with Babylon. In 586 BC Jeremiah's prophecies of doom were fulfilled. Jerusalem fell. Zedekiah, the last king of Judah, saw his sons murdered. His eyes were put out. He was carried to Babylon as a captive and imprisoned until his death. Hence the lamentations of Jeremiah.

The prophets who spoke to the Israelites from the time of Solomon's glory to the fall of the divided kingdoms of Judah and Israel were addressing specific contemporary problems, issues of moral, religious and political significance in their own time. Is it therefore legitimate to push their message any further? Henry Mowvley believes that we have to begin by locating them in their history. We have to see what they are saying to their own day. It is legitimate then to follow the process of interpretation and see what they can be saying to us in our day.

*

But which prophet can most effectively speak across the centuries? For Professor Rogerson there is no contest. Jeremiah finds himself in bitter conflict with the rulers of his day. His religious message is one they do not want to hear. He is branded as a traitor because he is faithful to the word that he thinks needs to be spoken. Also, he suffers deeply himself – we have those poignant parts of his book that we call the 'Confessions of Jeremiah'. When you take those things together, there is the further theological pay-off that the God who sends Jeremiah to speak these words and suffer in the way he does is not some remote God in a bunker, indifferent to what his servants are saying or suffering, but very much bound up with them in their sufferings. Jeremiah then brings us to the point where we see that it belongs to the prophetic office to speak the truth, even if it brings the prophet into conflict with authority, and that the suffering involved in doing that is a clue to God's own suffering in the world.

For Dr Rowland, the words of Isaiah of Jerusalem reach

beyond the 8th century BC. Their message of good news for the poor and liberty for captives is a political message for today. All of us, he says, find the prophecy of the second part of Isaiah an inspiration. They are words which are familiar to us through their use at Christmas. They rekindle in many people the hope for change, not just at the personal level, but also at the community and national level. In those passages the image of liberation, the exodus theme, is taken up again, reapplied in a new situation in the life of the people of God. That is what we too ought to be doing, because while we may not feel oppressed, we are a part of a political system which is doing its fair share of oppression in its relations with the Third World. Even in our own country liberation is needed, as much as in Brazil or any other Third World country.

For Lord Blanch, the story of the prophet Hosea who forgave his unfaithful wife and used his experience to teach others about the relationship with God and his people speaks as loudly today as it did in 8th-century Israel. Hosea is Lord Blanch's favourite prophet because he was not involved, like the others, in great events. Although he had things to say about politics and international affairs, he was not dominated by them, as Isaiah and Jeremiah were. In that sense he is more accessible to us. He is simply a man who had a clear calling from God to be a prophet, a minister to his people. No great miracles are associated with him and he delivered no great utterances about state policy. In fact his whole ministry is based, not on what he did, but on what happened to him. That makes him a sympathetic figure, because it is true for most of us. It is what happens to us, not what we do, that dominates us. Here was a man who had an unfortunate marriage. He learnt from it and compared the unfaithfulness of his wife with the faithfulness of God.

The prophets are best known among Christians for their Messianic prophecies, but have Christians read into ancient words a message that was not there? Were the prophets intent on identifying the Messiah? Henry Mowvley says they had no intention of doing so. They were concerned to prophesy about things that were close at hand. Most of the prophets before the exile, the ones whose books we now possess, were people who had to prophesy disaster. Their books are rather depressing in some ways, because they are consistently threatening the downfall of Samaria, the destruction of

Jerusalem, the exile of the people or the death of some king or other. But here and there there is a vestige of hope. In Jeremiah, for instance, there is always the hope that there will be something new beyond the exile. In the book of Jeremiah there is a passage about the new covenant. This is not something that Israel will perform but something that God will inaugurate when he takes up his people again after the exile. There is also talk in Isaiah about a new king, a new David, a son of Jesse. These were hopes that were born of their theology – of their understanding of God and of what God was doing with his chosen people. Some of the hopes were never fulfilled after the exile. But some were. The Israelites did return to their own land, though they did not acquire a new David. Yet they never gave up hope. Somehow what the prophets had said remained as a lasting hope in people's minds, and so the Jews in the time of Jesus were still looking for this Messianic figure mentioned by the prophets. The early Christians, when they met Jesus and saw what he had done and what happened to him, said, 'This is the Messiah, this is the new David, this is the one about whom the prophets were speaking.' So, with hindsight, they could look back and identify Jesus with the Messiah that the prophets were expecting, but it cannot be claimed that the prophets were expecting Jesus.

*

Why did prophecy stop? Lord Blanch says that, from the Christian point of view, the last prophet according to the scriptures would be John the Baptist. But, from the point of view of the Hebrew people, the age of the prophets has never ceased, although the great canonical prophets, as they are called, span a particular time in history, from about 1000 to about 300 BC.

Rabbi Magonet believes that prophecy ended because it was too dangerous. At some stage the rabbis became aware that prophets were far too anarchic. It is never certain where they will lead, so the rabbis of the past thought it better to close the canon. Instead, prophets are replaced by teachers – rabbis who interpret – which is safer, because they work within the establishment. But the reality is more complicated since Judaism has been a minority religion. Living under great empires, whether Christian or Islamic, Jews had to become more cautious. The few who have claimed to be either Messiahs or prophets, such as Shabbetai Zevi two centuries ago, have been so disastrous that they have been avoided. So there grew up a feeling that it was better – certainly safer – to stick to what was already known. New messages can be dangerous. But prophets keep on making themselves heard. The rabbis say that prophecy is closed, but it now comes in the babbling of fools and children.

Some would say the babbling can be heard in the charismatic Christian groups who prophesy in tongues. Can that have any relationship with the prophets of old? Mary Evans thinks that those who experience the gift of charismatic prophecy today wish to speak God's word for today. Often they speak in the first person, as though they are speaking from God and speaking what they believe God has given them to say. These are usually messages of challenge or encouragement. They seem to be saying, in the name of God, 'I want you to be encouraged about the fact that there is growth in your church', or, 'I want you to spend more time worshipping me.' If we accept the possibility of God's speaking in today's world, there is no reason why he should not speak through people, as he did in the past.

But is the role of prophet limited to that minority who feel called to prophesy? What about the wider church? Lord Blanch says that the Church today has a responsibility, a prophetic responsibility, to be involved in confrontation. It should show the world that it is falling short of what God requires of it. Clearly that is particularly true of the Church itself. There is a message for people who acknowledge God, but the Old Testament prophets, such as Amos in his first two chapters, make it clear that there is also a message for outside nations. There is a call for right behaviour, justice, righteousness, holiness. The Church therefore has a responsibility to speak out against the injustice, unrighteousness and immorality of society. The Church has a function there, and needs to speak out, as Bishops Sheppard and Jenkins have. If we recognise that God is God of the world, God is involved in politics. Because God is God of the world, involvement in politics is to some extent inevitable. That is certainly seen in the Old Testament prophets.

For Lord Blanch the prophets of Israel and Judah have a

message of justice which reaches out beyond the world they knew to the world known by us. The prophets are remarkably modern and contemporary, because they were primarily concerned with justice – 'Let justice roll down like rivers', and so on – and with the championship of the law. They stand in a tradition which is on the side of the oppressed, the weak and the powerless, and find themselves, as they would today, confronting the powers of government, culture and so on. That is their most important contribution today. They remind us that there is still a role for the prophet who will stand up for the poor and the oppressed and resist the inroads of government and all the other great powers of this world.

7. The Furnace of Affliction

2 Kings 25:8-30
2 Chronicles 36:15-23
Daniel
Lamentations
Ezekiel
Psalms 137
Ezra

There is a far-fetched story in the book of the prophet Daniel, the visionary and friend of lions. It concerns three young exiles from the broken kingdom of Judah and Nebuchadnezzar, the desolater of Jerusalem, the ravager of the Temple – a man who was the greatest ruler of the neo-Babylonian empire, a military leader who had cut a swathe of destruction from the Persian Gulf to the hights of Lebanon and the gates of Egypt. He was a dream-racked man, Daniel tells us, given to periodic insanity, when he would leave his palace and grow his nails until they bent over like the claws of a bird and his unkempt hair would flow as long as the feathers of an eagle.

Daniel and the three young exiles arrived in Babylon as part of one of the earlier waves of compulsory deportations from Judah before the Temple was destroyed in 586 BC. They were chosen by the chief eunuch of the royal palace to undergo a three-year training course in the language and culture of their conquerors to prepare them for privileged careers as court officials. At first all went well. Daniel was pre-eminent in the interpretation of dreams, and the other three, known by the Babylonian names of Shadrach, Meshach and Abednego, soon excelled in the wisdom of their adopted country.

But then Nebuchadnezzar commissioned an image of gold 90 feet high and 9 feet wide and issued a proclamation that all his subjects must worship the statue when they were within earshot of the sacred music, on pain of death by fire. A clash with the jealousy of Israel's God was inevitable, and unwelcome reports soon began to reach the King's ears:

'O King, live for ever! You, O king, have made a decree, that every man who hears the sound of the horn, pipe, lyre, trigon, harp, bagpipe, and every kind of music, shall fall down and worship the golden image; and whoever does not fall down and worship shall be cast into a burning fiery furnace. There are certain Jews whom you have appointed over the affairs of the province of Babylon: Shadrach, Meshach, and Abednego. These men, O king, pay no heed to you; they do not serve your gods or worship the golden image which you have set up.'

Then Nebuchadnezzar in furious rage commanded that Shadrach, Meshach, and Abednego be brought. Then they brought these men before the king.

Daniel 3:9-13

Shadrach, Meshach and Abednego were summoned to the King's presence and were unrepentant. Nebuchadnezzar's fury knew no bounds. The three were to be fed to the fiery furnace. The furnace, a giant kiln with an opening at the top and a door at the bottom, through which the king could watch the guilty burn, was heated to seven times its normal temperature, so much so that those throwing the three victims in at the top were themselves burnt to death. To the King's amazement, through the lower doors he saw Shadrach, Meshach and Abednego walking in the furnace unscathed by the heat. They were immediately released, restored to their old position of favour and given guarantees of religious freedom and new preferment in their official careers.

*

This story is often dismissed as a pious fiction, but there is more to it than that. The fiery furnace contains the only key to understanding the riddle of the exile.

The plain historical facts are these. When Jerusalem fell in 586 BC, defiled by famine-inspired cannibalism, its people had lost everything – their religious and political institutions, and any vestige of self-determination. Even their leaders had been shipped off to Babylon. They were finished. But the Israelites were about to break all the rules of history. The destruction of their kingdom would make them an indestructible nation. This is the contradiction threaded through and holding together the books of Lamentations and Ezekiel, the later Isaiah and Daniel, and the books of restoration, Ezra and Nehemiah. The account of the Exile, the reverse side of the Exodus, is one of the most remarkable in the Bible. It is a story about kings and queens, about astute immigrants and bizarre revelations, about doom-laden graffiti and a virtuous Gentile, but above all it is a story about a people strengthened by suffering, uniquely tempered, not tarnished, by the flames of affliction.

But why did Nebuchadnezzar take the Jews into exile in the first place? Was it common practice in the ancient world? Professor Lambert says that the practice had been started by the Assyrians, in about 1000 BC. The Assyrians had armies, but they had no civil administration and no police force. Their policy was to conquer brutally, by force of arms, which meant that the conquered people did not love them. So their problem was, how could they hold down these conquered people without a huge army? They hit upon a method of uprooting populations and moving them around. The uprooting usually served to destroy the national sense of identity of the uprooted people, but the Israelites were the exception. The Assyrians, and Babylonians after them, realised that it was important to remove the upper classes of society, those who had more influence. They tended to leave behind only the poorest. Those who were politically dangerous might either be killed or be taken away as prisoners. But populations *en bloc* were assumed to be relatively harmless, once removed.

The prophet Jeremiah had the bitter satisfaction of experiencing the suffering he had promised. He saw Jerusalem fall and was chained up to await deportation. But Nebuchadnezzar had given orders that the prophet who had counselled surrender should not be compelled to go to Babylon. He was given a choice, and he chose to stay in his defeated homeland. He claims that 4,600 Jews were carried off to Babylon in the three deportations: a conservative estimate by Biblical standards. The book of Kings suggests a figure of between 8,000 and 10,000 for one deportation alone, leaving the land virtually empty. Peter Ackroyd, Emeritus Professor of Old Testament Studies in the University of London, thinks it most unlikely, under the circumstances, that a conquering power would completely remove the population of an area, quite apart from the impossibility of doing so in an area like Judea. They did not all go into exile, and to talk about the exile as if the whole land had been left empty is an explanatory view of what happened, rather than what actually happened. The story in the Biblical text concen-

15. The burning fiery furnace

trates on those who were taken away to Babylon, and then on those who returned from Babylon. Of the rest, it either says loftily that the poor inherited the land, or, as in Chronicles, that the land was empty, having a complete rest. Neither of those observations will really quite do. It is quite evident that a considerable part of the population remained behind.

For those who were left behind, life was not easy. Gedeliah, a friend of Jeremiah's, was appointed governor of the vassal state of Judah. He lasted barely two months before he was assassinated. Jeremiah's opinion of those who remained in Jerusalem was not flattering – he considered them useless: as useless as inedible figs. The good figs had been taken to Babylon, but they would one day return. The exiles saw themselves as the guardians of the land they could no longer see. But how did they cope in their new home – with its canals, its moats, its processional walkways and its hanging gardens? Were the exiles in a state of culture shock? Professor Ackroyd says that up to a point this would be so because, clearly, an urban centre like Babylon was very different from the small, rather insignificant city of Jerusalem. We think of Jerusalem as an important city, but in fact it was minute. On the other hand, the more educated Jews would undoubtedly have been familiar with something of the wider culture of the ancient Near East. There was a good deal of commercial activity between Assyria and Judah and Babylon and Judah over the centuries.

But it is one thing to be a trading partner and another to be an enforced guest. Would the Judean exiles have felt at home with the Babylonians – with their odd predilection for unnecessary walking sticks, excessive use of perfume, monotonous music and strange habit of dividing the hours of the day by the figure 60? Were the Jews homesick? Dr Carroll suspects that initially some of them must have felt like that: the older people certainly, because they had lost their land, their roots and their family, and family ties to land were very strong in that culture. They must have felt completely lost. But the younger generations could hardly have missed the old land, and the second and third generations would not even have known the old land. For them therefore, Babylon was home, and by the second, third or fourth generation some of the exiles had set up businesses and possessed their own land. The Jews thrived in Babylonia until the 20th century, when the Iraqis started hanging them in public. There are not so many there now, but for a thousand years Babylonia was one of the great centres of Jewish culture.

From the earliest days of the exile, the Jews in Babylonia worked at perfecting a curious balancing act of loyalty. Encouraged by the excellent Babylonian postal service, they invented the concept of dual nationality. As Professor Bartlett of Trinity College, Dublin explains, they still lived as a community, or in communities. They were settled in groups. They would therefore still have their friends and relations around them – those of them who had survived. In an interesting letter in the book of Jeremiah, chapter 29, Jeremiah writes to one of the exiled communities, telling them to settle down in the place where they have been taken, to marry and to build, and to multiply. In particular he tells them to seek the welfare of the city into which they have been exiled because in its welfare they will find their own welfare. He expects them to settle down there and to live out their lives there.

*

But however much at home the Jews were, behind the walls of Babylon there was a large part of Babylonian life which they rejected out of hand. They played no part in the religious life of the city with its elaborate ceremonial of creation dramas, sacred marriages, oracles, astrology, magic and temple liturgy. (The Greek historian Herodotus records that the Babylonians managed to get through two and a half tons of incense a year.) There is even a prophet of the exile, the priest Ezekiel, the son of Buzi, whose dreams and revelations made sense of disaster and comforted the exiles with the promise of return. But the highly-strung Ezekiel (perhaps an epileptic) was influenced by the Babylonian religion he fought against. His extraordinary vision of God in a fiery chariot with four living creatures, part human, part eagle, part lion and part ox, reflects the mythical beasts of Babylonian temple remains.

Ezekiel and Jeremiah formed a morale-boosting pincer movement. In Babylon Ezekiel, who had been taken down into exile in the first exile of 597, was prophesying that God would not spare Jerusalem and elaborating details of the fate that was coming upon the city. Similarly, in Jerusalem itself, Jeremiah, at terrible risk and suffering, predicted that the city would fall because God was fighting against it. This prophetic witness, according to Professor Rogerson, should be read in the light of earlier stories: for example, that God had allowed the ark of the covenant to be captured by the Philistines when the Israelites were trusting in the object instead of him. There was a lively tradition that God could destroy symbols which people put in place of him. Therefore the pair of them were able, not only to prepare the people, but to preach and draw attention after the event to the fact that the fall of Jerusalem and the exile were not the great triumph of the gods of Babylon over the God of Jerusalem. Rather the God of Jerusalem was still the sovereign Lord, and the exile had been his will.

Ezekiel taught his people that, whatever happened, God was in control. Only *they* had been defeated, God was still victorious. Jerusalem was a ruin and the Temple a soot-blackened memory. Ezekiel countered that bleak despair with a vision of hopelessness, a vision of a valley of dry bones:

> The hand of the Lord was upon me, and he brought me out by the Spirit of the Lord, and set me down in the midst of the valley; it was full of bones. And he led me round among them; and behold, there

were very many upon the valley; and lo, they were very dry. And he said to me, 'Son of man, can these bones live?' And I answered, 'O Lord God, thou knowest.' And again he said to me, 'Prophesy to these bones, and say to them, 'O dry bones, hear the word of the Lord. Thus says the Lord God to these bones: Behold, I will cause breath to enter you, and you shall live. And I will lay sinews upon you, and will cause flesh to come upon you, and cover you with skin and put breath in you, and you shall live; and you shall know that I am the Lord.'

So I prophesied as I was commanded; and as I prophesied, there was a noise, and behold, a rattling; and the bones came together, bone to its bone. And as I looked, there were sinews on them, and flesh had come upon them, and skin had covered them; but there was no breath in them. Then he said to me, 'Prophesy to the breath, prophesy, son of man, and say to the breath, Thus says the Lord God: Come from the four winds, O breath, and breathe upon these slain, that they may live.' So I prophesied as he commanded me, and the breath came into them, and they lived, and stood upon their feet, an exceedingly great host.

Ezekiel 37:1-10

If the word of the Lord could make dry bones live, restoration of a homeland would be easily within his power. For Rabbi Albert Friedlander these are more than the words of an ancient religious fanatic: they are for the present and the future. He spent part of his life in Mississippi, and the spirituals of the black community – 'Dem bones, dem bones, dem dry bones' – were a marvellous revelation to him. They related him directly to the suffering of the black community. Walking with Martin Luther King, he felt that this was an affirmation of the Biblical vision, confirming that the Bible belongs to everyone, that the blacks had the same experience of exile and hope for redemption. So, he says, it is not that Jews claim a patent in exile experience, it is part of humanity's fate. Those who come back to the Bible and read this text find that it really is a book for our time.

Throughout the book of Ezekiel there is the growing idea that faith is possible anywhere. The God of Abraham was once again a wandering God, but this time he would *follow* his people and pitch his tent wherever exile forced them. After the fall of Jerusalem, Babylon was not the only place where a Jewish community took root, as Professor Bartlett explains. Some of the Jews escaped to Egypt. You can read all about that in Jeremiah 40-44; they took the prophet Jeremiah off with them. The interesting thing about that group is that they were soldiers, not the ordinary population. The group who

16. The valley of dry bones

escaped to Egypt were escapees, not deportees. They probably survived in Egypt by becoming mercenaries. We know that at a place called Elephantine Island near Aswan, up the Nile, a Jewish community was founded that built its own temple. The people who lived there seem to have been mercenary soldiers, and we actually have some correspondence, written from them to Jerusalem, in the last decade of the fifth century BC, in the years between about 440 and 400 BC. This particular community must have perished about 400 BC, in one of the revolts that happened periodically against the Persian empire. The Jews there as mercenaries were, in effect, a Persian garrison, holding down the southern end of the Persian empire.

> Preserve my life, for I am godly; save thy servant who trusts in thee. Thou art my God; be gracious to me, O Lord, for to thee do I cry all the day. Gladden the soul of thy servant, for to thee, O Lord, do I lift up my soul.
>
> Psalms 86:2-4

Psalm 86, a song celebrating God's love of Zion, puts forward the notion that it is possible to be part of Zion even if you are born elsewhere – a sophisticated idea. But how did the Jews manage to retain their nationality in the face of national defeat? Dr McKeating thinks they coped with it partly because it had been prophesied. If it had hit them out of the blue, they would have wondered what they could do about it. They would probably have gone under and lost their national identity. Nor is this guesswork, because when the northern kingdom fell in 722 or 721, they did lose it. Many of them were deported – the ten lost tribes: they are still lost, they have never reappeared. That could happen. But it did not happen in the 6th century when the southern kingdom of Judah was attacked. Its Temple was destroyed, it lost its king and many of its people were deported; but it did not lose its national identity, because the prophets had said, 'This is going to happen, but it doesn't mean that God has deserted you. It means he's keeping a close eye on you. It isn't pleasant, but it proves that God is alive and kicking, and at the moment kicking very hard.' That, Dr McKeating thinks, was the first impetus they had to make them see it in a positive light, and to believe the prophets when they delivered the second half of the message, that the God who had punished them by sending them into exile would actually bring them back. They went on believing that too.

*

The prophets of the exile not only promised restoration, they also predicted the end of the Babylonian empire; and their prophecies were vindicated. In 539 BC, less than seventy years after the first Jewish exiles had arrived, Babylon fell to Cyrus the Great, the founder of the Persian empire, a fair-minded man with a soft spot for the Israelites. He issued an edict permitting the return of the Jews to their homeland beyond the Tigris. They could rebuild their Temple, and those who did not want to return could contribute towards the building costs. Alone of all pagans, Cyrus is honoured by the Bible: as 'the shepherd of the Lord' and 'the anointed one'. However, the Jews might be returning to their homeland, but their God was plainly an international God who could inspire Jew or Gentile regardless of rank or location. The years of exile had been formative. Were the Jews who chose to return to Jerusalem therefore identifiably different from those who had been forced to leave? Professor Lambert says that when they got back they were certainly less tolerant in their ideas. In Ezra and Nehemiah we find conflict arising over questions like mixed marriages, and very severe lines were being developed. This was the time when the law of Moses, as we now know it, became the rule of life of the community. Before the exile, it had often been ignored.

When the exiles returned they gave a new, firmer shape to the faith which had survived in Jerusalem. The faith they brought back was adaptable because it was firmly delineated by law and not dependent on place. But to what extent was continuity with the old faith broken? Professor Ackroyd thinks he detects a build-up of something which eventually appears to be new. But it is largely a question of how they continue to use the material which is characteristic of worship: psalms, various forms of liturgy, sacrifices. If you no longer have the only place of worship where sacrifices should be offered, you have to ask the question, 'What do we do instead?', or 'How, if we revive it, can we be sure that what we are doing is still valid?' There was stress on bringing back the sacred vessels which had been taken by the Babylonians from the Temple. They were obviously taken, because some at least of them were of precious metals, and they were almost certainly destroyed, or broken or melted down for their value. But in spite of all the indications of that, we are told that the vessels were counted out and restored. The only reason for that must be that it validates what then goes on. This worship is in continuity with the past.

In spite of that prized continuity there had been changes. Before they went into exile, the Israelites were a political, independent kingdom, even though sometimes partly subservient in political matters to other powers. When they came back, says Professor Lambert, they were definitely subject to the Persian empire. They no longer had even the pretence of being an independent kingdom. Their religion served them both as a way of life – in the sense of providing social standards – and in holding them together where previously their political organisation had held them together. They went into exile as a nation which had been independent: they came back much more as a religious community.

It is easy now to look back on the exile as a salutary experience for the development of Judaism as a faith, but it must have been very different for those who went through the agony of losing everything that was familiar to them. Did the chosen people not feel in some way betrayed by the God who had chosen them and let them suffer? Sir Immanuel Jakobovits says that whenever Jews speak in their liturgy of being chosen they immediately add that they are being chosen for special duties. If these special duties also entail, as they have done, special suffering and special sacrifices, then so be it. Jews are ready to pay that price. They were warned that, if they did not keep up their part of the covenant, of the deal that they entered into at Sinai, they would be punished; and exile would overtake them. They would be driven out of the land, they would lose the blessings that were otherwise promised to them. And so it happened, twice over in their history, on a major scale. Since then they have often endured the humiliation, and certainly the disabilities and persecutions, of exile – purely because they were not worthy of the special blessings that would have been theirs had they kept up with this covenant – their side of the bargain. That is an intrinsic Jewish teaching. Sir Immanuel explains:

> We repeat it in our basic declaration of faith, every morning and every evening: that if we hearken to the word of God, all will be well and we shall prosper, and if not, we shall be driven out from off the good land, and we shall suffer.

Exile with all its connotations of defeat and powerlessness would become a shared triumph for the whole people of Israel – just as the exodus had been. Pharaoh's slaves had brought with them the gifts of faith and freedom. The exiles who returned brought with them a new liberating vision. Professor Bartlett thinks that what the removal to Babylon did was to open the Jews' eyes to the world around them. They suddenly had to cope with the fact that their own state, and their own God, had been conquered by another larger state, a state which was devoted to other gods, like Marduk. One of the interesting things about the exile was the way Israelite theologians rose to the challenge. In particular, the theologian we call Second Isaiah spent a great deal of effort working out how Israel should see itself in its new position. He emphasised the universal power of Israel's God Yahweh. The Israelites were worried that their own God, Yahweh, had lost out to the Babylonian gods. Second Isaiah was concerned to demonstrate to them that they had a God of power, a God who was the creator, who was responsible for the whole world, who had power over the nations, and power over the Babylonian gods whom he called useless nothings. He presents Yahweh as saying, 'Before me no God was formed. Nor shall there be any after me, I am the Lord. And besides me, there is no Saviour.' Isaiah projected this message to the Israelites in exile, teaching them to think that their own God was the only one who could save them, and this comes over strongly in his writings. The other thing he tries to project clearly is God's power in creation. The nations, he says, are so many drops at the edge of a bucket, like the dust on the scales before God. He is in full control of creation. Second Isaiah starts his prophecies by pointing to God's might in creation, and he goes on to challenge the Babylonian gods in a series of rather dramatic court scenes in which he puts them on trial, as it were, and demonstrates that they are absolutely powerless to change the world. Obviously the Jews have preserved this material because they found this powerful theology coming from the exile.

The captivity in Babylon had streamlined Judaism. The essentials that survived were, as Dr Carroll says, things they could travel with – like circumcision, a day off in the week, the idea of the divine word. Things they could not travel with, like temple and land, became symbols, and less important. They were probably not important at all. Otherwise the Jews would not have flourished in Babylonia and lived there for more than a thousand years. For when there were chances for them to return to Palestine few went back. There was no reason for them to – like the Irish in America, who probably love Ireland but would not want to live there.

For those who returned and for those who stayed away suffering was now more than a punishment, it was a privilege of faith. As Sheshbazzar, a prince of the Davidic line, led the exiles back to the glory of Jerusalem, a new vision of kingship was set before the people – a vision whose beauty has never been surpassed, a vision not of a king but of a suffering servant. Israel is to be the servant of God, and that servant is, as it were, to teach them God's Torah, his will, so that they can go out into the world, and the world can be *Shalom*, at peace, all united. The song of the servant from the unknown prophet is included in the last chapter of the book of Isaiah. Kingship, slavery, victory, defeat – all are turned inside out, pointing to a new sense of purpose for Israel.

*

The ideal has been tested in the face of prejudice and inhumanity many times since the three young men of the Babylonian exile survived Nebuchadnezzar's furnace. Its harshest test was in our own century, as Rabbi Friedlander knows from experience. There was almost a break then, he says, between the past and the present. There have been many times of suffering – in Biblical times, the exile itself, the suffering throughout history – but whereas Orthodox Judaism is more prone to say, 'We suffer because of our sins, we suffer because God wants to test us, mould us, shape us, in a furnace of affliction', many Jews today say that the holocaust was different from past suffering. It was just too big. We cannot put the holocaust into a framework of a divine plan. Many Orthodox Jews believe it is a part of the divine plan: others, Rabbi Friedlander among them, say that it is something we cannnot put into any of the Biblical promises, or earlier explanations: it is still a terrible enigma to us – we are not sure what it means. Some people who have been in the concentration camps have come out with a stronger faith, some with a faith destroyed. Rabbi Friedlander was in a German prison as a child in 1938, but he escaped. It has not destroyed his faith, he says, because doubt and questions and anguish are part of faith.

Professor Zwi Werblowsky of Jerusalem believes that the seeds of Jewish survival were sown both in the exile and in a 'remembered future'. The exile was something negative. He says it was the furnace through which you have to pass, and if you pass through you come out as stronger and better. That notion of being one people is something rooted not only in the past but, paradoxically, in the hope for the future. There will be a reunion. There will be what the prophets call an 'ingathering of the exiles', which means that the unity and the creativity which come out of this unity really incurred were not so much in the memory of the common past as in what we might call the remembered future. A remembered future is what theologians call hope.

8. A Framework for Eternity

Deuteronomy 5 – 6:25
Psalms 119:1
Ecclesiastes
Job
Proverbs
Jonah
Mark 8 – 9:38

Long after the sprawling city of Nineveh had fallen, leaving only its name embedded in the folk memory of the ancient world as a byword for wickedness beyond control and for luxury beyond reason, it received a strangely compassionate treatment in the book of Jonah – the most indigestible prophet in the Bible. The story of Jonah and his unwanted holiday inside a whale is one of the best known in the Bible. But it is not simply a misplaced fisherman's yarn. It was written for the Jews rebuilding their city, and without it any understanding of the law and wisdom of the Israelites in the years following their return from exile is incomplete.

Jonah's adventures begin with a summons from God to preach to the notorious Ninevehites. Jonah, who can recognise a thankless task when he sees one, hares off in the opposite direction as fast as the first available ship will carry him. A storm threatens to sink the ship and he is thrown overboard. He is swallowed by a passing giant fish, only to be regurgitated three days later. He gives in and goes to Nineveh. The people repent and, much to Jonah's disgust, God forgives them. Still hoping for the city to be destroyed, he goes outside the city walls and settles down to wait for disaster.

> And the Lord God appointed a plant, and made it come up over Jonah, that it might be a shade over his head, to save him from his discomfort. So Jonah was exceedingly glad because of the plant. But when dawn came up the next day, God appointed a worm which attacked the plant, so that it withered. When the sun rose, God appointed a sultry east wind, and the sun beat upon the head of Jonah so that he was faint; and he asked that he might die, and said, 'It is

17. Jonah vomited out by the whale

better for me to die than to live.' But God said to Jonah, 'Do you do well to be angry for the plant?' And he said, 'I do well to be angry, angry enough to die.' And the Lord said, 'You pity the plant, for which you did not labour, nor did you make it grow, which came into being in a night, and perished in a night. And should not I pity Nineveh, that great city, in which there are more than a hundred and twenty thousand persons who do not know their right hand from their left, and also much cattle?'

Jonah 4:6-9

This is more than a fairy tale about a bad-tempered hitch-hiker. Still less is it an excursion into marine biology. The most important animal in the story is hidden. It is not the whale but Jonah himself. His name is the Hebrew word for 'dove', a symbol of the children of Israel. Just as Noah dispatched a defenceless dove into the hostile world after the crisis of the flood was past, so in the same way after the crisis of the exile we have the story of Jonah. The dove is freed from his dark, watery prison and sent out in faith to a hostile world where he preaches the law, only to be surprised at its success and at God's mercy.

The exile had taught the chosen people how to survive pain and despair in an alien land, but the book of Jonah contains a new lesson. It offers a warning against the pitfalls of security and the dangers of complacency and exclusiveness. If the people of Nineveh could be moved by the word of God, anyone could be. The ancient law of Moses contained in Exodus, Leviticus, Numbers and Deuteronomy was collated and finalised after the exiles' return. In the future, wherever the wandering people pitched their tents, through force or free will they would always be secure in the knowledge of the law. They had a framework for eternity which would shelter them anywhere at any time. Add to that the commonsense and mysticism of Israel's wisdom, from the suffering of Job to the scepticism of Ecclesiastes, and they could take on all comers and win. In the Jerusalem of Nehemiah, former cup-bearer to the Persian king Artaxerxes and of Ezra the priest who was not keen on mixed marriages, there may well have been a new emphasis on legalism, but this must be balanced by the story of Jonah with its insistence on the power of God's law as a sign for the world as a whole and its reminder that the mercy of Israel's God exceeded all fine print.

*

The law of the Lord is perfect and sweeter than honey, says Psalm 119, the longest psalm in the Bible. It is devoted to singing the praise of the law. That exuberance and delight is something which seems far removed from our notions of law, or from those of any other peoples current in the fifth century BC. When Ezra conducted an eight-day session of reading and expounding the law, everyone in Jerusalem attended. Why was there such enthusiasm for something which restricted people's freedom of action? Professor Ernest Nicholson of Oxford believes that the law in ancient Israel was a remarkable humanising force in the life of the people. It was something that was put on to them, not as draconian laws, but as a good gift from God. At the very centre of it is the discovery of the worth of humanity, the abolition of all magic and superstition and emphasis on the decision of human beings to organise their own life and their own society rationally and well. People began to accept their solemn responsibility to choose between the right way and the wrong way. No magical forces come between them and the commands of God. They cannot fall back upon excuses for not obeying God's will or trying to behave like human beings. In that way the law rationalised life and humanised life.

At the heart of the law were the ten 'words', the commandments given to Moses at Mount Sinai when the Israelites chose freedom and a promise rather than the safety of slavery. Within the Bible, the commandments are accorded a status beyond all other words. They are not the mere inspiration of God, they are his handiwork written by his finger on two tablets of stone. It is therefore likely that these words more than any others were relayed from one generation to another with care. This would explain why, though the final touches were put to the books of the law after the return from exile, the ten commandments and the Mosaic covenant carry echoes not of the 5th century BC but of the long-forgotten world of the suzerain treaties of the ancient Hittites and Sumerians. There is one notable difference. In the laws of Israel's God, all men are equal. Even today the commandments remain a checklist for our better natures. Lord Blanch thinks the ancient prohibitions of Moses have survived because they make up a code which is old and new. He believes the code was in advance of its time, although great legal codes existed contemporary with it, notably the code of Hammurabi in the second millennium. He thinks that the ten commandments are commandments for atheists as well as believers. And that is why they have been in one way or another incorporated into law through most of the western world. On the whole it is still true that robbery and theft and disrespect for parents are regarded as bad. That is due entirely to the tradition inherited from the Jews.

But if the ten commandments are so all-embracing why are there any other laws? Professor Nicholson says that no Jew or Christian today would regard the ten commandments as the end of Jewish or Christian ethics. But they are not at all a bad beginning. They are signposts for society, and he laments the fact that they seem to be so little read or taught in schools, or indeed in church, these days. They are not the positive end of Jewish and Christian ethics, but they are certainly a good basis. They are remarkably succinct, summarising your duty towards God and your duty towards your neighbour. In that way, certainly for the Christian and the Jew, they still warrant attention. We are all in one way or another going to be forced to look at the question of how we honour our parents, the fifth commandment. The word 'honour' there has the sense of 'glorify', but also 'care for'. As our older generation live longer, we as a society and as individuals are going to have to do more about the way we care for them. We have become a very covetous society, and that may be the root of some of our problems. The tenth commandment, against covetousness, is ingeniously put at the end, as a way of saying, above all, 'Do not let the desires of your heart start to control you, because, if they do, you may break any or all of the foregoing.' The person who put that golden touch at the end was saying that much of the evil that men do begins in the desires of their hearts.

But Jesus condensed these commandments still further:

> And one of the scribes came up and heard them disputing with one another, and seeing that he answered them well, asked him, 'Which commandment is the first of all?' Jesus answered, 'The first is, "Hear, O Israel: The Lord our God, the Lord is one; and you shall love the Lord your God with all your heart, and with all your soul, and with all your mind, and with all your strength." The second is this, "You shall love your neighbour as yourself." There is no other commandment greater than these.'
>
> Mark 12:28-31

If no other commandment is greater than these, have the ten commandments of Moses been overtaken by Christ's two great precepts of charity, at least for the Christian? Lord Blanch thinks not. He says that the advantage of the negative commandments is that you know where you are. It is much more that you may find yourself in a situation where love for a neighbour can be is bad for him; if, for example, you decide to harbour or conceal a criminal act on the part of somebody else. You may say that that is loving your neighbour. On the other hand, is it really love of neighbour if it does not lead him to repent of his actions? It is a much more diffuse idea. It was not diffuse in the Hebrew mind, but it is in our minds. Love of your neighbour then meant care for his good, care for his faith, care for his membership of the sacred people. All of that would have been quite explicit in the Hebrew mind. It is when we use it rather vaguely, in a kind of wishy-washy way, 'Be kind to your neighbour and don't kick the cat, and don't ever criticise anybody else.' It is not sufficient to give us all we need.

*

In Judaism, the law is nothing if not explicit. The absolute ideals of the ten commandments are backed by a wealth of regulations and case law touching on every area of life. There are laws about food and fighting, and about what to do with an enemy's stray ass, and a proscription against tattoes, and endless refinements of what can and what cannot be done on the Sabbath. Would anyone aim at observing all the law? Rabbi Jonathan Sacks, Principal of the Jews College, London, would. Jews believe, he says, that if we do not take every single word of the Mosaic books with absolute seriousness our faith is compromised. They are the governing principles in our lives as Jews. They are essential to the survival of the Jewish people. Keeping a sabbath kept us to some degree economically distinct, keeping the dietary laws kept us to some extent socially distinct. Those laws which appear to be very little connected with ultimate concerns are probably, more than any other, the secret of Jewish survival.

In no area of life are the restrictions of Judaism more apparent to the outsider than in the preparation of food. Jews may not eat pork – a restriction they share with Moslems. A verse in Deuteronomy condemns the pagan practice of boiling a kid in its mother's milk – the liquid was then used as a fertility charm. This prohibition has grown into an insistence on cooking all meat and milk separately. Also, the faithful may not eat shellfish, quadrupeds without hooves or any animals which crawl, swarm or use their front two legs as hands – so no prawn cocktail, no rabbit pie and no kangaroo-tail soup. In a hot climate, it makes sense to steer clear of pork and seafood and to be careful of milk, so perhaps the dietary laws are a recipe for health, rather than for holiness.

Mickey Yudkin disagrees. Scholars throughout the ages, she says, have tried to prove that the strictures on various types of meat, foul and fish in Leviticus lead to the healthy life. This has been refuted. There is, however, an internal logic in the dietary laws. It is a way of proclaiming that you are a holy people. Over the ages it was thought that *kashrut*, which is the abstract noun for keeping the dietary laws, was a protest against the gluttony and the licentious habits of the Canaanites. This idea was developed particularly around the eating of pig flesh because the pig was supposed to be a symbol of gluttony and easy living. In the dietary laws we see a great striving to impose discipline in an area where there would probably be no discipline at all.

Self-imposed domestic discipline is one thing, but how can the Hebrew law of revenge, the *lex talionis*, reflect the justice of a merciful God? For Christians, has not the Old Testament 'an eye for an eye, a tooth for a tooth' been countermanded by Christ's injunction to turn the other cheek? Mary Evans says that in the Old Testament an eye for an eye was very much a positive statement – *only* an eye for an eye, as opposed to a *life* for an eye. Within that context it was a radical statement. So, although you cannot hold the two together, you can see one as developing the intention of the other. 'Turn the other cheek' is an expression of the theological principle that was contained in 'an eye for an eye'.

In all fairness, an eye for an eye was mild in the ancient world – and still is in the modern world. As recently as the last century the Gentile laws of England hanged men for stealing sheep and deported the hungry for stealing bread. There are countries even now where it is considered just to torture the dissident and mutilate the criminal. Yet throughout their long history the Jews have avoided mutilation as well as literalism. As Rabbi Sacks says, the Jewish tradition has never taken the verse 'an eye for an eye, a tooth for a tooth' literally. It always referred not to vengeance but to monetary compensation. One has to see the legal parts of the Bible through tradition, and that is the fundamental difference between the Jewish and some more literal Christian approaches to the Bible.

Down the centuries the Jews have kept their law alive by constant study and repetition. The law is a carrot not a stick – a source of protection not a threat. Dr Phillips believes that this unique concept of law was only crystallised after the return from exile. Before the exile, with the writer of the book of Deuteronomy, for instance, law was thought of very much as what God gives to the people. They know where they are: there are no surprises: God discloses his will. Indeed Torah, in Deuteronomy, comes to mean the complete expression of the will of God. It is the nearest thing we have to an incarnation in the Old Testament. After the exile, the law changes. The new writer recognises that man will always fail. He has to provide a way out, and he shifts the law. If you imagine God, and underneath him a line, and then Israel, that is the old position with the law hanging, rather as a threat, over the people. But the new writer shifts the position round, so that we have God above and Israel below, and the law is at the side. The God-Israel relationship is always assured.

The Israelites are the elect. All they have to do is to appropriate their election. The question this writer asks is: 'In this appalling disaster of exile will they have sufficient faith to appropriate their election?' But the law is placed round the side, as it were. It is what St Paul calls the 'fence of the law'. It surrounds the elect people. It no longer stands as a threat. It protects the elect community and God is above, beaming down his election on that community.

*

But there are also dangers in the law. Blind addiction to the letter of any law is one of the prime sources of bigotry and injustice. Professor Nicholson says that there is a great deal in the Old Testament which is acutely aware of the power of religion to alienate human beings. He speaks with some feeling, as someone originally from Northern Ireland, about the sadness in his own land. It is an example of the power of religion to alienate human beings, to dehumanise them, to make them behave on both sides of the sad divide there in an unholy way to one another, to do the most vile things that people can do to each other, often in the name of religion.

Law has to be applied with wisdom. For the Jews in Jerusalem, collating their laws, while Socrates shuffled towards hemlock, asking his endless questions of the youth of Athens, wisdom was not the preserve of an academic élite. It was a practical combination of common sense and human insight, offering answers not questions. In the third section of the Hebrew Bible – the Writings – we find the books of wisdom, the homely advice of Proverbs with its warning against adulteress's eyelashes, the cynicism of Koheleth and the conundrum of one man's suffering posed by Job. But is this all rather small-scale compared with the rest of the Bible? How do the wise men fit in with the grandeur of the law and the fire of the prophets?

Dr Carroll says that what he likes about them is that they are so diametrically opposite to the prophets. The prophets rant and rave, and shout and scream, call down fire and brimstone, and curse everybody. The wise man says, 'We've been around for thousands of years and the world's going to be around for more. You get by by seeing how it works. Certain things you don't do – if you're invited out to dine with a great man, a king, you don't gobble your food. If you're married to a loud woman, you go quietly, and if you have options, you avoid anything that will lead you into trouble.' It is all very sagacious, but built on pragmatic experience. There is very little theory there. It is designed to teach people how to live ordinary lives, not how to deal with a crisis. You could say that prophecy is something for crisis. The Assyrians and the Babylonians are knocking down the walls – what do we do now? The prophet turns up with something to say. The wise man simply gets on with how you live a normal life, and that is how most people actually live, outside crisis.

> Act with righteousness as long as you live. Wipe away the tears of the mourner and protect the widow. Respect the inheritance a son gains from his father. Let him be on his land. Deal justly and carefully with officials. Take care that you do not punish without cause. Do not kill – it will do you no good.

That is not the work of an Israelite but an instruction to the Egyptian king Merikere in 2100 BC or thereabouts. The Jews came late to wisdom. The wise men of Egypt and Babylonia had been at it since the third millennium. So was Hebrew wisdom merely derivative? Was there anything that distinguished it from the ancient wisdom of the two countries in which the Israelites had been held captive. Professor Davidson thinks that the wise men in Egypt and Babylon say more or less the same things about human life, because what they were saying was based on shrewd observation of what went on in the world about them. But in Ancient Israel there had to be an attempt to integrate this wisdom, as there was an attempt to integrate everything else, into the context of a belief in the God of Israel. Wisdom therefore tended to be identified with the fear of the Lord. Wisdom develops a personality which is then closely linked with God.

Throughout the wisdom literature of the ancient Near East there are two approaches. There is the thoughtful probing of the human condition in the Babylonian 'Praise of Wisdom', the Egyptian 'Dispute over Suicide' and the Biblical books of Job and Ecclesiastes. The second school is harder to take seriously. It is the sound, hoary advice represented by the book of Proverbs which seems to be waiting to be cut up into calendar mottoes. Can observations about the industry of ants and the social acceptability of lizards represent the summit of Jewish wisdom? Of course not, says Sir Immanuel Jakobovits. Although Jews call certain parts of the Biblical canon the 'wisdom literature', including notably the book of Proverbs, we have certainly never assumed that the human capacity for the original use of intelligence has been exhausted and that wisdom is a finished chapter. On the contrary, we are charged to use our intellect constantly for the interpretation of the divine will for the further research and study of our ancient sources − our Biblical sources, our post-biblical talmudic sources − and thereby exercise the capacity of wisdom with which we are endowed. This is to enable us with each successive generation to penetrate further into life's purposes, God's will and the application of timeless teachings to every particular age. All this is part of wisdom.

It is the Hebrew Bible which has given the world a patron sage of wisdom. The reputation of Solomon, the son of David, overshadows the Egyptian Amenemopet and the nameless sages of Babylonia. In all probability Solomon was responsible for gathering a nucleus of wise men at his court. The book of Kings says that he was wiser than all the kings of the east, a reputation which even reached south to Sheba and its queen. Solomon has been credited with writing 3,000 proverbs, the Song of Songs and the book of Ecclesiastes − all of which is one way of saying that he was the undisputed king of wisdom: a glory unchanged for a thousand years until someone gave it away to some lilies growing in a field. Dr McKeating believes that even the work ascribed to Solomon which is not in the canon of the Bible is ahead of its time. Read, for instance, the Wisdom of Solomon in the Apochrypha and you will find that there is nothing primitive or home-spun about it. There is some rather sophisticated thought going on there, some rather clever critiques of religion. Read what the book of Wisdom says about idolatry and you will find explanations of how idolatry arises which were not re-invented until some time in the 19th century. It is very sophisticated thinking.

*

18. Job abused by his wife

The book of Job, dealing with the problem of undeserved suffering, was considered by Luther to be the greatest book of the Bible, and the text of Ecclesiastes is familiar to many who have not read it. Is their eminence deserved? Dr Carroll considers Job a book that can stand alongside any of the great writings of world literature – with Greek tragedy or Shakespeare. It may have been a response to the crisis of exile: it is difficult to date. Perhaps somebody looking at the exile wondered about some of the traditional beliefs about punishment from the deity and thought, 'That's not good enough, that's too corny. Let's tell a story, an old story, which you can find in Mesopotamian literature, about Job.' They tell the story and all the arguments are rehearsed, though they do not resolve the matter, because, for the writer of Job, God is beyond good and evil. So in that sense the crisis may also have compelled the wisdom writers to rethink certain ideas.

Job's problems are far beyond his control. One day, while he is quietly and piously minding his own prosperity in the land of Uz, he becomes the subject of celestial debate. God praises

Job's fidelity to Satan, the adversary. Satan replies that Job's faith is a fair-weather faith, which will be turned by any squall of misfortune. Job's fate is then sealed. He is put to the test and has become a byword for meek suffering – an improving caricature which misses the real point of the story. Sister Nilda Pettanuzzo says she wonders sometimes about the validity of the patience of Job. Some people, she says, stop at the first two chapters with their stoic acceptance – 'The Lord gives, the Lord takes away' without proceeding to chapter 3 where Job curses the day he was born. Job becomes angrier and angrier with God. Then God speaks, and in a sense his conviction that God will be in relation to him is answered. God says: 'Hey, Job, stand up. Act like a man. Where were you when I created the world?' Job more or less says, 'Oh, I'm sorry I spoke.' So he gets no answer, except the answer of God's presence. It speaks to her, Sister Nilda says, of a deep faith in the reality of God and the ultimate triumph of goodness.

But Job still complains:

> I loathe my life; I will give free utterance to my complaint; I will speak in the bitterness of my soul. I will say to God, Do not condemn me; let me know why thou dost contend against me... Are thy days as the days of man, or thy years as man's years, that thou dost seek out my iniquity and search for my sin, although thou knowest that I am not guilty, and there is none to deliver out of thy hand? Thy hands fashioned and made me; and now thou dost turn about and destroy me.
>
> Job 10:1-2, 5-8

For Dr Clines the vehemence of Job's reactions marks him out as the world's best sufferer. There is more than one Babylonian story of an innocent sufferer who laments in much the same words as Job, but none come anywhere near the coherence and majesty of the book as a whole. The Babylonian poems show no kind of advance in thought, or psychology, on the part of the sufferer, whereas the Job of the Bible is in every speech constantly shifting his ground psychologically and theologically. He is developing a dialogue with God which God only belatedly enters into, but there is constant movement in Job's position and there is the presence of the other friends which makes the whole book into something more like a seminar than a simple lament. It is a much deeper book.

Above all, it is an attack on bad religion. Job's friends Eliphaz, Bildad and Zophar are certain that suffering must be merited – and with comforters like that, who needs enemies? The unlovable trio are a send-up of shallow mechanical religion which is still alive today. Job tells us that illness and poverty are not a sign of God's anger any more than success is a proof of goodness. The thought is echoed in Ecclesiastes – God is ruler over all and the man who thinks he can understand the world is a fool.

But is there any insight for today's world that can be derived from such negative wisdom? Sister Nilda says she is conscious of being shocked out of pious platitudes by phenomena like the famine in Ethiopia, or by the sight of a child dying, while at the same time living with an absolute conviction of the reality of God and the joy of life. They resonate with her own readiness to doubt, and what she finds marvellous is that within the Bible this doubt has been canonised in the book of Job. The Lord says to Job, 'You have spoken well', even though Job has literally waved his fist in the Lord's face. She says, 'I am quite encouraged, because I often wave my fist in the Lord's face.'

The scribes and scholars who collated and edited the law and wisdom of the Israelites from the fifth to the second century before Christ were performing a unique trick. While the rest of the ancient world merged its cultures in a race towards Hellenism, the Jews, a tiny nation, borrowed freely from all surrounding cultures, but they adapted the insight of Egypt, of Babylon and even of Greece to their own purposes. They had built a framework for eternity which could be added to but not destroyed, and which would offer shelter in many countries through many centuries far beyond the fashions of a dying classical age. The beginning of wisdom was the fear of the Lord. By obeying the laws and studying with wisdom, the Israelites would become like Jonah – a sign to an unbelieving world. They were secure in the knowledge that some human questions could not be answered, that failing was a bridge to the one God; and to Job's unresolved problem of suffering the answer is – a hippopotamus.

As Dr Clines says, Job does not need comfort in the sense of being patted on the head and hearing, 'There, there, it's all going to be over before long.' He wants something more serious than that: he wants an answer to an intellectual problem that has become an existential problem for him. He wants to know why he, a righteous man, is suffering and, by implication, why every other righteous man who suffers is suffering. God gives him his answer. He spends his speeches describing in loving detail the cosmic menagerie of wild animals that he has created. Some of them are quite delightful animals, like the stupid ostrich who hides her eggs in the sand, and that seems to have nothing whatever to do with the problem of suffering. But the climax of God's speeches are his descriptions, running into two chapters, of the crocodile and the hippopotamus. God is saying, 'In the world that I created, there are not only wild animals that do not make any sense to humans and that are completely useless to humans. There are also wild animals that are positively hideous, and frightening and dangerous to humans. But I made them. They are in my world and, believe me, I have my reasons.' That is an argument on the cosmic plane, and Job is meant to understand it on the moral plane. He quickly realises that the meaning of that speech is that suffering is a hippopotamus. It makes no sense to us, but it makes sense to God.

9. Cries in the Wilderness

There is a Jewish legend unimpeded by evidence, or even by likelihood, which tells of a secret journey undertaken by Alexander the Great, a romantic youth with a loose grasp of geography and a fondness for drink, a soldier who put entire cities to the sword without a qualm but wept inconsolable tears over the death of his favourite horse. For a brief span of years in those five centuries which separate Malachi, the last prophet of the Hebrew Bible, and John the locust eater, the first prophet of the New Testament, Alexander moulded the culture of half Europe and Asia. He ruled an empire which he himself had won that stretched from Northern Greece to West Pakistan.

In 331 BC, after gaining control of the small country of Palestine as well as the larger prizes of Egypt and Syria, Alexander took time off from ruling the world to go on pilgrimage to the shrine of the Egyptian god Amun in the Libyan desert – so much is attested by the reliable, if unimaginative, historian Arrian. That pilgrimage quickly became encrusted with rumour and fable. Alexander had received a special oracle. Perhaps he had been promised immortality, perhaps death. Perhaps he had been told that he was not the son of Philip the deceiver of Macedon, but of the god Amun himself. But among the Jewish communities of the eastern Mediterranean another story quickly gained credence. The visit to the priests of Amun had been a blind. Before he had set foot in Egypt, Alexander had made a lonely detour to Jerusalem to see the High Priest, and as the young master of the old world set eyes on the priestly diadem bearing the words 'sacred to the Lord' he had fallen down in awestruck reverence.

That untrue story is important. In Jerusalem the Temple had been rebuilt and the law had been collated and consolidated, but this was not enough to withstand the new and insidious dangers of Alexander's world. Alexander had a vision of a world united by a single culture. His successors would declare war on the exclusiveness of the God of the children of Israel. This would force the hand of many Jews. Some, like those who manufactured the Alexander story and those who wrote the Sibylline oracles, took on the Greek world at its own propaganda game and turned their separateness inside out. They produced literature insisting that the one God should be worshipped by Jew and Gentile alike. Others responded with heroism, martyrdom and violence. Still others fled to the desert to wait for the final conflict between the sons of darkness and the sons of light.

*

The story of the four centuries before John began baptizing in the river Jordan is a story of bigots, rebels, Temple politics, insane hopes, visions of the end and a pagan world fascinated by eastern saviour cults and the enigma of the nameless God of the Jews. Our understanding of those years when the Bible began to be translated out of Hebrew and made available to the wider world is hampered by the fact that much of the evidence has literally been 'hidden away'. The Greek word is 'apocrypha', the title given to fourteen books of prayer, patriotism, gentle fiction and ferocious apocalypse that belong to this period.

The books are traditionally included in Roman Catholic Bibles but are often missed out of Protestant Bibles. Does this omission matter? Professor Bartlett thinks it does, and that to omit them is to miss out on a great deal. It really is necessary, he says, to read widely if you want to get a fair picture of the Judaism of the last two or three centuries BC, which was the cradle of Christianity. One of the problems has been that the Protestant tradition, as seen in the Authorised Version and other translations, has ended its Old Testament with the book of Malachi and the promise at the end of that book of the coming of Elijah. Most readers have then turned over one blank page and found themselves in the first chapter of Matthew. In doing so they have turned through 500 years of history without ever noticing what is there.

The Old Testament contains some material which belongs between the period of Malachi and the time of Jesus, but the general tendency has always been to ignore it and pass on to John the Baptist.

What lies between Malachi's promise of the forerunner of the Messiah and Matthew's account of the ancestry of a child born in awkward circumstances in the reign of Herod the Great is a welter of sectarian controversy and sharpened religious conviction. These were not years of calm and silence; Judaism was at boiling point. Dr Rowland thinks that most people who write on the Judaism of the Second Temple period – the period culminating in the destruction of the temple in AD 70 – think of the situation as one of intense religious ferment, with a variety of different ideas and interpretations of the Jewish religious inheritance. There were people who wanted to impose a particular view on all Jews, but it proved to be remarkably difficult, and we know now, particularly as a result of the discovery of the Dead Sea Scrolls, that within Judaism there could exist an enormous variety of interpretations and attitudes. One of the great contributions of Judaic studies over the last thirty years has been to show that Judaism at the time of Jesus was far from being a monolithic entity.

The divisions between the legalistic Pharisees and the more worldly Sadducees (who had doubts about life after death) are well attested in the Gospels, but they were only part of the picture of conflict. There were also the ascetic Essenes, the freedom-fighting Zealots, and the shadowy covenanters of Qumran waiting and praying for the Messianic age. All these groups contributed to the religious climate into which Jesus was born. It is important to remember that, however different they were, they all held the same purpose and grew from the same source. Their loyalty was to the Torah, the law of God, and their roots lay deep in the bloody soil of the years of persecution that followed Alexander's death in 323 BC.

*

At first, everything had gone well. Palestine had passed to the Egyptian Ptolemies. Ptolemy Auletes had commissioned the first translation of the scriptures into Greek and had spoken in glowing terms of the wisdom of the Jewish sages. Jews in Palestine chose without compulsion whatever they wished from Greek culture. But in the year 198 BC all that changed. The Syrian Seleucids took control of Palestine. Acceptance of Greek culture was now no longer an option. The God of Israel was under attack. Some Jews responded with the pen, some with the sword; but as the books of the Maccabees (from the Apocrypha) and recent findings from Qumran show, for all of them the final line of defence was the law.

This was a period of great intellectual activity. Enormous stress was laid upon the interpretation of the law. Sects such as the Essenes arose, and members of the Qumran sect spent much of their time and energy interpreting the Biblical books. The books of Maccabees are a fairly late, 2nd-century BC description of how the Jews resisted the attempt to Hellenise Israel and the wars in Maccabees are presented as a struggle for the law against those who would subvert it.

The struggle was vicious and the tactics were not pretty. The Seleucid king Antiochus Epiphanes, 'the god manifest' – or Epimanes, 'the slightly barmy', to give him his less official title – believed he was divine and knew he was short of money. He had the bright and blasphemous idea of auctioning the office of High Priest. This did not go down well in Jerusalem. There were riots and Antiochus was furious. In 168 BC he marched into Jerusalem and outlawed Judaism. Circumcision was forbidden and the Sabbath abolished, and anyone found in possession of the Torah could be put to death. In the Temple itself Jews were forced to sacrifice pigs to an image of Zeus – whose face, it was said, bore more than a passing resemblance to Antiochus.

The book of Daniel dates from this period. It encouraged the pious, the Hasidim, with old stories about Nebuchadnezzar. It could be read on two levels: as a tale from the past or as a veiled message for the present about the triumph of faith over tyranny. The books of Maccabees are more straightforwardly historical. They describe the bitter resistance of Jews forced to offer pagan sacrifice.

The first spark of revolt was struck in the village of Modin by an old priest called Mattathias. The king's officers came to the town of Modin to see that sacrifice was offered, and many Israelites went over to them. Mattathias and his sons stood in

19. Mattathias kills an idolatrous Jew at the altar

a group. The king's officers spoke to Mattathias:

> You are a leader here, a man of mark and influence in this town, with your sons and brothers at your back. You be the first now to come forward and carry out the king's orders. All the nations have done so, as well as the leading men in Judea and the people left in Jerusalem. Then you and your sons will be enrolled among the King's Friends; you will all receive high honours, rich rewards of silver and gold, and many further benefits.

To this Mattathias replied in ringing tones:

> Though all the nations within the king's dominions obey him and forsake their ancestral worship, though they have chosen to submit to his commands, yet I and my sons and brothers will follow the covenant of our fathers. Heaven forbid we should ever abandon the law and its statutes. We will not obey the command of the king, nor will we deviate one step from our forms of worship.
>
> 1 Maccabees 2:17-22

As soon as he had finished, a Jew stepped forward in full view to offer sacrifice on the pagan altar at Modin in obedience to the royal command. The sight stirred Mattathias to indignation; he shook with passion, and in a fury of righteous anger rushed forward and slaughtered the traitor on the very altar. At the same time he killed the officer sent by the king to enforce sacrifice and pulled down the pagan altar. Thus Mattathias showed his fervent zeal for the law. 'Follow me,' he shouted through the town, 'every one of you who is zealous for the law and strives to maintain the covenant.' He and his sons took to the hills, leaving their belongings behind in the town.

Mattathias died soon after. His sons Judas, Jonathan and Simon continued his work. The temple was rededicated in 165 BC, three years to the day after it had been first defiled. The victory is still remembered every year by the Jews celebrating the feast of Hannukah.

The Maccabees had won a considerable and unlikely victory and Israel was once again politically independent, but all was far from well. The wider world could not be kept away. Israel was caught between a mundane unsatisfactory present and an implausibly glorious future. Dr Rowland believes that she had also developed a cultural inferiority complex. Israel, he says, became more conscious of being a country which had to be subordinate in various ways to the super-powers of its own day, and that must have been a difficult position to be in for a group whose religious ideology stressed the supremacy of their God, and of his promises to them and for the whole world. To be regarded as a fourth- or fifth-class nation, rather than the centre of the universe, was extraordinarily difficult for them. We find contrasting responses. On the one hand there were those who taught that they just had to live with the fact and do the best they could to practise their religion, preserve the Temple and maintain piety at the individual level. Others still clung to prophetic hopes for the future – for liberation and change, and the renewal of the cosmos. A tension developed within post-exilic Judaism between those who looked forward to change and regarded the prophetic oracles as an inspiration and those who were content to make the best of a rather inadequate situation.

Given that feeling of inferiority, it seems strange that the triumphalist story of Maccabees finds a home only in some Christian Bibles but is excluded from the Hebrew canon. Why did the rabbis decide that their Bible was closed? Rabbi Friedlander says that in one way the Bible is never finished. In the first century, the rabbis established the canon, determining which books belonged and which did not. They excluded some, like the books of Maccabees, not because they were unholy or improper, but because they were too close, too contemporary.

There were other contemporary writings. The pious of the Qumran thought they were living in the end-time foretold by the prophet Habakkuk. They believed that the long-dead prophets of the defunct kingdoms of Judah and Israel had a specific message for their time. Dr Rowland thinks that their sense of urgency and their reworking of the Old Testament are a valuable key to understanding the New Testament. He believes that they have helped us understand the period when Jesus conducted his ministry because they enable us to see how a group with eccentric views – with firm convictions about their own calling and identity over against other Jews – could have existed as part and parcel of the fabric of 1st-century Judaism. One of the staggering conclusions that come across when we read the Dead Sea Scrolls, is the clear-cut conviction that not only were they members of a new covenant, but their co-religionists outside were in some sense beyond the pale. It was this group who followed the words of the teacher of righteousness mentioned in the Dead Sea Scrolls who could really comprehend the scriptures and gain true insight into God. It is that kind of insight which enables us to understand something of what was going on in the minds of Paul and the early Christians.

*

But where does academic interest end and faith begin? Is it necessary to understand the arcane religious fervour of the last centuries BC to grasp the domestic parables of a wandering carpenter? Professor Bartlett says that that depends on whether we are talking about an understanding of Christ as our saviour in a personal religious sense, or about a historical understanding of the background of Christianity and a deeper understanding of the work and meaning of Christianity. The two cannot, and should not, be divorced entirely. Most people who have the former want to have some sense of the latter. You cannot understand what Jesus and his contemporaries are saying unless you have some idea of the Judaism from which Jesus springs. You need to understand the literature he knew and to be able to read it through his eyes – as far as that is possible, given the gap of nearly twenty centuries.

To understand the development of Christianity in the Mediterranean world you need to understand the Hellenistic world in which Christianity developed. The last three centuries BC were the great age of Hellenism, and Hellenism had affected Judaism. It affected the Jews who were settled in the Hellenistic towns on the Mediterranean shores, and it is among those Jews in their synagogues in all these towns around the Mediterranean shores that Christianity developed.

There are further clues to the religious climate in which Jesus was born. Apart from the Apocrypha, there are the Pseudepigrapha, or 'false writings', so called because the books were written under the names of Israel's ancient patriarchs, between 200 BC and AD 200. Over the years they have become the waste-paper basket into which anything that does not fit the Hebrew or Christian canons has been thrown. One of these, the book of Enoch, written within the first two centuries BC, consists of revelations about the Messiah. Margaret Barker, an authority on the book, believes that it is essential to look in the Biblical waste-paper basket if we wish to understand Jewish Messianic expectations.

She thinks that many of the ideas about the Messiah are to be found in the Pseudepigrapha. They are not there explicitly, but they are clearly understood as the basis upon which many of these books are written. If we are to understand what the New Testament meant by the Messiah, we have to look at books other than the Old Testament. We cannot assume that the Christians invented it all, or that they suddenly had a completely new inspiration. They were working with material that was already there. This is most clearly seen in the book of Enoch, which has survived in the Ethiopian Church, and we now know that it was a pre-Christian book because remnants of it have been found at Qumran.

The central section of the book of Enoch gives us a clear description of a Messianic figure, and if we look at some of the traits of this figure the most obvious source for them would have been the old royal cult. If we read the New Testament on the assumption that many of the ideas in it were originally rooted in the old cult of the king, much of the early Christian imagery becomes readily understandable: for example, the ideas of exultation, exorcism, healing, which were thought to be part of the old role of the king. The tradition of Enoch claims that angelic beings could become incarnate in human form. Anyone reared in that tradition would therefore not have found it hard to cope with the idea of incarnation.

*

As the Hellenistic world became weaker and the Roman empire gained in strength there was an awakening of religious awareness. Throughout the Mediterranean eastern mystery cults became popular – cults which spoke of rebirth and after-life and deification. In Israel, now the Roman province of Palestine, ruled over by unloved puppet kings, the expectation of a Messiah was much less mystical. As Rabbi Friedlander says, the idea was of a political Messiah: a leader who would create justice, serve to bring the world to peace and redeem those who suffered. It was because of all these concepts relating to the Messiah that the Jews in that time did not recognise Jesus as more than a teacher. They saw him as a profound and good person, but not as a Messianic figure.

There was also a larger vision – a hope for a golden age which could be gleaned from even the most pessimistic prophecies. Dr Rowland has no doubt at all that the greatest influence on Jesus, and indeed on the whole of early Christianity, was what might loosely be called the eschatological tradition: in other words the hope expressed in the writings of the prophets, and indeed of the Torah itself, that God would bring about a reign of peace and justice on earth. It is those ideas which had most influence on Jesus and the early Christians. There were various expectations concerning a future Messianic figure or deliverer. While it is true to say that many people looked forward to the coming of a descendant of David who would liberate the people of God by armed struggle from the bondage of Rome, there were many other views as well. It is not all that obvious that a Jew looking at Jesus would have said that he did not conform to the pattern. There were many patterns, many models, of future Messianic, prophetic figures.

The Messiah would be a cornerstone, a tent-peg, a battle-bow, a source of security and defence, a shepherd for his people, a priest and a king. The final chapters of the book of the prophet Zechariah, probably written in the time of Alexander, contain another curious image: that of a king not of war but of peace, who rides not in glory but on the back of a donkey:

> Rejoice greatly, O daughter of Zion! Shout aloud, O daughter of Jerusalem! Lo, your king comes to you; triumphant and victorious is he, and having salvation: lowly, and riding upon an ass, even humble and riding upon an ass...and he shall command peace to the nations; his dominion shall be from sea to sea, and from the River to the ends of the earth.
>
> Zechariah 9:9-10

Coupled with this belief was a conviction held from Rome to Babylon of the promise of a golden age of peace and prosperity. Those Messianic hopes are part of Christian history, but they are still part of the Jewish present, as Rabbi Magonet explains. When we get into Jewish and Christian debates about Messianism, it is the future, he says, that is present – potentially present. This is what is really being talked about. It is only later that it becomes historicised and pinned down in chronology. Within the Jewish way of reading the matter these are all things continually *in potentia*. They are not past or future: they are there, present, potential at any moment, and the Messiah may walk through the door.

*

So far in the Bible story, Jews and Christians have been walking hand in hand. They have shared the same writings and merely read them in a slightly different order. For anyone, Christian or non-Christian, it is folly to try to understand Jesus the Jew apart from the scriptures which were part of him. But having said that, is the Hebrew Bible, with all its vengeance and bloodshed, compatible with a God of love? Rabbi Sacks thinks it is:

> When I read the Old Testament, or what I call the Bible, I find it full of love. In every page I find it a book of love. We read in the synagogue last week the line from Isaiah, 'Like one whom a mother comforts, I comfort you, says God.' Here, instead of a stern father, we have God as a comforting mother. The week before, we read the words of Amos, which reminded the Jewish people forcibly that the God who had love for Israel was also the God of the Philistines and the Syrians and the

20. Zechariah preaches the coming of the Messiah

Ethiopians. On our holiest day, the day of Atonement, we read the book of Jonah, where God tells Jonah he has to love the inhabitants of Nineveh, even though they are not of his people and they have a history of corruption behind them. The Bible is shot through with love, but love in a particular context: namely, how do we translate that love into a national constitution? What implications does it have for economic systems? For political structures? For the conduct of war? If my enemy strikes me, I can turn the other cheek, but what if he's about to strike my wife, or my child? One of the great differences between Jewish spirituality and Christian spirituality is that whereas the New Testament is concerned with the salvation of the individual, the Jewish Bible is concerned with the salvation of the people as a whole and of society as a whole. So I see them both as traditions of love, but love in a very different context.

In the past not everyone has been so broadminded. The early Christian heretic and manic subeditor Marcion insisted that the entire Hebrew Bible was worthless. His views were roundly condemned, but Professor Moltmann thinks that the prejudice lingers on. He believes that the Old Testament is *the* scripture, and that the New Testament is a Christian commentary on the scripture. Usually we understand it the other way round and call that book the Old because we have, in our possession, the New. But this is altogether wrong. It was a heretic from the old church who brought the terminology into use, to speak about the Old and New. In reality we read the Old Testament alongside the New Testament and the New Testament alongside the Old Testament.

In practice many Christians are not so even-handed. Lord Soper, former President of the Methodist Conference, says this means they are in danger of losing the background which makes the New Testament comprehensible and Jesus intelligible. But, he admits, it would also save the Church a great deal of trouble because, although the Old Testament is one of the most impressive and important documents in history, it can be more trouble than it is worth when Christians try to square what it says with what they feel they should believe in the light of the teaching of Jesus. In many respects, says Lord Soper, the Old Testament is a dangerous document because it serves the purposes of those who are concerned in the first instance with particular propositions, rather than with the evaluation of the eternal truth which, he holds, is manifest and finalised in Jesus.

But Rosemary Ruether, Professor of Applied Theology in Illinois, thinks that the very use of the words Old and New has become a dangerous value judgment. She says they suggest that the Jewish Bible is somehow surpassed; that it is only a preface, or something pointing towards Christianity. That is not an appropriate way to understand the book. The Hebrew Bible is more than a preamble. What tends to be missed, or simply put aside as though it were not fully Christian, is the strong this-worldliness of Hebrew scripture. It presents a system in which religion and politics are intimately related and in which the message is very much of justice here on earth. Christianity has the model of being a religion of the spirit of the other world and has tended to hold that the Hebrew model is mere materialism when in fact it contains an important message about justice which many Christians are only waking up to now.

But if Christians take a few tips from the practicality of the Hebrew Bible, is that not enough? Does a Christian have to make the whole Old Testament part of his journey? James Barr, Regius Professor of Hebrew at Oxford, thinks that the story of the beginnings of the world and the first wanderings of the fathers of the nation of Israel is important for our picture of the world in which we live and the relationship between man and God. The wanderings of the people teach us that God operated through a particular small society of people with whom he lived in an intimate relationship, and that he set before them a purpose which was to be fulfilled at a later time. That planned purpose and promise is central to the expectations of Christianity.

The antiquity of the Jews could not save them from the cruelty of history. In 63 BC the hard-won Maccabean independence crumbled when the Roman general Pompey stormed into the Temple and claimed Palestine as a subject nation. Roman rule was a double curse, bringing with it the hated Herodian kings who, coming from Edom, were not even properly Jewish. The old heroes of the Bible took on a new contemporary meaning.

When you were under Roman oppression, says Rabbi Magonet, you did not talk directly, for example, about the Romans; you talked instead about Esau. Esau became the symbol of Rome, because of his other name, Edom, which stood for Rome. So you could tell all manner of stories about Esau, and read the Bible stories as paradigms of your political struggle against the Romans. The stories were not allegorised. They were not past, but living sermons, living homilies, living people to whom you would turn to understand the nature of what was happening to you.

Special loathing was reserved for the Herod the Great. Medieval mystery plays were to paint him as a raging paranoid tyrant, and his contemporaries were not much fonder of him. He married Mariamne, a descendant of the Maccabees, but spoilt the gesture by murdering her. Herod's family life was complicated: he had ten wives and tended to kill his relations. The Roman emperor Augustus had no illusions about the quality of his family life. It is safer to be Herod's pig, he remarked, than his son. Herod and his successors scandalised and repelled the people they tried to rule. During their reign the ascetic communities of Qumran enjoyed a new lease of life. There has been much speculation that John the Baptist had been part of their community, but Dr Rowland thinks this theory overlooks one important difference between John and the Qumran community. As far as we know, the people who lived in the Qumran felt that they had to cut themselves off completely from society. From what we know of John, while he was definitely on the fringes of society he was keen to inculcate the truth of his message and persuade people to go out to him to the river Jordan to be baptized, repent and await the coming kingdom. He may have been influenced to some extent by the writers of the Dead Sea Scrolls, but unlike them he was convinced that the time of fulfilment was already at hand.

John's message of the corruption of the house of Herod was eventually to cost him his life. But his promise of a new kingdom, and of One who was to come, would outlive the cunning of all the Herods and the deadly dancing of Salome. His voice crying in the wilderness repeating the ancient Messianic promises of the prophet Isaiah would be the first notes of a new song which has been sung by Christians down the centuries. John believed that the early years of the 1st century AD were the time of fulfilment, a conviction embedded in faith and, Professor Bartlett believes, also in historical plausibility. Professor Bartlett says that all we can do is look at the historical circumstances which favoured the rise and spread of Christianity. First was the fact that in the 300 years before Jesus, the Jews had encountered the Hellenistic world. The Jews were spread out everywhere, from Babylon in the east to Alexandria in the south and Rome in the west. Secondly, in the 1st century AD eastern religions were of interest in the west: the Roman poet Juvenal wrote of the eastern river Orontes pouring into the Tiber. There was a great deal of exchange between east and west. Communications were good, and that was all part of it. Thirdly, Judaism itself was in crisis once again. Rome was suppressing the more nationalistic tendencies of Judaism, and the Jews, under Pharisaic leadership, were in the process of evolving a more pietistic form of religion. While this was happening on the Jewish front, in the Hellenistic world too people were seeking their own forms of salvation – the word salvation is well-known to Hellenistic Jews and others of the 1st century AD. There were many people looking for salvation from the slings and arrows of outrageous fortune, which they called Tychê or Moira, fate.

People were anxious to find ways of avoiding fate, and so Jesus was proclaimed in two ways. He would be proclaimed to Jews as someone who fulfilled the Old Testament scriptures, and he would be proclaimed to the Gentile, Hellenistic world as someone who could bring them salvation. He was a *sôtêr*, a saviour (various Hellenistic kings were called *Sôtêr*) and to call Jesus *sôtêr* or saviour was to suggest that he was a figure who had importance for the non-Jewish world of his time. Clearly the times were favourable, although the idea of God involving himself in human affairs must be appropriate in any age. Jesus was obviously a person of his time, and we cannot pinpoint that moment in God's chronological chart and say, 'Well done, God. You got it right.' We can only observe that certain movements were about, working in their own way to the advantage of a new faith which would one day be known as Christianity.

10. A New Song

Matthew
Mark
Luke
John

Every day in the backstreets of Calcutta young women dressed in coarse cotton saris thread their way through the hot damp stench of a poverty beyond despair. They seek out those with the least hope of life and take them back to an old Hindu temple, where they care for them until they die. In the Soviet Union sane men and women profess beliefs which they know will lead them to the drugged nightmare of the psychiatric wards of prison hospitals. In Latin America priests, pastors and church workers speak out for the losers from whom everything is taken and by doing so consciously court the macabre fate of a mysterious disappearance. Even in Britain and the United States many who are well-off are surprisingly uneasy about their comfort and question the apparent certainties of success.

All these patterns of thought and behaviour, which are only distant relations to commonsense, share a single motive: the conviction that it is possible to walk in the footsteps of a Jew of the 1st century AD who was born in the reign of Herod the Great and was put to death under the procuratorship of Pontius Pilate. What was so special about Yeshua-bar-Joseph, the healer with allegedly magical powers accused by the rabbis of leading the children of Israel astray? Why is Aisa, the gentle teacher, the son of Mary, remembered in the Qur'an as the beloved of Allah? And why do more than one and a half billion people believe that Jesus of Nazareth, the son of God and the son of Man, was the promised Messiah and is still alive today?

*

The Gospels, the first four books of the New Testament, tell us that Jesus proclaimed a confusing message of love. God, said Jesus, was the prodigal father waiting for, not demanding the return of, his children. The Almighty would not coerce even the powerless. The followers of Jesus grew used to contradictions. They were told about a kingdom where poverty was wealth, where the first would be last and the way to gain life was to lose it.

It is not surprising that the words of Jesus have been mangled down the centuries and that a message of love has often been twisted into an excuse for violence and hatred. But however much Jesus has been misinterpreted, there can be no doubt that he existed. In addition to the four Gospels, written by his friends, there are references to him by his enemies. Who in their right mind would bother to blacken the name of someone who never existed? The death of Jesus is remarked upon by people who did not care one way or the other, men like the Roman historian Tacitus, the Jewish historian Josephus, and the letter-writing Younger Pliny, a man who may have been a toady but was not a liar.

All these non-Christian sources present a unified picture. They testify that Jesus of Nazareth died the sordid death of crucifixion, a punishment normally meted out to the lowest criminals, and that oddly enough he still had a following after his death.

As you would expect, the Christian writers present a more complex picture. In the Gospels of Matthew, Mark, Luke and John, we have four parallel and sometimes divergent accounts of Jesus' life and ministry. Matthew, Mark and Luke clearly shared the same sources, but each sees Jesus from a different point of view. For Matthew, Jesus is above all the fulfilment of the prophetic promises of old. For Mark, he is the obedient servant with a message reaching beyond the Jewish community. Luke, the best journalist of the four, seems to have done his own research to produce a polished account which emphasises Jesus' humanity. The last Gospel, ascribed to John, the disciple whom Jesus loved, the son of Zebedee the fisherman, is the most mystical and theologically challenging. Jesus, says John, is the true vine, no more nor less than God's word made flesh.

But why were four competing versions written? Was that not a certain recipe for holy chaos? Professor Küng says that the Gospel writers did not quarrel about it among themselves.

They did not want a uniform doctrine about Jesus, but tried to interpret him as well as they could. The four Gospels in the New Testament did not contradict each other: they just said that one witness saw him in one way and another in another. They also gave him different titles. Some called him the Son of Man, others the Son of God. Yet others preferred the word Messiah. The Greeks said Christos. All these words and titles had different implications. The reality of Jesus himself is greater than the titles. The reality of his life and death and new life is greater than all these theories. The first Christians were much more concerned about what it means to be a Christian in practice than to have a theory. There is no theory about Christ in the New Testament. Afterwards, the Christian churches were much too concerned to have a theory about Christ, and they have sometimes forgotten what it means to follow him.

The accounts of Matthew and Luke suggest that Jesus was born several years 'before Christ', most probably in about 6 BC. The fact that the entire modern world is several years behind itself is the fault not of the Gospel writers but of Dionysius Exiguus ('the dwarf'), a 6th-century monk with a tidy mind but a poor head for mathematics.

*

The story of the birth of Jesus, beginning with an angel appearing to Mary and ending in a cave in Bethlehem, may puzzle many Christians today. To the Jews of the first century the claims were sacrilegious. The man dared to call God his father, and his words marked him out as a blasphemer and a troublemaker.

The Gospels avoid the innocuous facts we would expect to find today in any devotional biography of a religious leader. We do not even know what Jesus looked like. The earliest description we have is probably spurious. It is supposed to have been written by Lentulus, a Roman official on Pontius Pilate's staff. Jesus, he claimed, had a reddish face, expressive eyes and no spots. Later traditions would claim that Jesus was short and had a limp. By the fourth century the Bishop Epiphanius was sure that he had been six feet tall, had a long nose and looked like his mother.

All these inventions are attempts to fill the Gospel gaps.

21. The Annunciation

Why do the four evangelists miss out elementary biographical detail but include stories which are bound to cause trouble? The Rev. John Drury, Dean of King's College, Cambridge, believes that the evangelists never thought they were writing a bald, historical chronicle. They were writing books which were meant to appeal to the imagination and show people how to live, an aim that has always been achieved by symbols. A good example is the scene of the baptism of Jesus in Mark – which is adapted by the others. Mark says that when Jesus came up out of the water, the sky split open, God spoke certain audible words in Greek and the Spirit came down like a dove descending. The sky cannot split. *They* thought it could, *we* know it cannot. God does not speak audibly. These are legends. They are religiously powerful, but they are pictures. It is a symbolic narrative.

Jesus himself was clearly aware of the power of symbols. The four Gospels concur in pointing to a man who was the greatest teacher the world has ever known. He uses himself as a visual aid. His actions reinforce his words. He teaches his

followers that God is Lord of all – stronger than a storm on the
Sea of Galilee. He tells them that the only leadership which
counts is service – they began to understand when he washed
their feet. He forgives the sins men cannot see and heals the
wounds which are only too visible. The impact of his actions
was immediate and memorable, allowing time for the
meaning of his words to sink in.

The Gospels are more than diary accounts: the writers have
had time to stand back and reflect on all that has happened.
The Gospels are the unashamed beneficiaries of hindsight –
but of how much hindsight? When were the Gospels written?
According to the tradition of the Church, it was while the
apostles were still alive. Matthew, Mark and Luke were
written before AD 70 and John a little later. But, as Dom
Bernard Orchard says, modern critics prefer to date them all
post-70, and argue that they were written between AD 70 and
AD 100.

The dating of the Gospels has been a matter of considerable
dispute. The earliest date suggested for the first Gospel is AD
45 and the latest for the last AD 145. Both extremes are
unlikely, but even if the latest possible dates are taken the
Gospels are firmly placed in the earliest years of the Christian
community. By the standards of the ancient world the sources
for Jesus are highly respectable. Our historical knowledge of
the intrigues which brought the emperor Augustus to power
are based on the work of historians who wrote a good century
after the events they were describing. But by modern
standards how accurate is Gospel reporting? Dom Bernard
Orchard believes that the Gospel of St Mark is a verbatim
reconstruction of an eye-witness report.

Much of the religious thought of Jesus' time was bound up
with a future hope and with visions of the end. Jesus spoke of
a kingdom that was more than a promise or a warning. It was
as present as a grain of mustard-seed or a lost coin discovered
by a woman sweeping. Those who listened to him were
uncertain who he was. Perhaps he was one of the prophets
from the past who had come to life again. Perhaps he was
Elijah, the messenger of the future destined to prepare the
way for the Messianic kingdom. He referred to himself as the
'Son of Man', but what does that mean?

Morna Hooker, Lady Margaret's Professor of Divinity at
Cambridge, says that the title goes back to an Aramaic

phrase. That much we know. In the time of Jesus it was probably a phrase that could be used to refer to a person, or to oneself. Clearly Jesus used it in a way that impinged on people's memories. They remembered that he had used it, and they thought it significant. There is an interesting instance in the book of Daniel (7:13) where it is part of the imagery used by the author when he is talking about the vocation of Israel. The figure who is 'like a son of man' is said to represent the saints of the Most High, who are God's people, Israel. Perhaps what Jesus was doing in using this phrase was deliberately linking himself and his followers with this image of the vocation of Israel, which was to be obedient to God. That would involve suffering, and in the end it would involve glory, because God would acknowledge his people.

Jesus also claimed not only that he was the 'Son of God', but that the Temple was the house of his Father and that his ministry was his Father's business. 'Son of Man' was a familiar title in the Jewish world, but 'Son of God' reached out into the non-Jewish world. As Don Cupitt, Dean of Emmanuel College, Cambridge, says, the phrase 'Son of God' has a long pedigree in the Jewish tradition. It could be used just to mean a righteous man, or someone close to God, or it could stand for the people of Israel as a whole, or for the king. It also had meanings in the Graeco-Roman world, where the king was often thought of as Son of God, in the sense that he was a kind of mediator between the earthly and the heavenly world. When the Gospel was taken out into the Graeco-Roman world, the phrase 'Son of God' grew in significance. Jesus would have thought of himself as 'Son of God' in the sense of 'servant of God'.

By itself, the title was not remarkable. In the early centuries of the Christian era Messiahs were in fashion. The pagan philosopher Celsus complains to the Christian Origen that everywhere you trip over people claiming to be the son of God – even in the market place. What was unusual about Jesus was the intimacy he claimed with God. When he prayed he used the word 'Abba' – an informal word more like 'Dad' than 'Father'. Jesus left his followers little room for manoeuvre, and inevitably his words scandalised the religious establishment.

Many, particularly the Pharisees, the spiritual descendants of the Hasidim who had fought for Jewish independence against the Seleucids, found Jesus' words at best unfathomable and at worst threatening to the whole fabric of Jewish belief. What Jesus did *not* believe in caused as much scandal as what he proclaimed. As Professor Küng says, Jesus was not interested in ritual correctitude. Only purity before God, he said, bestowed purity of heart. Nor did he cultivate asceticism or fasting. He allowed people to call him a glutton and a drunkard. Nor was he scrupulous about sabbath observance – the human being is the measure of the sabbath and the law. All these questions are disputed again today in Jerusalem: whether a human being has to follow the letter of the law mechanically, or whether the spirit of the law, the will of God, is decisive.

It is easy to build up a politically chic image of Jesus – the anti-capitalist who caused a scene at the Temple, the demagogue with no time for the religious élite, the social iconoclast who broke up families and suggested that the dead should be left to bury their dead. But was Jesus a revolutionary? Professor Dunn of Durham thinks that the various attempts to piece together the story of Jesus as a revolutionary do not really work. Too much of the evidence fails to fit in and too much has to be forced to fit in. Jesus did not see himself as in any way setting out to challenge the establishment. If we consider the situation of the time it was all unrealistic. We, in our modern, democratic days, have a reality of political power which, in those days, was impossible for the ordinary person.

Much to the frustration of those of his followers who wanted to see the Romans thrown out of Palestine, Jesus never made any bid for political leadership. The emperor could receive his taxes – in the kingdom of God the widow's mite outweighed all the imperial revenues. Herod and Pilate were safe – Jesus appealed to a power-base older than the city of Rome, or the house of the murderous Hasmonaens. Professor Ruether says that Jesus was obviously not a Christian, but a Jew, and he operated out of a Jewish prophetic tradition. We have not read Jesus in his own Jewish context. A prayer like the Lord's Prayer is fully within a this-worldly framework of justice. It is not a prayer that we should go to heaven, but that heaven – the place where God is present – should come to earth. 'God's kingdom come' means 'God's will be done on earth'.

Even when he spoke about the kingdom that belonged to his

22. The Good Samaritan

Father Jesus always used this-worldly imagery. Was this because he wanted to avoid religious language, or was the social message a goal in itself? Have the parables a social purpose? Professor Dunn says yes, in two senses. One is that the context of the parables, the pictures he is using, is social, set firmly in the social context of the times. In that sense all the parables are social comment, or social description. But, in the sense that there is social criticism, the best example is the parable of the Good Samaritan. Those who are criticised for not helping the man who has fallen among thieves are the religious bureaucrats, the priest and the Levite. The hero is the Samaritan, who is despised. He is a social, political, religious, racial half-breed, and yet he is the star of the story.

*

Jesus' chief enemies were clearly the priests, the priestly circle which held such power as was held within the Jewish state by the Jews. He obviously created problems with the

Pharisees. The Pharisees saw themselves as the separated ones, who needed to be separated from the common, unclean, everyday things of life, in order to keep a proper purity and holiness for God. That concern was impressive and laudable in many ways, but it was its corollary that Jesus reacted against: the view that there are those who are inside and others, the sinners, who are outside. Jesus said that this attitude showed a misunderstanding of the way God looks on people. He therefore broke through the boundaries.

Jesus also broke many of the social rules of his day. He urged that one should follow the spirit not the letter of the law. He was not fastidious about the company he kept. Yet there was one social taboo he did not break. When he began his ministry, the twelve he summoned were all male. Professor Ruether believes that this aspect has overshadowed a more important message running through the Gospel stories. The Gospel writers, particularly Luke, have a tendency to present the good news to the poor in terms of the women who responded to the message. The tendency had nothing to do with feminism, as we know it today, but was an instinctual recognition that, if women are the most deprived members of groups that are already deprived because they are, for example, Samaritans, the most dramatic way of highlighting good news to the poor is to represent the poor in the shape of a woman, especially an unclean woman, or one whom society regards as a sinner. What we need to do is to see how the principle is applied to our own times.

Outside Palestine, exotic mystery cults were much in vogue. Ceremonies and secret formulae learnt by initiates ensured them life after death. Jesus spoke of a different sort of secrecy. The truth was hidden from men's eyes simply because they refused to open them. When God spoke they chose not to listen. The truth was more startling than magic. Mark, according to John Drury, sees the secret of the Gospel as quite other-worldly, but it suddenly erupts into this world. Somebody – a madman – shouts out in a synagogue, 'You are the Son of God', and it is true. Or at the very end, when Jesus dies, the centurion for no apparent reason says, 'This was the Son of God.' And the high priest, when Jesus is on trial before him, suddenly realises the same. The disciples, not understanding, emphasise that this divine truth has no continuous life in the world. It comes from elsewhere and explodes suddenly into the world.

In Judaism through the ages there have been many wonder-working rabbis teaching within the fold of orthodoxy. When Jesus healed the paralytic, it was not the miracle that shocked the onlookers, but the personal authority that lay behind the promise 'My son, your sins are forgiven.' For Rabbi Sacks that claim of authority marked the parting of the ways between Jesus and the covenant into which he had been born. There are, he says, a number of discontinuities between Jesus and the Jewish tradition. The first is the feeling, already evident in the sermon on the mount and highlighted by Paul, that one person has the authority to announce a new revelation, a new covenant and the abrogation of the old. That was a definite parting of the ways because the Jewish people regard their covenant with God as something that can never be broken or transcended.

Jesus failed to conform to Jewish hopes for a kingly Messiah. Matthew and Luke both claim royal genealogies for him. They saw, but did not see, that he had chosen another genealogy, older than David's Jerusalem. The king who would wear a crown of thorns chose another line of descent – a line of servants, not of kings. Professor Rogerson says that there is a whole series of servants of God who suffer. Abraham in Genesis 22 is asked to sacrifice his only son. Moses is rejected by the people he has brought out of slavery. Jeremiah is imprisoned, accused of being a traitor and whispered against and shouted at by the people of his own home village. Then there is the anonymous prophet referred to in Isaiah 40-53, and the writer of such psalms as Psalm 22. All through the Old Testament it is clearly shown that people who are caught up in the work of God as the servants of God will be involved in suffering; because that is what God's attempt to break through to men without violating their freedom implies. It foreshadows the New Testament, where Jesus is the suffering servant par excellence.

When Jesus rode into Jerusalem in triumph on his way to Calvary, he was welcomed as a second David. For Dr Gordon, the differences between David and Jesus are as important as the similarities. It is striking, he says, how the coming of Jesus into Jerusalem on Palm Sunday is deliberately contrasted with David's arrival at Zion as described in 2 Samuel 25. He comes, as we know, riding on a donkey.

Matthew tells us that when he arrived at the Temple the lame and the blind came to him and were healed. The verse (21:5) stands in isolation. But if we go back to 2 Samuel 5, we find some strange events involving the lame and the blind who, according to one understanding of the text, would be sufficient to ward off the Israelite attack led by David, and we are told that the lame and the blind are hated of David's soul. We are told also of a current saying that the lame and the blind shall not go into the house, which presumably means the Temple, when it is built. But Matthew, portraying Jesus as the son of David, sees a contrast between the militarist approach of David and the irenic, peace-making advent of Christ.

Christ's kingship, Dr Gordon believes, starts with Christ himself, the kingdom in person. Christ is proclaimed king by Christians, and yet his kingly rule in the world is not in evidence – or not very much. That is quite different from the national, ethnic kingship represented by David, and by Judah and Israel, in pre-Christian times. In other words, Israel was intended to be a messenger, a servant, to the nations. That was clearly seen by some of the prophets, even though they had their nationalistic moments. The essence of Christ's kingship is his appeal, world-wide, not on a social or ethnic basis, but through his message of forgiveness and a new beginning, his personal presence, the acknowledgement of him in human hearts and its translation into practice.

*

Jesus, the night before he died, behaved very strangely. Before crossing the Kidron Valley to the Garden of Gethsemane, he had a meal with his friends in an upper room. He took bread and broke it. He gave it to his disciples and told them to eat – it was his body. He lifted up a cup of wine and told them to drink from it – it was his blood. For Christians these strange actions are a living link to a man who died for them. For John Drury as for the early Christians and St Paul, the most important part is the Last Supper and the death of Jesus, because Jesus gave himself away freely. He did not write a book, as people do who wish to make a mark in the world. Some people do believe that God wrote a book, but to John Drury that does not seem to be a very clever idea:

23. The Last Supper

Jesus was a speaker. Then, in the end, in this last scene, at the Last Supper, he gives away all that he has left to give away, which is his body. That is enormously impressive. It was handed down in the church, as we can see in Paul's letters. On the night on which he was betrayed he took bread. I, like other priests, repeat that action several times a week. I believe we come nearest to Jesus in that action. It is presenting to people symbolically what I believe to be no less than the secret of life.

Throughout the Last Supper, Jesus tried to prepare the apostles for the shock of his death, and as usual they struggled to understand. When the meal was over, he made his way to the Mount of Olives just outside the city walls, where he was betrayed by a friend's kiss. The path to Calvary had begun.

On the following day he was interrogated by Pontius Pilate. Like many after him, Pilate wanted to know exactly who Jesus was.

'Are you the king of the Jews?' he asked.

'My kingship is not of this world,' Jesus replied.

Bewildered, Pilate washed his hands of the matter. Jesus'

fate was sealed. He was mocked and flogged, and his body was broken on a cross between two common thieves.

For many this final suffering was too much. The Docetists, as we have seen, would claim that Christ the son of God was not nailed to a cross, only Jesus the man. Later the followers of Muhammed would say that Allah loved Jesus too much to let him suffer pain and disgrace – a man who looked like Jesus was crucified in his stead.

But what of the Gospel writers? How could a crucified, vilified teacher be in any way related to the promised Messiah? Dr Frances Young of Birmingham thinks that the fundamental conviction of the writers of the New Testament was that Jesus was the fulfilment of God's promises. They honoured him and expected different things, and yet they found that somehow, although he did not fit their preconceived picture, he was the one who fulfilled all their hopes. That conviction is important, and the reversal of human values is compelling. There are all kinds of insights in this kernel of Christian faith, centred on the scandalous and criminal execution of someone who was innocent, which compel one to realise that God's way is not the way we expect.

Jesus' followers mourned him and did not expect to see him again. But three days after he died a wild rumour spread through Jerusalem. Jesus who had died was alive; his tomb was empty. His friends were as incredulous as any contemporary theologian. For the Christian, is belief in the resurrection an option?

John Drury says:

> Believing or denying that the resurrection took place makes no difference to what happens in our lives. If we read the Gospel sympathetically and attentively, which people rarely do, we see the enormously disturbing power of this symbol. Jesus was often transgressing things – he was often breaking taboos, breaking boundaries, and the greatest boundary that we know, the most terrible boundary, is the boundary between the living and the dead. Religion often marks that boundary – burial services are elementary in all religions – so the empty tomb, which in Mark they run away from in terror, is a sign that what is to us the most important boundary, between the living and the dead, can be broken. This is the climax of his transgressions, that he even walks across the boundary between the dead and the living.

The Gospels of Matthew, Luke and John give details of Jesus' many appearances in the forty days after his resurrection.

24. Jesus with two disciples on the road to Emmaus

What is striking about the appearances is their ordinariness. Jesus does not appear in a puff of smoke, he just turns up on the road to Emmaus or in a closed room. He performs no magic, but grills some fish for his friends. For Professor Hooker, it is wrong to limit the risen Jesus to forty days – the resurrection contains a promise for today. She believes that what Mark is saying to those who read his Gospel is, 'Look, follow Jesus. That is where you will see him. You do not need to rely on appearances. Just get on with being a disciple and, by being a disciple, you will meet him.'

Down the ages many people have walked the road to Galilee. With the resurrection, Jesus steps beyond the history of the 1st century AD. For Romeo Tiongco, a Christian worker in the Philippines, the fact of the incarnation means that Jesus of Nazareth, son of God and son of Man, asks to belong to each day:

The incarnation has always meant for me that God almighty, the all-powerful, the infinite, decided to become man. And when he became man, he was imprisoned in time, in place, in history. And yet, he is supposed to be a saviour of all peoples, of all times, of all places. So that, in imprisoning himself within time and within space, he has said, 'I need you, I need your hands, I need your person to continue the work of salvation.' That is the way I understand the mystery of the incarnation.

11. To the Ends of the Earth

Acts
Romans
1 & 2 Corinthians
Galatians
Philemon
1 Timothy

For the first few years after Jesus the troublemaker from Nazareth had died a public and shameful death on a hill called Golgotha, belief in him remained a local problem – a demonstration of Jerusalem's ability to sustain religious eccentricity. As a rule, false messiahs, once dead, lost their appeal, but not Jesus. Less than two months after his crucifixion his followers had regrouped and were openly proclaiming that their teacher was the promised one, the Christ, and that he had died and now lived beyond death.

They compounded that sacrilege by making grandiose claims for the future. They said that the last time Jesus had spoken to them, some forty days after he had died, on a hill where his memory is now venerated by a mosque, he had told them that they would spread his teaching not only in Jerusalem and throughout Judea and Samaria but to the ends of the earth. A few days later they claimed that their faith had been confirmed by the gift of the spirit of the Lord visible as tongues of flame burning over their heads. This had given them the courage to preach and heal in the name of Jesus.

According to the Acts of the Apostles, the fifth book of the New Testament, the followers of the Way, as the apostles and their converts were first known, became part of Jerusalem's religious life. They met regularly in Solomon's portico. Peter the coward was now Peter the miracle-worker. Stretchers carrying the sick were strategically placed in the hope that his healing shadow might fall on them. But those who believed in Jesus were still emphatically Jewish, both in nationality and religious practice. The apostles still went to the Temple to pray. The tension within the early Christian community

149

between the hellenised and the non-hellenised was a Jewish problem.

*

All that was about to change. In the year 36 the infant church suffered its first martyrdom when Stephen the deacon, a voluble young man, was stoned to death. Luke, the most probable author of the Acts of Apostles, weaves into his account of that black day and its consequences two clues about the future of the faith Stephen had died for. He points to the silence of an insignificant coat-minder and the miscalculation of a famous magician:

> Then they cast him out of the city and stoned him; and the witnesses laid down their garments at the feet of a young man named Saul... And on that day a great persecution arose against the church in Jerusalem; and they were all scattered throughout the region of Judea and Samaria... Now those who were scattered went about preaching the word. Philip went down to a city of Samaria, and proclaimed to them the Christ... But there was a man named Simon who had previously practised magic in the city and amazed the nation of Samaria, saying that he himself was somebody great. They all gave heed to him, from the least to the greatest, saying, 'This man is that power of God which is called Great.' And they gave heed to him, because for a long time he had amazed them with his magic. But when they believed Philip as he preached good news about the kingdom of God and the name of Jesus Christ, they were baptized, both men and women. Even Simon himself believed, and after being baptized he continued with Philip. And seeing signs and great miracles performed, he was amazed.
>
> Now when the apostles at Jerusalem heard that Samaria had received the word of God, they sent to them Peter and John, who came down and prayed for them that they might receive the Holy Spirit... Now when Simon saw that the Spirit was given through the laying on of the apostles' hands, he offered them money, saying, 'Give me also this power, that any one on whom I lay my hands may receive the Holy Spirit.' But Peter said to him, 'Your silver perish with you, because you thought you could obtain the gift of God with money! You have neither part nor lot in this matter, for your heart is not right before God. Repent therefore of this wickedness of yours, and pray to the Lord that, if possible, the intent of your heart may be forgiven you. For I see that you are in the gall of bitterness and in the bond of iniquity.' And Simon answered, 'Pray for me to the Lord, that nothing of what you have said may come upon me.'
>
> Now when they had testified and spoken the word of the Lord, they returned to Jerusalem, preaching the gospel to many villages of the Samaritans.
>
> Acts 7:58 8:1,4-5,9-15,18-25

25. The stoning of Stephen

Simon the magician is never mentioned again in the New Testament, but he was well-known in the ancient world as Simon the Magus, the illusionist, the Samaritan from Gittae who founded a school of magic at Alexandria and made men believe that he could fly. After he died he was credited as the founder of Gnosticism, one of the earliest heresies which promised enlightenment only to the few. In later years the story of the confrontation between Simon Peter and Simon Magus would become the stuff of folk tale, complete with conjuring tricks and talking dogs. But here the bare account in Acts is intent on making only two points: first, that the Kingdom could not be forced by bribe or personal ambition (there were no secrets to be bought or personal advantages to be gained), and secondly, that the simplicity of faith in Jesus could survive outside Judea and triumph over the most polished practitioners of Gentile occultism.

*

After the foray into Samaria, the followers of Jesus would become world-travellers. Local traditions from Spain to southern India, from Ethiopia to Armenia, would boast of entertaining or killing apostles. But there was one missionary whose work and energy would overshadow the efforts of all the other apostles. Saul, the coat-minder, the persecutor, would out-travel and out-preach all those who unlike him had followed Jesus before the brutality of Calvary. Saul, the scourge of Christians, would become Paul the letter-writer, the apostle to the Gentiles, the second founder of Christianity.

That transformation took place on the road to Damascus, on a journey undertaken in a spirit of predatory hatred. Saul knew that the independent city of Damascus had sheltered religious refugees before. It was a reasonable assumption that followers of the Way were skulking there.

We do not know precisely what happened on the Damascus road. In later life Paul would insist that he had seen the Lord. There are three accounts of the incident in Acts, all mentioning a blinding light and the voice of Christ asking, 'Saul, Saul why do you persecute me?' Given the inconsistencies about whether Paul's companions heard anything, is it possible that the whole incident was not so much a transforming vision as the fruit of a highly strung and perhaps guilty imagination? Dom Edmund Flood, a Benedictine monk and writer on Paul, says that some have suggested that Paul may not have seen Christ on the way to Damascus. Several theories have been advanced, none of them totally convincing. But the whole weight of evidence is that he did. The whole Christian experience is impossible to account for if people did not see Christ, not just as a person, but as someone who showed the kindness of God and gave people the opportunity and the task of personal transformation. If you look at Paul's allusions to his conversion experience, the stress is on transformation and on light to all people. He never spells it out clearly. It is not something he wants to ram down your throat. It is something he alludes to, and alludes to in terms of people's experience. When he saw Christ on the Damascus road, we have to remember that he gave up everything. He gave up his race, his family, his religion – everything he valued. If that isn't a revolution, what is?

Paul's enemies were now his friends – though some of them were understandably cautious about accepting his change of heart. The light on the Damascus road was to do more than

26. Paul's conversion

turn Paul's life upside down, it was to transform Christianity. Paul, who was intensely proud of his Jewishness, saw with a convert's enthusiasm that Christ's message of the kingdom of God must be taken to the non-Jewish world. For the next thirty years his exploits dominate the story of Christianity – the word itself was first used of the Gentile church he co-founded in Antioch. The Acts of the Apostles are full of his adventures, his escapes and imprisonments, his brushes with the law and his contests with paganism. Two-thirds of the letters of the New Testament are his. Even today Christian theology cannot but bear the stamp of his mind.

*

So what was Paul the man like? F.F. Bruce, Emeritus Professor of Biblical Criticism and Exegesis at Manchester, believes that he was a human tornado, a man of strong emotions, but the impression that is uppermost, when we read his letters carefully, is his capacity for friendship, which has become proverbial. Paul was a man who aroused strong antipathy in some but equally strong affection in others. There are many names of people in the New Testament of whom we should not know anything at all but for the fact that they had been friends of Paul and have been immortalised either in his letters or in those parts of Acts that tell of his ministry.

According to the evidence of the ancient world his appearance was unprepossessing. Even the pious author of the second-century 'Acts of Paul and Thecla' has to admit that he was small, bald and bandy-legged. His nose was large, and his eyebrows met in the middle. On the positive side, he could look like an angel and his words were as captivating as a spider's web.

Paul's temperament is less of a conundrum. His letters show a competitive man quick to approve or condemn. He was not above sarcasm and could give vent to some vicious name-calling – being Christ-like did not come naturally to him. On the island of Cyprus, Elymas the magician would find that Paul was more inclined to blind his enemies than love them. At times he had a chip on his shoulder about his lack of ability as a public speaker – people from his native town of Tarsus were renowned for their abominable Greek. He felt he was cut down to size by a mysterious thorn in the flesh which impeded his work and from which he asked three times to be released. Long-distance diagnoses have variously suggested malaria, sexual frustration, depression, failing eyesight and intermittent epilepsy.

More obviously, pride was his constant problem. But then he had much to be proud of. He had been born into a chosen people. While a Pharasaic student-rabbi he had been taught by the great teacher Gamaliel. By their own endeavours his family had gained the rights of Roman citizenship. Paul himself was well-educated enough to salt his letters – which were all written in Greek – with references to the poets Aratus and Menander. He could feel at home in the three worlds of the ancient Mediterranean. He was a Jew by faith and race, a Roman by constitutional right and a Greek by cultural absorption – and yet none of this was enough. For him life was a daily death, and only death would bring the life for which Jesus had died and risen. Paul's letters contain what is probably the earliest written testimony to the resurrection. Jesus, he told the Corinthians, had appeared to Peter, and then to the Twelve, and then to a group of 500, and finally to him. No details are given about the process of resurrection, so what precisely did he expect his readers to understand from his account?

Professor Hooker thinks it was certainly far more than any suggestion that the ideas of Jesus lived on. It was quite clearly a belief that they were experiencing a person. Jesus was alive for them. Although the people to whom Paul was writing could not claim to see Jesus, they nevertheless experienced the risen Lord among them. Paul would not have inherited any understanding of life after death, in the sense of a person's continuation after death. Paul was a Jew, and he was a Pharisee. He would have believed in resurrection, and that meant that he would have looked forward to the resurrection at the end of the world when everyone would be brought back to life. So it was natural, or inevitable, that he thought of his experience with Jesus in terms of death and resurrection. That was the framework of his belief. What is remarkable is that he was convinced that Jesus had been raised already and had not had to wait for some future event.

Paul's acceptance of the resurrection has been constantly questioned and misunderstood. Even in his own time the Athenians assumed that the resurrection – the anastasis – he preached about was some new eastern goddess, perhaps the Anat from Tarsus. He slowly learned to make his message plainer and not to assume that his non-Jewish listeners had any grounding in the religious roots from which Jesus had grown. So all along the northern Mediterranean seaboard the committed, the curious and the unconvinced received their first ideas about Jesus from someone who had never heard him teach. But was Paul's information accurate? Did he know enough about Jesus for the job he undertook?

Professor Dunn suspects that he knew a fair amount. Paul does not speak very much explicitly of Jesus' life, but there are two things we can build on. One is that he says himself that he spent a fortnight with Peter in Jerusalem three years after his own conversion, and the verb he uses means that he went there to get to know Peter. Peter's main reputation was as the chief disciple of Jesus, and so to know Peter you must have to know about Peter's time with Jesus. The other factor is that, in much of his ethical teaching and exhortation in the second half of his letters, Paul again and again seems to be echoing things Jesus said. For one reason or another they did not think it necessary in the early church to quote Jesus' teaching as 'Jesus said, therefore do it'. It had a more immediate and authoritative dimension. So they formulated their ethical teaching under the influence of things said by Jesus but not explicitly attributed to him. From that we know that Paul knew a good deal of Jesus' teaching.

However much Paul learned about Jesus the man, who spoke to outcasts, slept rough, healed lepers and washed the feet of his friends, the Jesus he proclaimed was the fulfilment of Hebrew scriptures standing outside history and beyond domestic detail. The death and resurrection of Jesus the son of David were now more important than sentimental anecdotes about his life. Why? Professor Hooker says that it was natural for Paul to start from where he was, as it were; and his meeting with Jesus on the Damascus road was with the risen Jesus. He did not himself know Jesus before his death and resurrection. And it was because of the impact of that meeting, and his experience of Jesus afterwards, that he concentrated on the death and resurrection of Jesus. Perhaps he did not feel the need to search into the history of Jesus, the teaching of Jesus. But there may well be more references to the teaching of Jesus in Paul than we recognise. There are many echoes, and there may well be influence there though we do not always recognise it.

Without charity – that is, without love – says Paul, his words are worthless. But even with charity, words can be misleading. Modern readers have not been the only ones to fail to recognise Jesus behind Paul's words and actions. In the city of Lystra, in what is now Turkey, Paul healed a cripple, and he and Barnabas were immediately hailed as the gods Hermes and Zeus respectively. Garlands were brought to them, the local priest of Zeus came running out to them with oxen, and the people begged to be allowed to offer sacrifice to the reluctant gods. The muddle was ended by some visitors from nearby Iconium, and everything returned to normal. Paul's disappointed devotees threw stones at him and cast him out of the city for dead.

Paul was to grow used to such rejections. He would boast of the number of times he had been stoned, flogged and imprisoned for his message about Jesus. But was Paul also a

27. Paul and Barnabas perform miracles

victim of his own prejudices? Does his message agree with the good news of the gospel? Professor Küng believes there is an important difference. It is the difference between the message *of* Jesus and the message *about* Jesus. Between the two is his cross, his execution, his death and what we call the resurrection. There is obviously a big difference between what he had to say and what was said about him, but they are not necessarily contradictory.

*

Down the centuries Paul's understanding of Jesus was to be used to plug the philosophical holes in the Gospels. His letters were to be cited as the final court of orthodox appeal by most of the heretics in the early Church. The Docetists, certain that Jesus was god not man – his body, they said, was a superhuman phantasm – applauded Paul's lack of emphasis on Jesus' humanity. The Arians, loath to admit the divinity of Jesus, combed through Paul's writings and pointed out that he had never specifically said that Jesus was God. So why did Paul write in such a way that diametrically opposite ideas could be derived from his words? Is not the reliability of his letters thereby seriously undermined? Dr Thiselton of St John's College, Nottingham thinks the answer is as simple as a telephone call. Paul's aims within the Christian communities are the same, but the letters he writes are quite different. They are like one side of a telephone conversation. For example, 1 Corinthians is written in response to a letter from Corinth and a set of enquiries from Corinth. Paul takes the topics raised one by one and answers them. We hear his side, but we do not hear the other side of the conversation. We have to reconstruct what the other side would be.

It is important to remember that Paul addressed all he said to specific situations. Some of those situations are different from our own, and there may well be parts of the Epistles for which we have to wait for the right moment for them to speak to us. But the closer we look at the relationship between Jesus and Paul, the clearer it becomes that Paul rightly interpreted what Jesus' work was. Dr Thiselton is totally confident of Paul's picture of Jesus.

But Professor Bruce believes that Paul was more than a faithful reporter. At point after point, he says, we can compare the teaching of Paul, in a very different literary medium, with the teaching of Jesus as given in his parables, and see that the picture of God in both is the same. Jesus, in his way, and then Paul in his, proclaimed the Gospel as good news for outsiders. The outsiders, in Jesus' case were the tax-collectors and riff-raff of society. In Paul's case they were the Gentiles, those lesser breeds without the law, from the orthodox Jewish point of view. But the message of both Jesus and Paul is the same: one of good news for outsiders.

The Eleven who had wandered with Jesus before the arrest in Gethsemene may well have heard their master's final instruction to go and teach all nations, but it was largely left to Paul to work out the practical implications. From the earliest days of the mission to the Gentiles there had been sharp contention about whether it was necessary for converts to become Jews before they became Christians. According to Luke's account of the first council of the Church, held in Jerusalem in AD 50, Paul drew on his experience of the success of Gentile Christian churches to insist that it was not necessary for Christian converts to be circumcised or to observe the full detail of the Mosaic law. It should hardly be surprising that Paul, the former Pharisee, emerges from this debate as a liberal. His mind had been formed by Gamaliel, the successor of the great rabbi Hillel who had insisted that Gentiles had a place in God's plan and should be offered the chance of conversion. Hillel was a liberal and a reformer, though not where women were concerned. A badly cooked meal, he said, was adequate grounds for divorce. Did these ideas affect Paul? Was Paul the first Christian misogynist?

*

Professor Hooker thinks that the description of Paul as a misogynist is totally unfair. Paul refers to women who laboured with him in the Gospel, and there are references to women who appear to be, in Paul's understanding, apostles. He allows women an equal place. For example, when he is writing to the Corinthians, he talks of women taking part in the service, and prophesying and praying. That is the famous passage about the covering of women's heads. People have always been concerned about this notion. They have not noticed that Paul is assuming that women take a real part in church worship. That was revolutionary. To 20th-century Christians, Paul's attitudes seem hopelessly conservative, but in the 1st century they would have appeared radical.

But what is revolutionary or radical is not always easy to detect. Women, Paul explains to Timothy, should never be allowed to teach men. They should not preen themselves, or have elaborate hairstyles or expensive jewellery. They should learn silence and in old age not drink too much. That was the theory. In practice some women broke the mould and had positions of authority. In Romans Paul mentions Phoebe who was deaconess at Cenchreae. Nor was there any sexual hierarchy in friendship. Prisca, the tent-maker, has precedence over her husband Aquila, and at the end of the letter women's names jostle with men's in the list of those Paul asks to be remembered to.

Paul believed that wives should obey their husbands and slaves should obey their masters, but he also stressed that those in authority should be worth obeying – a dangerous idea which Dom Edmund Flood believes holds the key to an understanding of Paul. Paul, he says, believed that Jesus was Brother, just as Christians were brothers and sisters. There is an enormous stress on equality, because everyone is meant to be the human projection of God. If we look at the main thrust of evidence, we see that women had the top leadership positions in the church. At Galatians 3:28, the experience of baptism, Paul says that when you become a Christian the great divisions that divide us – sex, class and race – fall away. We know that this was so in the Pauline churches. Take the letter to Philemon about Onesimus, the runaway slave. Imagine a clergyman in the 19th century writing to a landlord in the Deep South, saying, 'Your slave has bunked off with the cash. Have him back. Call him brother. And I don't want just *you* to decide, I want your Christian community to decide that.' The clergyman would get more than a flea in his ear. Paul took it for granted that that was the Christian way. He believed that Christianity was about not keeping to a system – about free transformation. The letter about Onesimus was written from a prison cell. As with all the letters, there is no reply. All we know is that forty years later a man called Onesimus is once again prominent in the Christian community – this time as bishop of Ephesus.

The fact that a Christian community had taken root in Ephesus at all was testimony to Paul's courage as well as to his effectiveness. Preaching Christ in Ephesus must have been like sowing seed in mildewed soil. Ephesus was the black-magic capital of the Mediterranean. Any occult writing in the ancient world was referred to as '*Ephesia grammata*', Ephesian writing. The city was also the centre of worship of Diana of the Ephesians – not the chaste goddess of hunting but a rawer Magna Mater, a fierce mother hung with multiple breasts and animal heads. When Paul went to Ephesus on the last of his missionary journeys he knew there would be trouble. By the time he left, the city was in a state of barely contained riot, but the Christian community was established.The elders of the church at Ephesus travelled down to the port of Miletus to see him off. He was full of foreboding, and his address to them was his last missionary speech.

And when they came to him, he said to them:
'You yourselves know how I lived among you all the time from the first day that I sat foot in Asia, serving the Lord with all humanity

and with tears and with trials which befell me through the plots of the Jews; how I did not shrink from declaring to you anything that was profitable, and teaching you in public and from house to house, testifying to Jews and to Greeks of repentance to God and of faith in our Lord Jesus Christ. And now, behold, I am going to Jerusalem, bound in the Spirit, not knowing what shall befall me there; except that the Holy Spirit testifies to me in every city that imprisonment and afflictions await me...' And when he had spoken thus, he knelt down and prayed with them all. And they all went and embraced Paul and kissed him, sorrowing most of all because of the word he had spoken, that they should see his face no more. And they brought him to the ship.

Acts 20:18-23, 36-38

*

In Jerusalem Paul's worst fears were realised and the martyrdom he seemed to long for began. He was arrested on a charge of taking a Gentile into the court of Israel, part of the Temple forbidden to all non-Jews. The penalty was death. For two years he waited in prison at Caesarea able only to keep track of his work by letter. These were dangerous years for the Christian community. At first Christianity had been seen, rightly, as a Jewish sect, but slowly the realisation grew that the Christians, with all their secret signs, cannabalism and donkey worship, were distinct from and potentially more sinister than the Jewish community.

The first Christians came from the poorest sections of society, and from slaves, who did not even have the freedom to be poor. Because the sect took root among those who had every right to be disaffected it came to be seen as a threat. It could blight careers and earn official disapproval, but that was part of its strength. Paul used his prison cell as a lesson for his converts. He was a prisoner not of Caesar but of Christ; any suffering which they experienced was part of their Christian life. Paul signs off one letter by passing on greetings from 'the saints of Caesar's household'. Even gaolers could become Christian.

It is easy to present an idealised picture of the first Christians. Paul's letters make it clear that there were tensions and jealousies, right from the start. But perhaps Paul was a hard task-master. Does it make any sense to talk of a golden age of early Christianity? Professor Bruce says not, if we mean an age when everything was perfect. There never was such an age. The early chapters of Acts contain the story of Ananias and Sapphira, who at an early date tried to get credit for greater generosity than they were entitled to and came to a sticky end on that account. The Christianity of which we read in the New Testament is Christianity as we know it today, as lived and transmitted by very ordinary and fallible agents.

Paul taught people that, no matter how lowly they were, they belonged to the only kingdom that mattered. They might not be chosen, but they could choose. For Professor Dunn, Paul's impact as a teacher sprang from his conviction that he lived at a time when the whole framework of belief in one God was changing. In the past it had been focussed explicitly on the Jews. Now, since the coming of Jesus, it was open to the whole world – to all the people, all the nations, the Gentiles. Much of Paul's work is as a Jew, who is an apostle to the Gentiles, trying to break down the barriers between Jews and Gentiles and to open the Gospel to the whole people of God. That is at the heart of his theology. In two of his main letters, to Romans and Galatians, he is dealing with this very problem, with people who say that the promise was given to Abraham and to Abraham's children, i.e. the Jews. That is how the Gospel has to be understood. Jesus is the Jewish Messiah, and Paul is saying that the promise to Abraham is a promise to all the Gentiles, to all the peoples. Therefore hedging round the Gospel with Jewish elements, like circumcision and food laws, is to misunderstand the final purpose of God, the stage of God's purpose that has now been reached.

The point about Jesus was that he was breaking down the barriers within Israel, within Judaism, between Pharisee and sinner. Paul is extending that to the barriers between Jew and Gentile.

Paul was transferred to Nero's Rome, and after a few years in prison he was released. He is believed to have gone on working in Rome among the ordinary fallible people who made up the Christian community. In AD 64 Rome was ravaged by fire. The rumour quickly spread that Nero himself had ordered the fire and used the flames as a backdrop for a thin-voiced recital about the fall of Troy. The rumour proved too persistent for comfort. Nero needed scapegoats and he chose the Christians.

There is a tradition that both Paul and Peter lost their lives in the persecution that followed. Some Christians were dressed in animal skins and torn to pieces by hungry dogs. Others were crucified. Others were used as human torches lighting the smouldering city by night. But Christianity would outlive the Julio-Claudians and the empire of Rome itself. Paul's lesson of Christ crucified has proved more powerful than any tyranny.

Romeo Tiongco says that when Jesus accepted death on the cross, he changed the meaning of death. Death, as a symbol of defeat and failure, became the symbol of success and triumph, in the sense that it was the supreme witness that he gave to us. We are pilgrims of earth and we should not lock up our hearts with material possessions and power but make God the source of our joy. And it is only in this true worship of God, when we no longer worship Mammon, that justice and peace and love can exist.

The challenge now is that Christians are being asked to live the paradox of the cross in their own lives. God is saying:

> This is the challenge for you: to love and defend justice, but become the victims of injustice; to love and defend life, and yet be deprived of it; to love and defend freedom, but end up in prison; to love and be committed to non-violence, and yet become the victims of the violence we have rejected; to accept death, because this is still today the witness that is demanded of the people of the earth.

Many of the earliest pilgrims of the Christian Church lived lives of poverty and danger under the bright shadow of faith. They were taught to live in the world but not to cling to it. They were told that, wherever they came from, they were the sons and daughters of Abraham, and that the riches of Judaism were theirs. They had a home in Zion, but Paul, the apostle of the Gentiles, had turned that image inside out.

Dr Phillips believes that in the writings of Paul we have a lesson of crucial importance, at once growing from and at odds with the teacher's Jewish roots. Paul is saying that in Christ the wall is broken down. Christianity has built into it the whole idea of mission, something not in the Hebrew scriptures. Dr Phillips explains: 'The Hebrew picture is of Israel sitting on Mount Zion, on Jerusalem, the High Mountain, to which all the nations come up. They don't actually come out to the nations – the nations are drawn to them – you remember the phrase, "like a light to the nations"

– the nations, like moths, are drawn up to Jerusalem to receive God's will.' Christianity, on the other hand, went out from the beginning with Paul and converted the Gentiles. So the Gentile mission expanded and expanded, and from Paul's work Christianity has spread the word to the whole world.

12. The Book as Battleground

Revelation

There is an ancient battlefield in the modern state of Israel called Megiddo. It was celebrated in an exultant victory song by the prophetess Deborah as the place where kings fought but gained no spoils of war. It was remembered more soberly as the place where Josiah the Devout, the sixteenth king of Judah, was fatally wounded by the soon-to-be-defeated Pharaoh Neco. By the time of the prophet Zechariah it was a byword for anguish and the bitter harvest of battle.

But its greatest notoriety derives from an event yet to come, which some believe is imminent and others say will never happen. Armageddon, the mount of Megiddo, the hill of plagues, is the most famous name in the history of the future. It has come to mean disaster beyond repair, the final conflict in which defeat is guaranteed to all.

And that is only part of the story. Armageddon, no matter how terrifying, is only a fragment of a larger vision unique in the Bible for the savagery of its warnings and the ferocity of its promises. The final battleground belongs to the book of Revelation, the Apocalypse, the last book of the Bible, which weaves an intricate web of allegory, hidden meanings and cryptic numbers to entrap man's instinctive fear of a future doom and turn it into irrational hope.

*

There are many mysteries in the book of Revelation, with its horsemen and its whore, its seven-headed beast and its woman clothed with the sun. It is a journey into the beginning of eternity and to the end of time. It starts in a cave on the island of Patmos where John the Divine saw the past and the future rolled into the present:

> I John, your brother, who share with you in Jesus the tribulation and
> the kingdom and the patient endurance, was on the island called

165

Patmos on account of the word of God and the testimony of Jesus. I was in the Spirit on the Lord's day, and I heard behind me a loud voice like a trumpet saying, 'Write what you see in a book and send it to the seven churches, to Ephesus and to Smyrna and to Pergamum and to Thyatira and to Sardis and to Philadelphia and to Laodicea.'

Then I turned to see the voice that was speaking to me, and on turning I saw seven golden lampstands, and in the midst of the lampstands, one like a son of man, clothed with a long robe and with a golden girdle round his breast; his head and his hair were white as white wool, white as snow; his eyes were like a flame of fire, his feet were like burnished bronze, refined as in a furnace, and his voice was like the sound of many waters; in his right hand he held seven stars, from his mouth issued a sharp two-edged sword, and his face was like the sun shining in full strength.

When I saw him, I fell at his feet as though dead. But he laid his right hand upon me, saying, 'Fear not, I am the first and the last, and the living one; I died, and behold I am alive for evermore, and I have the keys of Death and Hades. Now write what you see, what is and what is to take place hereafter...'

Revelation 1: 9-19

It is still possible to visit the cave, now called Aghia Anna, where John looked upon an emerald rainbow and a crystal sea. The cave of the vision is surrounded by the plain ramble of a white-washed monastery. The spot where John's head lay, while his mind was full of monsters, trumpet calls and a new Jerusalem, is encircled by a simple band of metal. The only other feature in the cave is a desk formed out of the natural rock where, according to the local monks, John's disciple Prochoros took down some of the most unfathomable dictation ever given.

John tells his readers that he has been exiled on Patmos for preaching the word of God. That much fits with historical possibility. Exile was a favourite punishment for trouble-makers, and Patmos with its deadly barrenness was a favourite place for dumping political exiles throughout the 1st century AD. That is where historical certainty ends. Until 250 AD there was no doubt that John the Divine was John the son of Zebedee, the disciple whom Jesus loved, and the only disciple credited with achieving a non-violent death. Jerome says that John survived into extreme old age. Finally, unable to preach, he had to be carried to services and would just say, 'Love one another, that is enough.' Irenaeus, one of the best theologians of the 2nd century, knew people who had known John the Beloved in his last years in Ephesus, and was sure of

28. The seven-headed beast

Revelation's apostolic authorship. Melito of Sardis, Justin Martyr, Clement of Alexandria, Tertullian and Hippolytus all shared that conviction.

But the book has always attracted controversy. Luther and Erasmus did not like it. The heretical sect, the Alogi, found its teaching too harsh and so attributed its authorship to Cerinthus, another heretic. The most reasoned doubter was the 3rd-century Dionysius of Alexandria, who pointed out quite rightly that the book bore little resemblance to the style of the Gospel of John. So either the book of Revelation was written by John the Divine, the apostle in his old age and in language markedly different from the Gospel of John, or it was written by John the Divine, not an apostle, a Jewish Christian with detailed knowledge of Asia Minor who happened to fall foul of Rome and ended up in exile on Patmos.

Whatever the doubt about authorship there was never any doubt about the identity of the vision-bearer, the one like the Son of Man with eyes like flame and a two-edged sword issuing from his mouth. John was certain it was the Word of God, present at the beginning of time, present at its end and made visible to him as the risen glorified Christ whose words are like the sword of wisdom brought down on a corrupt age.

*

But which corrupt age? When precisely was the Patmos vision written down? According to Dr Sophie Laws, the generally held view is that it was in the reign of the Emperor Domitian at the end of the 1st century. This is not just a guess by 20th-century scholars. It was stated as early as the 2nd century by Irenaeus, and there is a good deal to support it. The book anticipates an attack on the Christian communities launched by the Roman state, and part of that attack comes through the consistent demand of the state that the emperor, who represents the state, should be worshipped. It is emperor-worship that provokes the crisis for the churches, and we know that the emperor Domitian towards the end of his reign did go off his head and require to be addressed as God. The cities of Asia Minor responded enthusiastically to this hint. A massive temple was built to Domitian, the living god, in Ephesus, a city very much associated with John. We may imagine the impact on a 1st-century Asian Christian of the erection of this massive temple on the main street of Ephesus, which was to contain a statue of the emperor as god about seven metres high. Imagine the shock, the emotional and religious horror, of being confronted with that in your own city, your own province. What the state is requiring is the worship of a living man as god. What the church is developing is the worship of a man who lived and died and rose again. There is a head-on religious collision here.

The book of Revelation is about more than the clash between a madman's empire and a kingdom which belongs to fools and children. However much he loathed Rome and all it stood for, John does not begin on a note of self-righteous hostility. His vision opens with a practical, and at times critical, message for the Church itself. With a voice like rushing water, the figure of the glorified Christ warns seven local Christian communities in what is now Turkey about their imminent trials and past failings.

The church at Pergamum, he says, must stand firm against false teaching. The church at Thyatira has been beguiled by a prophetess as corrupt as the evil Jezebel. The Christians of Ephesus, Sardis and Laodicea must revive their lukewarm love and compromised faith. Only the churches of Smyrna and Philadelphia are praised for their energy and belief.

These messages to local churches pave the way for a more startling vision. John describes nothing less than the majesty of God who is older than time. Heaven shines more brightly than the most precious jewels known to man. It is more fragrant than incense burning in golden bowls, and at its centre angels and elders worship not a symbol of power but a sacrificial lamb bearing the wounds of death conquered. From beneath the altar of the Lamb, the souls of the martyrs cry for vengeance.

Is such imagery with its insistence on revenge completely Christian? Is it a throwback to Daniel and to the more violent visions which comforted the Jews persecuted a hundred and sixty years before Jesus was born? Dr Carroll thinks that though it may look like a throwback it is more than that. When you are facing the Romans (and, he points out, they were not Christian gentlemen, in spite of what Paul writes in Romans), you need something stronger than 'the magistrates are ordained of God'. You need something very much stronger. The old visions that were created to oppose the Greek invasion were revitalised in Christian terms. So the slain lamb leads his people against the enemy and defeats them, and Rome ends up in ruins. That goes right back to the attacks on Baal in Isaiah and Jeremiah. It is almost unchanged, and clearly represents a deep need. It is important either to believe that your enemies are going to suffer or to entertain visions in which they do, because, even if they do not, at least you still have the visions to keep you warm at night, or in prison, or at the stake. It is a way of transforming and giving a voice to those who now have no power.

But why was it necessary to express comfort to the persecuted in such arcane and terrifying language? John paints a nightmare canvas of the disasters which alone will loosen mankind's grip on this world. He promises a future at the mercy of conquest, war, famine and death – the four horsemen of the Apocalypse.

For Professor Dunn the problem of the interpretation of this vision is the mirror image of a question posed much earlier in the Bible. When you come to the New Testament equivalent of Genesis, he says, which is the book of Revelation – the end, as Genesis is the beginning – you have the same problems, because you are dealing with the outer edges of history. Just as, in Genesis, there is dispute about how you understand the language, so in Revelation you have the problem of how to understand the symbols and the bizarre imagery. Christians have had widely divergent views on that for centuries.

From its earliest days there has been contention over the book of Revelation. Many have felt that its description of the last days, when the sun would turn as black as death and the moon as red as blood, and the sky would vanish and the mountains move, was too brutal and fantastic to be included in the New Testament. However logical its position at the end of the Bible may seem to us now, after generations of scholars have explored its symbolism and its promise of a tree of life which would undo the harm of the tree of knowledge, Sophie Laws believes that John was allowed the last Biblical word by default, not by human design.

It is an accident of history, she says, that Revelation is at the end of the Bible. It is because so many people of a more scholarly turn of mind felt uncomfortable with it. Although they were bound, by its popularity, to include it in the Bible, they tucked it as far away as they could. It is a book that people either read obsessively, and know everything about, or have never touched. It is an unloving book. There are only two references to the love of God or Christ in the whole of its twenty-one chapters. On the other hand, it is a salutary book. It leaves one at the end of the Bible regarding this world as provisional, and it is perhaps as well to end on a note of discomfort.

John sees a dying world where power has become meaningless and even kings and great men lie cowering in caves and rocky fortresses longing to be no more. For those from the tribe of old Israel, and those from the new Israel gathered from all the nations, all that will matter is the seal of faith, the only guarantee of a new life beyond the horror of a ravaged earth. When the final seal on the scroll of destiny is broken by the Lamb, there is even silence in heaven.

*

29. The four horsemen of the Apocalypse

How can modern theologians swallow John's vision? Is not Jesus the healer, who taught his friends how to pray, all but obliterated in John's vision of a Lamb transformed into a symbol, not of gentleness, but of fearsome majesty? Dr Thiselton says that Christ is actually prominent in the book of Revelation, but it is not the pre-resurrection Christ of the Gospel stories, it is the living Christ through whom God rules his Church. So Christ is there, but not as we see him in Matthew, Mark or Luke.

John was not the only one to believe that the world will come to a sudden and violent end. It was an intuition shared by the Gospel writers. In Mark, Jesus warns of a time of wars and rumours of wars. Famine and earthquake will herald the beginning of the end. In Matthew, Jesus says that false Messiahs and false prophets and the coldness of men's hearts will be a sign of the close of the age. Death, in the final days, according to Luke, will be unpredictable and certain. The last days will be beyond human understanding, coming, says the writer of Peter's second letter, like a thief in the night.

John the Divine tries to prepare his readers for the worst that persecution or disaster can throw at them. He gives his imagination free and fruitful rein. In the last days seven trumpets will announce three woes. The natural world will be destroyed. Trees will be shrivelled up by fire, the sea will turn to blood, the fresh water of rivers will be polluted, the sky will be darkened by smoke from a bottomless pit, monstrous locusts will ravage the earth and horsemen armed like the Parthian cavalry, riding beasts with lions' heads and serpents' tails, will cut a swathe of destruction through men longing for death. No matter how fevered John's imaginings, Professor Dunn believes they are necessary for the balance of the Christian message. It is, he says, a recognition of the wholeness of the human person and human society. We cannot simply function on the level of the mind and body. There is an element of imagination, and it is important for any religion, for Christianity in particular, to have scope for that imagination, that ability to perceive and speak in a vision, because it is operating on a different level from the purely cerebral.

Nowadays we are more cerebrally inclined. Geologists, astronomers and ecologists who explore John's world of the final days are read compulsively. Doom is a bestseller. Theological naivety may have replaced John's scientific naivety and his paranoid hatred of the Roman emperors who killed believers and counterfeited divinity, but the impulse of fear and curiosity is the same. There are times when John seems more mad than inspired, but his vision of the end has a fascination which has outlasted the more tangible successes of his enemies.

Dr Carroll says that the apocalyptic strand is always topical. Some people think the centre of the old Bible is the apocalyptic part, the exodus. There is something to be said for the apocalyptic, because it allows people to go to the Emperor, like the old Quakers who would wear their hats in the presence of the King, and say: 'OK, you can get us now, but we will get you in the end.'

When John saw his vision, the world annihilation he promised could only be the figment of fanatical imagination. It is an index of man's shame, not of John's clairvoyant skill, that in this century we recognise total destruction as

something within mankind's ability. For all his violent
foreboding, John never foresaw that human ingenuity could
make the four horsemen of the Apocalypse redundant. John
planted his feet on the threshold of eternity. That means he
belonged to the present, not the future. He was firmly rooted
in the first century AD, and his aim was to bolster the
Christian community battered by a hostile empire. But why
should anyone think that images of terror could be
encouraging? Dr Thiselton believes that much of the message
of the Revelation is that, as far as God is sovereign, questions
about judgment belong to God. The book of Revelation never
says that Christians should make judgments. It says that
Christians may be confident that the world and history are in
God's hands. There are some very beautiful passages in the
book: for instance, the passage about the river of the water of
life that flows on the tree of life whose leaves are for the
healing of the nations.

Much of the violence in Revelation belonged specifically to
John's own age. When he speaks of a woman clothed with the
sun giving birth to a child, he is drawing on the Jewish
tradition of the Holy Spirit as mother overlaid with the
metaphor of chosen Israel as God's bride. The child is the
Messiah, but there theology ends.

The monsters who are its enemies are only thinly disguised.
They represent all the powers who have persecuted Jews and
Christians from Nebuchadnezzar to Nero. John is anxious
that his meaning will be clear. The monster seals people on
the hand or the head with the number 666, the mark of the
beast, described by John as a human number. In ancient
times letters were used as numbers. John's clue would have
been obvious to anyone familiar with Hebrew or Aramaic. 666
is *Neron Kaisar*: that is, Nero the Emperor.

*

So is there a case for using John the Divine merely as a coded
commentary on the past? The Rev. Jerry Falwell, leader of
the Moral Majority, disagrees. He believes that Revelation
contains the message of an escape route for believers. He
believes that it is basically a prophetic book. Chapter 1 deals
with the past. Chapters 2 and 3 deal with the present, with
what is going on today through the Church of the Lord Jesus

Christ. The seven churches of Asia Minor each represent a particular time period in church history. Chapters 4 to 22 have to do with the future. Many, he says, believe that when Jesus comes, all who have ever believed in him as Lord and Saviour and who have accepted the cleansing power of the blood of Christ shed at Calvary will be caught up to be with the Lord. Then will begin seven years of tribulation on earth, described in chapters 6 to 19 as an awful and terrible time. During that time God will purge the earth and prepare it for the establishment of his Kingdom. The second coming of Christ, says Falwell, is in two phases. First, at the beginning of the seven-year tribulation period, Christ will come to carry away or *rapture* his church. At the end of it he will return to earth with his glorified church. He will sit upon the throne of his ancestor David and reign in perfect peace for 1,000 years.

Many fundamentalists, particularly in the United States, believe that they will avoid the death-throes of the earth and will return after the world carnage to enjoy 1,000 years of peace – a dangerous thought in people whose government has a nuclear capacity.

Was John seeing things he could not understand? Is it significant that the literal translation of Chernobyl is 'Wormwood', the falling star that makes the water bitter? Was John predicting World War III? Sophie Laws thinks not. John, she says, speaks in images. He is not concerned to provoke the imagination. He does not believe that the world will end simply as a result of human wickedness. He does not accept that man can destroy the world by being wicked. He believes that the world will end because God will vindicate his own people against human wickedness. What brings the end of the world is God's redemption of his own.

Revelation concludes with a vision of the new heaven and the new earth and a vision of a future life in the presence of God. That message of a new life has also been interpreted at an individual level. For believers, the last things will stand on the brink of eternity. Over the years there has been much debate about John's precise meaning. After Armageddon John paints a lurid picture of a whore dressed in scarlet and adorned with gold and pearls. She rides a seven-headed beast and, in the manner of the prostitutes of ancient Rome, she bears her name written on her forehead. She is Babylon the Great, the Mother of Abominations: at one level a byword for

30. The new Jerusalem

occultism and materialism, at another the Jewish apocalyptic codeword for 'Rome'.

Down the centuries Christians have accorded each other the dubious privilege of identification with Babylon. Anti-Christ and the False Prophet, the other two members of John's satanic trinity, are constantly being re-identified. Indeed our own century, disfigured by Nazism, has provided all too convincing contenders. John's message is ultimately victorious: Christ will return and conquer all that is evil.

The book of Revelation is constantly being re-interpreted. Is there any way we can pinpoint the events it describes? Jerry Falwell believes that we cannot be certain that we are *not* living in the last days. Jesus warns us, he says, against date-setting. He specifically tells us that no man knows the day or the hour. Those in the past who have presumptuously set dates have all been embarrassed. However, he says, we are given certain signs of the Lord's return. One is the re-gathering of the Jewish people into the land of Israel, which since 1948 has been a reality. Another is the increase of knowledge and travel – the past hundred years have seen a dramatic revolution in communication and transport. As Jesus said, we can know the times and the seasons, but not the day or the hour, so that it is right to preach that the Lord's coming is imminent, that he could come at any time, and we should live and work as though we were planning for the next generation. We should plan and establish equity and peace on earth for our children and our children's children, but we should also live with a consciousness that this may be the crowning day when we meet the Lord face to face.

John's warnings about false prophets and fraudulent religion have turned the Bible itself into part of the Armaggedon armoury. One American professor has gone so far as to maintain that the Anti-Christ will be somebody like Professor Albert Schweitzer, who will convincingly throw doubt on the literal truth of the Bible. An untenable view, according to Professor Barr at Oxford, who argues that if you take every word in the Old Testament literally you will prove that it is not true, because there are many things within one part of the Old Testament, or within one part of the New Testament, which do not agree exactly and literally with some other part.

There is all the difference in the world between taking the Bible seriously and understanding every word mechanically. If literalism were taken to its logical conclusion, no translations or variants of the Bible should be allowed. Jerry Falwell believes in the inheritancy and infallability of scripture. With so many translations, words may be different; but in the general meaning and intention of most of the translations, they are all quite accurate. The Bible, he says, can be relied upon whether it is speaking to theology, geology, biology, history, or any other study.

There is a middle way of interpretation – of evaluating each book in the Bible and developing preferences and priorities. But Clive Calver, General Secretary of the Evangelical Alliance, thinks there are dangers behind this picking and choosing. Many people try to do that, he says, and they are very good at it. One of the difficulties is that the Bible actually claims that it is a totality of content, that the Old and New Testaments go together and that the stories contained within the Bible are a coherent unity. The Bible claims that it speaks as a single entity, and therefore you cannot pick and choose.

He believes that the events described did take place, and that what we have in the Bible is men speaking what they understood to be the word of God as the Holy Spirit inspired them. But critical belief is not such an impossibility. Dr Thiselton says that the analogy is the difference between the reader and the critic. There is a sense in which the reader steps into the world that the book opens up and simply receives. There is a sense in which the critic is making judgments and assessments. They are not the same activity, but the student who is also a person of faith combines the two roles. We might call him a critical reader. He is both a reader and a critic. 'I want to say of myself, I am both a Biblical critic and a Christian believer. I find no contradiction between those two things.'

Many early Christians, including John, felt that the last days were at hand. Our own last days always are. The last book of the Bible looks forward beyond death to a new heaven and a new earth, where man's wickedness has burnt itself out, and day and night are no more. In the final chapter John the visionary points to a paradise restored where the tree of life heals all the wounds of the tree of knowledge – where there is no need for a temple or a church because everything is alight with the living God.

The message behind John's nightmare vision is one of peace. A place called Armageddon is not the last staging-post of the Bible journey. The destination of those who walk from Eden's garden is a new city, which John calls the heavenly Jerusalem.

A Last Word

Long after the fire of Rome and the fall of the old Jerusalem, and many years after John the Divine had described his vision of the last days and of the new Jerusalem of paradise restored, a soldier from Illyria, now Yugoslavia, murdered his way to the Roman imperial throne. His name was Decius and for two bigoted and bloodstained years in the third century he declared war on the Christians, that odd group of people who based their lives on an amalgam of old Hebrew scripture about an unseen God and some allegedly good news about a man who died on a cross.

Those who called themselves the new Israel were allowed a taste of the persecution which had been meted out so often in the past to the old Israel. Decius insisted that all his subjects must sacrifice to the official state gods. It was a trial not so much of faith as of political loyalty. Local gods who knew their place and could be slotted into the Roman pantheon caused no problem. The god of the Hebrew Bible and the risen Lord of the Epistles and Gospels made claims which dared to rival the power of Rome. Christians who placed their own religious beliefs before their civic duty to sacrifice risked death – seen variously as the proof of stubborn treachery or the palm of martyrdom.

The Decian persecution of AD 250 was not a success. It made martyrs who are still revered today and, if anything, it gained public sympathy for the Christians at the time. But the respite was short-lived. Fifty years later another emperor from Illyria, Diocletian, dealt with the Christian problem more astutely. Egged on by his henchman Galerius, he decided not to test individual courage but to hack away at the tap root of the Christian faith.

Diocletian issued an edict against the Christians. Their churches were to be destroyed, but the believers themselves would be left in peace provided they surrendered any books they had containing Christian or Jewish scripture. The importance of those writings, known simply as 'the books', was now an open secret.

In the years between the two emperors, while the theologians of the early Christian community argued over which Christian writings should be added to the Hebrew scriptures, another movement gripped the early church. Men and women sought out the lonely places and tried to find God in the fierce clearness of the desert where no man-made lights dimmed the stars and no shade hid the strength of the sun. They lived lives of extreme simplicity, spending their time in manual work, in prayer and in reading the scriptures, and they adapted to the timelessness of the desert. They used the Bible not as a tool of debate, nor as a shield from thought, but as a source of living water for a dead world. It was not something simply to be read through, it had to be absorbed and revered like water in the desert. Those first monks and nuns meditated on – that is, kept on repeating – the Bible until it became part of them. One phrase might take a year. There was no hurry: the Bible was a journey through a life which would never end. Many others thought they were mad.

So seventeen hundred years ago there were nearly as many ways to approach the Bible as there are now. It was a threat to the powerful, an arena for debate among theologians and a constantly developing source of revelation for those seeking God. No one has ever had, or ever will have, sole rights to the Bible. The believer has no right to withhold it from the unbeliever. In the passage of time it has become more, not less, important. As Dr Cupitt says, it is the chief document of the ancient way of thought that has made us what we are and should be studied as a kind of history of the human spirit. It covers over a thousand years. It makes the transition from a primitive tribal society, through the Israelite monarchy to the exile, and then to the emergence of the Jewish synagogue. There follows an extraordinary kaleidoscope in which everything shakes into a new pattern, and a movement of the faith out into the early European world. The Bible covers several stages in the history of the human spirit. It is the crucible from which we have come.

The Bible does not fall easily into a single category. It contains law, poetry, history, prayer and parable. Its message about God and man unites its disparate books, from Genesis to Revelation. Piecemeal quotation to prove points reduces it to the level of holy scrabble. It was written for understanding not for selective quotation, and this is nowhere truer than in the arena of theological debate, as Professor Küng points out. Its use in debate is misguided, if it is drawn on merely to knock down an adversary. We should look at it together and discuss. We have different opinions, but we should not use the Bible as a weapon.

The impact of the Bible on individuals is far from uniform. It nourishes many wildly differing beliefs and practices. Does this plurality detract from its credibility? Rabbi Sacks recalls the wonderful story of the Tower of Babel – all mankind sharing a single language and culture. The first thing men do is to over-reach themselves to secure a place in heaven. By a simple act of confusing languages, so that one culture is no longer able to talk to another, God brings it about that each of us in our own culture finds his or her own way to God. As long as we don't compromise anyone else's way to God, that is the prescription for religious behaviour.

There are many roads to God. The Jewish way is the way for Jews. The Islamic and Christian ways are equally valid for them. But that is not the crux of the matter. The crux is, can our great religious traditions find a place for traditions that are not our own?

Are we penalised for not living in the time of the patriarchs, or of the prophets, or of Jesus of Nazareth? Lord Soper thinks not. He is sure that God did not stop speaking to his world when Jesus was crucified, or when he came back to his disciples. He certainly did not stop speaking when the books of the Bible were finally available as one documentary entity. He is speaking the whole time, and therefore we have to listen carefully to a world which demands answers to questions that our fathers knew nothing about.

If God is still talking to his people, is it possible for the Bible to have too much attention paid to it and for it to make people God-deaf? Clive Calver thinks it is. He believes that those of us who would hold a high view of the Bible have to be careful that we do not fall into a trinity of Father, Son and Holy Scripture. We have to recognise the Biblical trinity of Father, Son and Holy Spirit and allow the Holy Spirit to interpret the word of God to us. We need to recognise that Jesus was the word of God, that in the Greek the whole context is of a 'spermatic word', the word of life, the word that gives life, and that Jesus himself gives that life. The scripture merely gives us the foundation on which we can build, the line against which we can actually measure our experience and understanding of God. In other words, we are not building a salvation that is of the book, but a faith that is measured against the book.

But is it right to examine the Bible in the same way as any other ancient document? Or is this merely to arouse people's curiosity without leading them to faith? Professor Barr believes that you cannot force people into faith by saying, 'The Bible is true. Therefore you have to believe in it.' You have to become a believer before you can understand why the Bible is authoritative. Faith comes before scripture. On the other hand, from the point of view of checking on faith and asking the question 'Is this reliable faith?' the Bible is set in a critical role, and it can say, 'This kind of faith isn't adequate', or 'It's better than another kind.'

Can we draw lessons from the Bible without having faith? Clive Calver believes that it is a mistake to divorce scripture from other disciplines. Theology and history need one another:

> I cannot accept a story about a Jesus who might have been. It has to be acceptable to me as historical fact before I am prepared to believe in Jesus today. That is why I feel that theologians are doing us great damage within the Church when they try to separate theology and history. They give us a philosophical Christ who never walked this earth, a God who saves by remote control. To me this is totally unsatisfactory. That is why I am thrilled with the way historians are increasingly confirming Biblical records for us, and why it is important for us to look seriously at what academic disciplines tell us about Christ. Otherwise we are throwing all our theology out of the window on a philosophical whim that has existed for a mere 200 years, and we think that we can get rid of 2,000 years of Church history in a puff of wind from one contemporary mind.

There is all the difference in the world between taking the Bible seriously and understanding every word mechanically. The message may be inspired, but does this mean that every word is inspired? Dr Cupitt believes that literalism applied to the Bible or anything else is a throwback to our more atavistic instincts. In the old days people thought that language was such an amazing thing that it must have been taught to us by a higher level of being, by invisible spirits, and that these spirits could occasionally move inside our heads and talk through our mouths. The view of the Bible as the inspired word of God reflects that primitive world view. Nowadays we know that language is purely human. It has evolved in human societies, and we cannot use the old idiom in quite the same sense. We know now that it is mythical, in a way that people did not know in the past.

The Bible deserves more than literalism. It is more often underestimated than overestimated. It should enlarge our faith, not confine it, and it should be questioned. Professor Levi says that we need six inches of interpretation for even the holiest of texts. No one sensible believes that the Bible was inspired word-for-word, as if by somebody writing in a magical, semi-conscious way. Indeed it is clear that the Biblical writers themselves did not think it was like that. But somehow, concentrated more in those books than in any other books, is a wisdom which is divinely sanctioned.

For Lord Soper, the humanity of the Bible is its greatest strength:

> The Bible is an inexhaustible source of spiritual inspiration and spiritual correlation. Whatever your condition, you can find someone in the Bible who has been up that same road. In that regard the Bible is the most important document that we have, because it is at one and the same time a progressive revelation of the love of God and the epitome of that revelation in the spirit and teaching of Jesus Christ, who is not only the man who died on the cross, but the living interpretation, the human photograph, of God.

The Bible was written across many centuries by many different people – poets, priests, exiles, prisoners, prophets and dreamers. Unintentionally they fell in step on a journey from the edge of the past to the brink of the future. Even the Bible's simplest stories contain questions with answers which are always one step ahead of our understanding.

Sixteen hundred years ago St Jerome, the great Biblical translator, the hermit of Bethlehem who gave up Cicero to follow Christ, answered those who criticised his meddling with the Bible in these words:

> I am not so foolish as to think the word of God needs correcting, but the manuscripts are imperfect and there can be mistakes in translation. The next task is to translate the words of holy scripture into deeds. As well as *talking* about holy things, we must *do* them.

The Books of the Bible
a summary

THE HEBREW BIBLE

A: *The Law* (Torah)
Genesis (Bereshith)
Exodus (Shemoth)
Leviticus (Vayikra)
Numbers (Bamidbar)
Deuteronomy (Devarim)

B: *The Prophets* (Nebi-im)
Former prophets
  Joshua
  Judges
  1 & 2 Samuel
  1 & 2 Kings
Later prophets
  Isaiah
  Jeremiah
  Ezekiel
  The twelve:
    Hosea, Joel
    Amos, Obadiah
    Jonah, Micah
    Nahum, Habakkuk
    Zephaniah, Haggai
    Zechariah, Malachi

C: *The Writings* (Kethubim)
Psalms
Job
Proverbs
The Festal Scrolls:
  Ruth, Song of Songs
  Ecclesiastes, Lamentations
  Esther
Daniel
Ezra/Nehemiah
1 & 2 Chronicles

THE CHRISTIAN OLD TESTAMENT

A: *The Pentateuch*
Genesis
Exodus
Leviticus
Numbers
Deuteronomy

B: *The Historical Books*
Joshua, Judges
Ruth
1 & 2 Samuel, 1 & 2 Kings
1 & 2 Chronicles
Ezra, Nehemiah
usually only in R.C. bibles:
  Esther, Judith, Tobit
  1 & 2 Maccabees

C: *Wisdom*
Job, Psalms
Proverbs, Ecclesiastes
Song of Songs
usually only in R.C. bibles:
  Wisdom of Solomon
Ecclesiasticus

D: *The Prophets*
Isaiah, Jeremiah
Lamentations
usually only in R.C. bibles:
  Baruch
Ezekiel, Daniel
The twelve
  Hosea, Joel, Amos
  Obadiah, Jonah
  Micah, Nahum
  Habakkuk
  Zephaniah, Haggai
  Zechariah, Malachi

The Old Testament

Genesis

The book of origins. It describes the story of creation and the earliest days of the world. It follows Adam and Eve out of Eden and into the harsher world of mortal men. Cain, the son of Adam and Eve, murders his brother Abel. Mankind multiplies and falls into sin – in their pride reaching up to heaven by the Tower of Babel.

Noah, the just man, is saved from the great flood by his obedience and boat-building. Terah, a descendant of Shem, one of the sons of Noah, decides to leave Ur of the Chaldeans to journey to the land of Canaan. He does not reach Canaan but instead settles down in Haran with his extended family, including his son Abram.

Terah dies and Abram, the first of the patriarchs, is called by the one unseen God to resume travelling. Abram sets out with his childless wife Sarai and his nephew Lot. God promises the land of Canaan to Abram and his descendants. Abram and his family prosper so much that the land between Bethel and Ai can no longer support all the livestock.

There is tension between the herdsmen of Abram and Lot. At Abram's suggestion they split into two camps. Abram stays in Canaan. Lot moves east as far as Sodom, a city notorious for its wickedness. Abram has a son, Ishmael, by Sarai's maid. God enters into a formal covenant with Abram promising him descendants as numerous as the stars. Henceforward Abram will be known as Abraham and Sarai will be known as Sarah. The covenant is sealed by the rite of circumcision.

Abraham entertains angels. The impossible happens: Sarah conceives in her barren old age. Her son is called Isaac. God warns Abraham that he plans to destroy Sodom and Gomorrah because of their inhabitants' wickedness. Abraham pleads with God to be merciful. God relents and says that if there are ten just men in Sodom he will not punish the city. Meanwhile the disguised angels who stayed with Abraham arrive in Sodom and receive hospitality from Lot. All the inhabitants of Sodom turn against Lot, demanding that the strangers be handed over to become the victims of gang rape. Lot refuses and is told by his mysterious guests that the city will be punished by destruction at the hand of God. They tell Lot and his family to flee without even giving the city a backward glance. Lot's wife disobeys and turns to look at the city being ravaged by fire and brimstone. She is turned into a pillar of salt. Lot shelters in a cave in the hills of Zoar and is seduced by his daughters.

Meanwhile Isaac, the son of Sarah and Abraham, thrives and Abraham accedes to Sarah's insistence that Ishmael and Hagar be cast out into the wilderness. God then tests Abraham by demanding Isaac as a sacrifice. Abraham obeys but an angel stays his hand and Isaac is saved. Sarah dies in advanced old age.

Abraham sets about finding a wife for Isaac. He sends a trusted servant back to the Haran area. In the city of Nahor by the well the servant sees Rebecca, Abraham's great-niece. She agrees to return to Canaan to become Isaac's wife. She is childless for many years.

Isaac prays for children and Rebecca has twin sons, Esau, a hunter, and Jacob, a quiet man and his mother's favourite. Esau, the elder, does not value his birthright and sells it to Jacob for a dish of lentil stew. The sale is confirmed when Rebecca and Jacob conspire to trick the blind Isaac into bestowing his blessing on Jacob instead of on Esau.

Under pressure from Rebecca Isaac tells Jacob to go to Haran to find a wife from his mother's family. Jacob agrees and sets out. As night falls he settles down to sleep. He dreams of a ladder connecting heaven and earth. The Abrahamic covenant is renewed.

Jacob continues his journeys and meets the family of his uncle Laban. He falls in love with Rachel, Laban's younger daughter, and agrees to work for her father for seven years to win her hand. Laban tricks Jacob by substituting Leah, Rachel's elder sister, on the wedding night. Jacob has to work a further seven years for Rachel. Leah bears Jacob six sons – Reuben, Simeon, Levi, Judah, Issachar and Zebulun. Jacob has two more sons, Gad and Asher by Zilpah, Leah's maid.

Rachel remains childless for a long time but finally bears Jacob his two favoured sons: Joseph, the dreamer, and Benjamin, the child of his old age. In time the twelve tribes of Israel will take their names from, and trace back their descent to, the twelve sons of Jacob. At the ford of Jabboh, Jacob wrestles with God. From then on Jacob is also known by the name Israel.

Dinah, the daughter of Leah, is raped by Shecham, the son of Hamon, a Canaanite. Simeon and Levi wreak terrible vengeance, at first appearing to agree to intermarriage between the Hamonites and their family on condition that circumcision is accepted by all the Hamonites. Once the operation is completed, Simeon and Levi put the Hamonites to the sword. Jacob is worried by their tactics.

More trouble is brewing. Joseph, Jacob's favourite son, with a coat of many colours, is sold into slavery by his ten older brothers, who are angered by his dreams implying his superiority. The brothers trick Jacob into believing that Joseph has been killed by wild animals.

In Egypt Joseph works in the house of Potiphar, one of Pharaoh's officers. Through his diligence he is promoted as overseer of Potiphar's master's house. All goes well until Joseph rejects the amorous advances of Potiphar's wife. In revenge she accuses Joseph of attempting to assault her. He is thrown in prison.

Joseph gains his freedom by using his skill at dream interpretation on Pharaoh's behalf. Pharaoh rewards Joseph with high office, an Egyptian name and a high-born wife. Contact with his brothers and father is regained when bad crops force Jacob to send his sons to Egypt to buy corn. There is a reconciliation. Joseph secures Pharaoh's favour for the family, who settle in Goshen in north-east Egypt.

After seventeen years in Goshen, Jacob dies. He is embalmed in the Egyptian fashion but is buried by Joseph in the land of Canaan. Joseph returns to Egypt and dies in old age. He too is embalmed and put in an Egyptian coffin. His last words look forward to the exodus, predicting that one day his bones will be carried away from Egypt.

Exodus

The book of slavery and liberation. A new pharaoh comes to power who does not remember Joseph. The descendants of Jacob, the children of Israel, find that they have overstayed their welcome. They are enslaved and persecuted. An edict is passed ordering that all Hebrew male infants be killed. A Hebrew woman called Jochebed hides her baby son in a basket in the bulrushes. He is rescued and adopted by Pharaoh's daughter and is called Moses.

As an adult Moses throws in his lot with his downtrodden people, killing an Egyptian whom he sees flogging a Hebrew slave. He is now a wanted man. He escapes eastwards into the Sinai desert. Pausing in his flight, he helps some women who are being bullied by shepherds at a well. He is taken back to their father Jethro, priest of Midian. He marries Zipporah, one of Jethro's daughters. While looking after his father-in-law's sheep on Mount Horeb he hears the voice of God speaking to him from a burning bush. He is charged to lead his people out of slavery and into the danger of freedom. God encourages him by signs and wonders. His rod turns into a snake and back again.

Reluctantly Moses accepts the commission and, with Aaron his brother, gains an audience with Pharaoh. Moses and Aaron ask for permission for the Hebrews to undertake a three-day journey into the wilderness to hold a religious festival. Pharaoh refuses and deals even more harshly with the Hebrew slaves. All Egypt, apart from Goshen, where the Hebrews live, is struck by a succession of plagues.

Moses and Aaron return to Pharaoh's court. They work miracles.

Pharaoh remains adamant. The plagues begin. Moses tells Aaron to smite the waters of the Nile with his rod. The water turns to blood and is undrinkable. Plagues follow in quick succession: frogs, lice, flies, cattle disease, boils, hail, locusts and darkness. The final plague is the most terrible. The first-born of every household unmarked by the blood of the Passover lamb is killed. The Hebrew slaves escape, following Moses into the wilderness.

They are pursued by Pharaoh and his chariots to the edge of the sea. By the power of God Moses parts the waters. The Hebrews pass through dryshod. The waters close over the Egyptians.

Miriam, the sister of Aaron and Moses, leads the women in a triumphant singing and dancing. The children of Israel's wandering begins in earnest. They are sustained by migratory quail and manna, a sweet hoar-frost secreted by plant lice, and by water from a rock struck by Moses' rod.

In the third month of their wandering the Israelites come to the wilderness of Sinai. Moses is summoned by God to climb Mount Sinai where he receives the law, the Ten Commandments. Meanwhile at this solemn moment the Israelites backslide into idolatry with worship of the golden calf. When Moses descends he is enraged by what he sees. He smashes the tablets of the law, destroys the golden calf and punishes the guilty. The people repent and resume their journey to the promised land. Rules are made governing religious practice under nomadic conditions.

Leviticus

A priestly handbook. Laws are laid down about sacrifice, cleanliness, diet, vows and tithes. Aaron, the brother of Moses, and his sons are consecrated as priests. A religious calendar is formed, including the annual day of atonement and the idea of the sabbatical and jubilee years.

Numbers

The book of the census. The story of the desert wandering is resumed. This is the second year of flight from Egypt. Moses and Aaron count and organise the people.

Tension builds up over leadership. Moses marries an Ethiopian woman. Both Aaron and Miriam are highly critical of this and call his leadership into doubt. God defends Moses and punishes Miriam with leprosy for seven days. The march pauses while spies are sent to Canaan.

Next Korah, a Levite, rebels against the authority of Moses and Aaron. He and his followers are punished. The question of authority is tackled by Moses, who is told by God to gather rods from the twelve houses of Israel and place them in the tent of meeting. Aaron's name is placed on the rod from the tribe of Levi. As a sign of God's favour it blossoms overnight and bears fruit. Thus the Levites' priestly status and Aaron's own authority are confirmed.

Miriam dies and is buried at Kadesh. There is discontent among the Israelites. Moses brings forth water from a rock struck by his rod. The king of Edom refuses the wanderers permission to journey through his territory. Aaron dies and his priestly authority is passed on to Eleazar, his son.

The Israelites pitch camp on the plains of Moab. Balak, the king of Moab, panics and asks Balaam, a soothsayer, to lay a curse on the Israelites. God tells Balaam to refuse the commission. Balak becomes insistent. God tells Balaam to comply with the invitation but only say what God tells him to. On the way to Balak's court, Balaam beats his reluctant ass. To his amazement the ass rebukes him in human speech. Balaam sees a sword-bearing angel. He resolves to say only the words which God puts in his mouth. When Balaam meets Balak and his court he infuriates them by blessing the Israelites instead of cursing them.

At Shittim many Israelites begin worshipping Baal. They are punished for their faithlessness. Twenty-four thousand die. A second census is taken. Moses adjudicates over Zelophehad's daughters' claim to their father's estate.

God tells Moses he is to die within sight of the promised land. Joshua, the son of Nun, will be his successor. The Israelites fight the Midianites and kill their five kings and all the men. They take the women and children as prisoners. This angers Moses, who lays down the laws of warfare. The tribes of Gad and Reuben settle in Transjordan. More laws are recorded.

Deuteronomy

The three discourses of Moses. Moses lays down the religious and civil codes. He reminds the people of their history and their faith. He speaks of a great prophet who is to come and explains why God has told him that he, Moses, will not enter the promised land. He prepares the children of Israel for his death. He dies, having seen but not entered the promised land. The Israelites weep for him for thirty days.

Joshua

A book of struggle and conquest. Joshua takes over the leadership. He sends spies into the promised land, who are aided by Rahab the harlot. The children of Israel cross the Jordan. The city of Jericho falls, followed by the south and the north of Canaan. Joshua divides up the land. At Shechem the people reassert their loyalty to their covenant with the one unseen God. His work completed, Joshua dies.

Judges

A book of old sins and new leaders. After the death of Joshua the children of Israel have no centralised leadership. They look for inspiration from a succession of charismatic military leaders called the judges. The Israelites fall into a pattern of sin, punishment, repentance and deliverance.

Deborah the prophetess, the only woman judge, masterminds the Israelites' victory over Jabin the Canaanite, king of Hazor. Sisera, the Canaanite general, flees from the battlefield. He shelters in the tent of Jael, the Kenite woman, who lulls him into a false sense of security and then pierces his head with a tent peg while he sleeps. Deborah celebrates Jael's courage in a triumphant song. The Israelites are at peace for the next hundred years.

About a hundred years later a child is born to the previously barren wife of Manoah, a member of the tribe of Dan. The child is called Samson. In accordance with a vow made by his mother before his birth, Samson undertakes to live as a Nazarite pledged to God's service; he will neither drink alcohol nor cut his hair. Asceticism does not come naturally to Samson. He has a weakness for women and a violent temper. He kills 1,000 Philistines with the jawbone of an ass. He removes the city gates of Gaza with his bare hands and carries them to Hebron.

After this exploit he falls for the wiles of Delilah, a woman of Sorek in the pay of the Philistine chief. Delilah is bribed to find out the secret of Samson's strength. By determined nagging she wheedles Samson's secret out of him – his strength comes from his uncut hair. Samson falls asleep with his head in her lap. While he sleeps his hair is shorn. He wakes up to weakness and betrayal. His strength gone, his eyes are put out and he is put to work turning the millstone at the prison in Gaza. He becomes an object of derision. The Philistines summon him to mock him in the temple of their god, Dagon. Three thousand crowd in to laugh at him. But Samson's hair has grown back. Pretending to need to lean on the pillars, he pushes the two main supporting columns of the temple apart. The temple collapses. He and his three thousand tormentors are killed.

The other major, but less well known, judges are Othniel, Ehud, Bartak, Gideon and Jephthah. The minor judges include Shamgar, Tola, Jair, Ibzan, Elon and Abdon. The book of Judges ends on a note of idolatry, lust and violence only shakily contained.

Ruth

A book of gentleness and hope. In sharp contrast to the book of Judges, this is a story of loyalty and love. It is named after its heroine, a Moabite (i.e. Gentile) woman who protects her dead husband's mother Naomi and is faithful to the God of Israel. Ruth has not been born into the chosen people but is one of the first 'choosing' people. By her marriage to Boaz of Bethlehem she becomes Israelite. Her great-grandson will be David, the golden king.

1 Samuel

A book of transition. Eli and his successor Samuel are the last of the judges. The old tribal system of *ad hoc* leadership is breaking down. The ark of the covenant is captured. The children of Israel demand to be like other nations and have a king. With grave forebodings Samuel gives in and anoints Saul the first king of the children of Israel.

Saul begins well, but failure soon sets in. He is rejected by Samuel, who anoints David, the young shepherd harpist from Bethlehem. David kills the Philistine hero Goliath. A close friendship has sprung up between David and Jonathan, the eldest son of Saul. It survives Saul's resentment of David's popularity. Saul tries to kill David. Jonathan attempts to soothe Saul's anger against David and effects a temporary reconciliation.

But David's successes on the battlefield fan Saul's murderous jealousy again. David escapes and meets up with Samuel. Jonathan argues with Saul for David's life. He only succeeds in provoking his father's anger. Sadly Jonathan gives in. The breach between Saul and David cannot be healed. The two friends meet to say goodbye and promise eternal loyalty to each other. They go their separate ways.

Saul pursues David. David spares Saul's life twice. After consulting the Witch of Endor Saul arms for his last battle against the Philistines. The fleeing Israelites, including Jonathan, are killed on Mount Gilboa. Badly wounded, Saul acknowledges defeat and commits suicide.

2 Samuel

A book of family problems. David mourns the death of Jonathan and Saul. As king of Israel and Judah he makes Mount Zion his capital and brings the ark of the covenant into Jerusalem, leaping and dancing before it, much to his wife Michal's disgust.

David wishes to build a house for the Lord. Nathan the prophet tells him that this task will be only for his successor. David commits adultery with Bathsheba, the wife of Uriah the Hittite. David's family troubles begin. Amnon, David's eldest son, rapes Tamar, his half-sister. Absalom avenges the sister by hitting Amnon and falling into open conflict with David. Absalom is killed while fleeing through the woods of Ephraim. David is broken-hearted.

1 Kings

A book of glory and division. David dies, tended by Abishag the Shunamite. The kingdom is handed down to Solomon the son of Bathsheba. Solomon grows in wealth and wisdom. He is visited by the Queen of Sheba. Work on the Temple is begun. Solomon is tainted by the many gods of his foreign wives.

After his death the kingdom is divided. Rehoboam, his son, rules the southern kingdom, Judah. Jeroboam, a former court official, rules the northern kingdom of Israel. Rehoboam is succeeded by Abijah, Asa and Jehoshaphat. Jeroboam is succeeded by Nadab, Baasha, Elah, Zimri, Yibni, Omri and Ahab.

Ahab, a shrewd but idolatrous king, is married to the infamous Jezebel. After a disastrous drought Elijah, the prophet of the one God, challenges the priests of Baal to a fire- and rain-making contest. He wins. Ahab and Jezebel come to a sticky end. Ahab is succeeded by his son Ahaziah, who is no better than his father.

2 Kings

A book of degeneration. Ahaziah is succeeded by Jehoram. Elijah is lifted to heaven in a fiery chariot. He is succeeded by the bald miracle-working prophet Elisha, who anoints Jehu as the next king of Israel. Meanwhile Athaliah, the daughter of Jezebel, an adherent of Baal, has become queen of Judah. After a revolt led by Jehoida, the high priest, Joash, a follower of the one God, comes to the throne.

In the northern kingdom of Israel Jehu is succeeded by Jehoahaz, Johoash, Jeroboam II, Zechariah, Shallum, Menachem, Pekah, Pekakiah and Hosea. Despite the warnings of the prophets Amos, Isaiah and Micah, the northern kingdom degenerates irreparably. The Assyrians lay siege to Israel's capital, Samaria. In 722 Samaria falls to Sargon III.

Meanwhile in the southern kingdom of Judah king Hezekiah listens to the prophet Isaiah and destroys the pagan shrines of Asherah and Baal. His work is reversed by his son Manasseh and Manasseh's son Amon. But Josiah, the grandson of Manasseh, tries to bring Judah back to the worship of the one God. He finds the book of the law. He is killed by the Pharaoh Neco. Judah's days are numbered. King Johoiachim surrenders to Nebuchadnezzar. The last king of Judah is Zedekiah, a vassal king. Jerusalem, the capital of Judah, falls in 586 BC. The Temple treasures are carried off to Babylon. The deportation of people follows. The exile has begun.

1 & 2 Chronicles

Complementary books. These two books cover much the same period as 2 Samuel and 1 & 2 Kings. Their name in Greek is *Paralipomena* – literally 'things which have been left out'. They move from the death of Saul up to the exile. The final chapter of Book 2 tries to make sense of the exile. It ends on an optimistic note with the decree of Cyrus calling on the Jews to return to their homeland and rebuild the Temple.

Ezra

A book of homecoming. The return from Babylonian exile begins. Work on rebuilding the Temple is undertaken, interrupted and completed. Ezra, the teacher, arrives in Jerusalem. He campaigns against mixed marriages.

Nehemiah

A book of reconstruction. Under the guidance of Nehemiah, the cup-bearer, Jerusalem's walls are rebuilt. The community gathers at the Water Gate and Ezra reads out the law of Moses. The covenant is renewed.

Esther

A romantic tale of royal intrigue. King Ahasuerus of Persia is infuriated when his wife Vashti defies him by refusing to put in an appearance at one of his feasts. She is set aside. A kingdom-wide search begins for her successor. Esther, the adopted daughter of Mordecai, a pious Jew, is summoned to the court. Her beauty catches the king's eye. She becomes his queen. Mordecai advises her not to reveal her Jewishness. He then falls foul of Haman, the king's chief minister. Haman, a vindictive man, plots to have all Jews in Persia killed. Esther successfully pleads for the lives of her people. She and Mordecai undo Haman's plans. Haman is hanged on the gallows he has constructed for Mordecai.

Judith

A story of patriotism and head-chopping. Judith is the beautiful young wife of a rich farmer at Bethulia. Her husband dies of sun stroke. Judith does not remarry. An enemy army under the general

Holofernes threatens her city. The elders confer and decide that they will have to surrender, but Judith takes matters into her own hands. She infiltrates the enemy lines and then charms and beheads Holofernes. Holofernes' army is routed. Judith, the heroine, is praised by Joachim, the high priest of Jerusalem.

Tobit

A story of fish and angels. Tobit, a devout Jew living in Nineveh, is blinded by some sparrow-droppings. He sends his son Tobias to Reges in Media to collect some silver he left with his relation Gabael twenty years before. Tobias needs only a reliable travelling companion. He selects one – who happens to be the angel Raphael in disguise on a mercy mission to help Tobias' cousin Sarah, whose seven successive husbands have been killed by the jealous demon Asmodeus on her wedding night. Tobias fishes in the Tigris. He catches a fish. His travelling companion tells him to burn the heart and the liver. This exorcises Asmodeus. Tobias marries Sarah. Gabael comes to the wedding, bringing with him Tobit's silver. Tobias and Sarah return to Nineveh. Tobias (on Raphael's instructions) uses the fish's gall to cure Tobit's blindness. Raphael reveals his true identity. Everyone lives happily ever after.

1 & 2 Maccabees

Books of revolt. Mattathias and his sons John, Simon, Judas, Eleazer and Jonathan refuse to acquiesce in Antiochus Epiphanes' instructions demanding that Jews offer sacrifice to pagan gods. They take to the hills and form a resistance movement, destroying pagan altars and fostering hope among their people. Mattathias dies. Judas assumes leadership of the guerrillas and begins a bitterly fought campaign. The Maccabees enter Jerusalem and relight the temple candelabrum. Zion is fortified again. Judas defeats the Seleucid general Nicanor but is killed at the battle of Elasa. Jonathan, followed by Simon, takes on the mantle of leadership. Simon drives foreign overlordship out of the country. He is murdered by his son-in-law Ptolemy.

Job

A conundrum of suffering. Job is a pious, well-to-do man living in the land of Uz. God decides to test his faith. Job's wealth and family are taken away from him. He loses his health and his wife turns against him. He curses the day he was born. His friends comfort him with words of no comfort – only evil men suffer, they say. He knows he is innocent. God asks him why he is complaining. He admits there are things he cannot understand. His good fortune is restored. He lives to a happy old age.

Psalms

A book of prayer poems. It covers all human emotions from blind fury to the peaceful acceptance of the presence of God.

Proverbs

A book of homely wisdom. Wisdom brings mankind to a greater knowledge of God, as well as giving him more worldly rewards.

Ecclesiastes

A book of the worldly-wise. Life without awareness of God is the vanity above all vanities. Death, sin, uncertainty, misfortune and old age all prove that life by itself is pointless.

The Song of Solomon

A love poem. A Shulammite woman works in a vineyard owned by Solomon. Her skin is darkened by the sun. She works hard and is unnoticed even by her own family. A stranger visits the vineyard. She falls in love with him. It is Solomon. Later he returns in kingly splendour and takes her away as his bride.

The Wisdom of Solomon

A response to Hellenism. Wisdom is all praiseworthy and life is eternal. Idolatry means spiritual death.

Ecclesiasticus

A book of wise sayings by Jesus ben Sirach. Wisdom and love of God are inextricable.

Isaiah

The messianic prophet Isaiah (born in Jerusalem in the second half of the 8th century BC and living through the reigns of Uzziah, Jothana, Ahaz, Hezekiah and Manasseh) rails against Judah's enemies and his own people's weakness and material greed. He tells of a child who will be born, called Immanuel. The book also contains 'the Servant Songs', telling of a perfect servant who will suffer and pay for his people's sins by a guiltless death.

Jeremiah

The prophet of warning. Jeremiah (born in the village Anathoth, outside Jerusalem, in the second half of the 7th century BC and continuing through the reigns of Josiah, Jehoahaz, Jehoiakim, Jehoiachin and Zedekiah) attacks his people for their idolatrous ways. He is beaten up and put in the stocks. He continues to warn Judah that disaster is at hand. He is ignored. Jerusalem falls. The exile begins. Jeremiah advises his people to make the best of exile. He is given the choice of going to Babylon or staying behind. Initially he stays with Gedeliah, now governor of Judah. Gedeliah is murdered. Jeremiah flees to Egypt.

Lamentations

A book of grief. Jerusalem has fallen. The city itself weeps, sated with hunger and humiliation. Starving mothers boil their own children. Those who have died are happier than those who live. There is no joy in Jerusalem. Zion has become the home of jackals.

Baruch

A book of promise. Baruch the scribe prays for his fellow exiles. Jerusalem is grieving, but there is hope. One day there will be restoration. Chapter 6 is known as the 'Letter of Jeremiah'. It purports to be a letter from the prophet to Jewish captives in Babylon.

Ezekiel

The prophet of the exile. Ezekiel (the son of Buzi, born in the last half of the 7th century BC) is taken as an exile to Babylon with king Jehoiachin. His vision includes seeing the glory of God riding in a chariot moving on supernatural creatures. He tells of Jerusalem's doom. He relays the allegories of the eagle and the cedar, the two sinful sisters and the boiling pot. He has a vision of a valley of dry bones. He sees a day when the godless nations will suffer and Israel will be restored under a new covenant of peace. The Temple will rise again and God will dwell in the new Jerusalem.

Daniel

The prophet of the fiery furnace. Daniel (born at the end of the 7th century BC) is taken as an exile from Jerusalem and is trained for court service in Babylon. He interprets Nebuchadnezzar's dreams. Three young Hebrews survive the punishment of the fiery furnace. Nebuchadnezzar dreams again. Daniel interprets. The king becomes mad but recovers his sanity and before his death praises God. Belshazzar holds a feast. It is interrupted by graffiti. He is killed. Darius the Mede comes to the throne. Daniel ridicules idolatry. He kills a sacred dragon and spends a night in the lions' den. He recounts his apocalyptic dreams.

Hosea

The prophet of enduring love. Hosea (born in the middle of the 8th century BC) marries and loves Gomer, who is unfaithful to him. Hosea forgives his wife all her failings and, like God, will forgive Israel for her unfaithfulness.

Joel

The prophet of judgement. Joel (probably born in the 5th century BC) warns of a plague of locusts which will be a warning of the day of the Lord. He describes a terrible time when the sun will grow dark and the moon will turn to blood. The nations will be judged. Jerusalem will stand for ever.

Amos

The prophet of the plumb-line. Amos (a sheep-farmer of Tekoa in the second half of the 8th century BC) gives warning that the Lord will punish the Gentile nations for their violence. The kingdom of Judah will suffer because it has not kept God's law. Israel will be punished for its materialism and inhumanity. God will measure his people like a builder checking the trueness of a wall. They will be punished for their failings, but in the future all will be well.

Obadiah

The prophet of retribution. Obadiah (who probably lived in the 5th century BC) warns the people of Edom that they will suffer for their treatment of Judah.

Jonah

The prophet to the Gentiles. Jonah (8th century BC) is called to prophesy to Nineveh. He demurs and takes a ship to Tarshish instead. During a storm he is thrown overboard by a superstitious crew and swallowed by a passing fish. He is regurgitated and obeys God's repeated call to go to Nineveh. The city repents. Jonah is angry that Nineveh has escaped. God uses a castor-oil plant to teach him the error of his vindictiveness.

Micah

The prophet of protest. Micah (8th century BC) inveighs against the corruption and luxury of city life. God does not want ostentatious sacrifice but simplicity and justice. Only the future holds the promise of peace.

Nahum

The prophet of ruin. Nahum (7th century BC) warns that Nineveh's days are numbered. For all its worldly power it will be besieged and will fall.

Habakkuk

The prophet of indignation. Habakkuk (second half of the 7th century BC) puzzles why God allows injustice, but ends with a prayer of faith in the unknowable power of God.

Zephaniah

The prophet of repentance. Zephaniah (a contemporary of Habakkuk) says that God will destroy the paganism which has taken root in Jerusalem. God will judge the nations. A time will come when mankind's speech is pure, and all good fortune will be restored.

Haggai

The prophet of the Temple. Haggai (6th century BC) calls on the people of Jerusalem to concentrate on rebuilding the Temple and tells of a day when heaven and earth will be shaken.

Zechariah

The prophet of the shepherd. A contemporary of Haggai, Zechariah prophesies through visions rich in symbolism. He tells of a time of peace and a good shepherd, who will be rejected. After much suffering the kingdom of God will be established.

Malachi

The prophet of the messenger. Malachi (5th century BC) speaks of God's love and man's faithfulness. God will send a messenger to prepare the way. A terrible day of fire will destroy the evil and proud. Elijah the prophet will return to reconcile and protect God's children.

Synoptic Gospels

Matthew
Mark
Luke

The Fourth Gospel

John

Letters traditionally attributed to Paul

Romans
1 & 2 Corinthians
Galatians
Ephesians*
Philippians
Colossians
1 & 2 Thessalonians*
1 & 2 Timothy**
Titus**
Philemon

Judaeo-Christian, or general letters

Hebrews
James
1 & 2 Peter
1 & 2 & 3 John
Jude

Revelation

* Pauline authorship questioned
** Pauline authorship seriously doubted

The New Testament

Matthew

Good news about a Messiah king, written to the Jews. Joseph, a descendant of Abraham and David, discovers that Mary, the woman he plans to marry, is expecting a child. He has not slept with her. He decides on marriage followed by a quiet divorce to save her embarrassment. An angel reassures him that Mary's child is the son of the Holy Spirit. Joseph drops his divorce plans.

Jesus is born in Bethlehem. Wise men from the east seek him out. King Herod becomes alarmed at the prospect of a rival power bid. Joseph takes Mary and Jesus to Egypt for safety. Meanwhile Herod kills all male infants in Bethlehem. When Herod dies, Joseph brings Mary and Joseph back from Egypt. The family settles in Nazareth.

Time passes. John the Baptist begins preaching in the wilderness of Judea. He calls the people to repentance and tells them that the kingdom of God is at hand. Jesus is baptized by John in the river Jordan.

Jesus fasts for forty days and forty nights in the wilderness. He is tempted by the devil. John is arrested. Jesus begins to preach. He calls on the fishermen Peter, Andrew, James and John to follow him. They leave their nets.

Throughout the country Jesus' reputation grows. He attracts crowds drawn by his healing and teaching. He calls on Matthew the taxman to follow him. Matthew leaves his ledgers.

Jesus gives his twelve closest followers the authority to heal and cast out unclean spirits. He teaches in parables, speaking about a kingdom not of the earth but of heaven. He returns home and tries teaching there. The familiar people of Nazareth treat his message with contempt.

Meanwhile John the Baptist is thrown into prison because he has irritated Herodias, the grand-daughter of Herod the Great and current wife of Herod Antipas. Salome, her daughter, dances for Herod Antipas. She dances well and is offered a reward. She chooses the head of John the Baptist.

When he hears the news Jesus withdraws in a boat from the crowd round him. The crowd tracks him down. He heals them and distributes five loaves and two fishes among five thousand. Later that day the disciples see him walking on water.

Relations between Jesus and the religious establishment

deteriorate. At Caesarea Philippi Simon Peter identifies Jesus as the Christ, the anointed one, the son of the living god.

Peter, James and John climb a mountain with Jesus. At the summit they see him transfigured and suffused with light, talking to Moses and Elijah.

Jesus continues his teaching and begins to prepare his followers for his fate. He rides into Jerusalem on the back of a donkey. He is hailed as the son of David. He drives the money-changers out of the Temple. His teaching now includes messages about the end of the world.

At Bethany a woman anoints him with precious ointment. After this Judas Iscariot goes to the chief priests and agrees to betray Jesus for thirty pieces of silver.

It is the time of the Passover. Jesus eats his last meal with his friends. He blesses and breaks bread. They eat it. It is his body. He blesses the wine. They drink it. It is his blood.

They walk to the Garden of Gethsemane. Jesus is identified by Judas. He is arrested. False witnesses are brought against him. Judas regrets his action. He returns the thirty pieces of silver and hangs himself.

Jesus' passion begins. He is mocked and crucified. He dies. Joseph of Arimathea buries the body in a rock-hewn tomb. A stone is rolled over the entrance. The tomb is sealed and guarded.

On the third day after the crucifixion Mary Magdalene and Mary the mother of James and Joseph visit the tomb. There is an earthquake. An angel rolls the stone from the tomb entrance. Jesus is no longer there. He is risen and will see his friends in Galilee. Jesus appears to the women. They tell the eleven apostles. As promised Jesus meets them in Galilee.

Mark

Good news about a servant written for Romans. John the Baptist, preaching in the wilderness, says he is the messenger of one who is to come whose sandal he, John, is not worthy to untie. Jesus is baptized by John. A voice is heard affirming the divine sonship of Jesus.

Jesus withdraws to the wilderness where he is tempted for forty days. John is arrested. Jesus begins preaching. He calls Simon Peter, Andrew, James and John to be his apostles. They follow him.

They go to Capernaum. Jesus heals a man of an unclean spirit. He cures Simon Peter's mother-in-law. Jesus' reputation spreads. He continues healing and teaching. Jesus eats with tax collectors and sinners. He shares his authority to preach and heal with his twelve chosen apostles. He speaks in parables about the kingdom of God. He quells a storm and sends the unclean spirit from a Gerasene man into a herd of pigs. He heals the daughter of Jairus.

John the Baptist is put to death by an unwilling Herod Antipas at the request of his step-daughter Salome, who chooses John's head as her reward for dancing well. Now Herod fears that Jesus is John the Baptist raised from the dead.

Jesus walks on the water. At Gennesaret he heals many people. He feeds the four thousand. The scribes and pharisees come to question him.

At Caesarea Philippi, Peter states that Jesus is the Christ. Jesus orders his apostles not to tell anyone.

Peter, James and John follow Jesus up a mountain where he is transfigured before their eyes. Moses and Elijah appear.

Jesus begins to prepare the apostles for his death. He rides into Jerusalem on the back of a colt and is hailed as the son of David. He curses a fig tree. It shrivels. He throws the money-changers out of the temple.

In the temple he speaks in parables to the chief priests, the scribes and the elders. The Sadduccees question him about the resurrection. He teaches Peter, James, John and Andrew about the signs of the end days.

At Bethany in the house of Simon the leper, much to the apostles' indignation, a woman anoints Jesus with expensive nard. Jesus defends her extravagance. Judas Iscariot goes to the chief priest and agrees to betray Jesus.

It is the time of the Passover. Jesus eats his last supper with the apostles. He predicts he will be betrayed. He blesses bread, breaks it and tells the apostles to eat it. It is his body. He blesses the wine and tells them to drink it. It is his blood.

They sing a hymn and go out to the Mount of Olives. Jesus prays in the Garden of Gethsemane. Peter, James and John keep falling asleep.

Judas arrives and betrays Jesus with a kiss. The apostles flee. Jesus is taken to the high priest. Peter skulks in the courtyard. As Jesus had predicted, Peter denies him three times.

Pilate, the Roman governor, asks the people whether they would prefer him to release Jesus or Barabbas. They choose Barabbas and shout for Jesus to be crucified. Jesus is scourged, mocked and crucified. Joseph of Arimathea, with Pilate's permission, buries Jesus in a rock-hewn tomb. A stone is rolled over the entrance.

Three days later Mary Magdalene, Mary the mother of James, and Salome go to the tomb to anoint the body. They are worried about how they will roll the stone away.

When they arrive there the stone is rolled back and Jesus' body is no longer inside. A young man in a white robe instructs them to tell Peter and the other disciples that Jesus is risen and will meet them all in Galilee.

Jesus appears to Mary Magdalene and to two other disciples but the rest of the disciples remain unbelieving. He appears to the eleven and orders them to teach the whole world. Jesus ascends to heaven. The apostles begin their work.

Luke

Good news about Jesus, the Son of Man, written for Gentiles. While Zechariah the priest is burning incense in the Temple the angel Gabriel appears to him and tells him that his childless wife will conceive a son who will be called John and will exercise the power and spirit of Elijah. Zechariah is literally struck dumb.

Zechariah's wife Elizabeth duly conceives a child. In the sixth month of her pregnancy the angel Gabriel appears again – this time to Mary, a young girl in Nazareth betrothed to Joseph. Gabriel tells Mary that through the power of the Holy Spirit she is to become the mother of a holy child, Jesus, the son of God. Mary accepts God's will. Gabriel tells her that Elizabeth, her cousin, is also expecting a child.

Mary goes to visit Elizabeth. Elizabeth greets Mary as the mother of the Lord. Mary breaks into a hymn of praise. She stays with Elizabeth for three months.

Elizabeth gives birth to a son. Zechariah, still struck dumb, writes on a slate that the child must be called John. Immediately his power of speech returns and he praises God.

There is a census. Joseph who belongs to the house of David has to go to Bethlehem to be enrolled. Mary goes with him. Jesus is born in Bethlehem in a stable because all the inns are full. Angels appear to nearby shepherds and tell them of a saviour child who has been born in Bethlehem. The shepherds seek out the child and tell Mary and Joseph about the angels' message.

Mary and Joseph take Jesus to Jerusalem for the rite of circumcision. The aged Simeon blesses Jesus and recognises in him the sign of God's salvation. The prophetess Anna also speaks about the hoped-for redeemer.

Mary and Joseph return to Nazareth and live uneventfully there for the next eleven years. Every year they go up to Jerusalem for the feast of the Passover. When Jesus is in his twelfth year he gives Mary and Joseph the slip and stays up in Jerusalem after the annual pilgrimage. Mary and Joseph look for him for three days. Finally they find him in the Temple questioning the teachers. Jesus is unrepentant. They should have realised, he says, that he would have been in his father's house.

Time passes. Jesus' cousin John the Baptist, the son of Elizabeth and Zechariah, begins to cause a stir preaching and baptizing in the wilderness. He tells of one who is to come who will baptize not with water but with the Holy Spirit and fire. He baptizes Jesus and a voice from heaven is heard describing Jesus as 'my beloved son'.

Herod puts John in prison for his outspoken criticism of royal family life. Jesus' public ministry begins in earnest. For forty days he prays and fasts in the wilderness and is tempted by the devil.

He returns to Nazareth, goes to the synagogue and reads Isaiah's messianic prophecies. He tells the congregation they have heard those ancient promises being fulfilled. The people are furious. He escapes from their anger.

He goes to Capernaum. He teaches, heals and casts out unclean spirits. The fishermen Simon Peter, James and John leave their nets and follow him, as does Levi, the tax collector. These three are among the twelve apostles he choses out of all his disciples.

He continues interpreting the law and teaching in parables. He heals the centurion's servant and brings the widow of Nain's son back to life. At a Pharisee's house, a woman of sinful reputation washes Jesus' feet with her tears and anoints them with nard. The Pharisee is scandalised. Jesus rebukes him.

With the twelve apostles and some women followers Jesus travels through the country preaching and healing. He gives his apostles the power to heal and cast out unclean spirits. They disperse to take the good news of Jesus to villages throught the land.

Jesus' reputation reaches Herod, who fears he might bring the beheaded John the Baptist back from the dead. At Bethsaida Jesus feeds five thousand with five loaves and two fishes.

Peter acknowledges that Jesus is the Christ. About a week later Jesus takes Peter, James and John up a mountain to pray. He is transfigured by their eyes. Elijah and Moses appear and talk to him about what will happen in Jerusalem.

Jesus sends out a further seventy or so followers to spread the good news. He teaches his followers how to pray and warns them about the hard times to come.

He rides into Jerusalem on the back of a colt. The people bless him and hail him as king. At the temple he drives out all those buying and selling. He is questioned closely by the scribes and pharisees and later by the Sadduccees. He predicts the fall of Jerusalem.

As the feast of the Passover draws near, Judas Iscariot agrees with the chief priests to betray Jesus for money. At the Passover supper, the last meal Jesus has, he blesses bread and gives it to his apostles. It is his body. He blesses the wine and gives it to them. It is his blood.

In sombre mood, he predicts that Simon Peter will betray him three times before cock-crow. He goes to pray on the Mount of Olives. His disciples follow him and they fall asleep. Judas appears with a crowd of supporters. Jesus is seized and arrested.

Peter follows at a distance. He loiters in the high priest's courtyard. A maid identifies him as one of Jesus' followers. Peter denies it. Someone else says the same thing. Peter denies it. An hour later the accusation is started by someone else. Peter denies it. A cock crows. Peter breaks down in tears.

Jesus is mocked by his gaolers and cross-examined by the chief priests' council. Pilate questions him and finds him innocent, but hearing he is a Galilean passes him over to Herod.

Herod, disappointed that Jesus will not work wonders for him, mocks him and sends him back to Pilate.

Pilate asks the people whether they would rather have Barabbas or Jesus freed. They chose Barabbas and call for Jesus' crucifixion.

Jesus is crucified between two criminals. One jeers at him, one asks to be remembered in the kingdom. Jesus comforts him.

After three hours Jesus dies. He is laid in Joseph of Arimathea's new rock-hewn tomb. Three days later, some of Jesus' women followers visit the tomb hoping to anoint the body. To their amazement the stone is already rolled away and Jesus' body is gone. Two men in dazzling white clothes tell them that Jesus has risen from the dead as he told them he would.

The women bring the news back to the apostles. The apostles do not believe them. Jesus appears to two of the disciples walking from Jerusalem to Emmaus. They recognise him in the breaking of bread.

They immediately return to Jerusalem to tell the eleven apostles. They find that Jesus has already appeared to Peter. At that point Jesus appears among them and eats some boiled fish. Jesus explains the scriptures to them. He tells them to stay in Jerusalem until they receive power from on high.

Then Jesus and the apostles walk as far as Bethany. He blesses them and ascends into heaven. The apostles return to Jerusalem rejoicing.

John

Good news for all believers. The Son of God belongs to both history and eternity. Jesus the word is the living expression of God who was and is and will be.

John the Baptist, the forerunner and witness to the light of the Messiah, is questioned about his identity. He tells of one who is to come whose sandal he, John, is not worthy to untie.

Jesus comes to the Jordan to be baptized. John hails him as the 'Lamb of God', the one who is to come. John sees a dove descend over Jesus. Andrew, a follower of John, listens to Jesus. He tells his brother Simon that Jesus is the Messiah. Jesus invites Philip to follow him. Philip brings Nathaniel.

At a marriage feast at Cana, Jesus obeys his mother's prompting and changes water into wine. Jesus goes to Jerusalem and drives the money-changers out of the Temple. He tells Nicodemus, the

Pharisee, that to enter the kingdom of heaven a man must be born again.

Jesus and his disciples set to work in Judea. John baptizes at Aeron near Salim. His disciples ask him whether he resents Jesus' popularity. John replies that it is right that Jesus should increase and he decrease.

Jesus leaves Judea and goes to Galilee via Samaria. At the well of Sychar he talks to the Samaritan woman about the living water which is eternal. Jesus reveals himself to her as the Messiah.

He goes to Jerusalem and infuriates the religious authorities by healing on the sabbath. He further scandalises them by speaking of God as his father. On the shores of the Sea of Galilee Jesus feeds the five thousand. That evening his disciples see him walking on the water.

The people seek Jesus out and he teaches them about the bread of life, the only food which will never fail. Jesus tells his followers they must be ready to eat his flesh and drink his blood. He is the bread of life. The disciples find this hard to understand.

Jesus goes up to Jerusalem and continues his controversial teaching. Some acclaim him as the Christ, others want him put in prison. Jesus teaches in the Temple and saves a woman caught in adultery from death by stoning. He is accused of being a Samaritan and a devil and only just escapes a stoning himself.

He heals a man born blind on the sabbath. Martha and Mary of Bethany summon him to the deathbed of their brother Lazarus. Jesus delays two days and then goes there. Lazarus is already in the tomb. Jesus brings him back to life.

News of this latest miracle reaches the Pharisees. They are alarmed. If Jesus gains too many followers the position of the Temple will be weakened. Their faith and national status will no longer be able to demand respect from Rome. For the good of everyone Jesus must be put to death.

Six days before the Passover Jesus returns to Bethany. Mary anoints his feet with a pound of nard. She dries his feet with her hair. Judas Iscariot is disgusted by the extravagant gesture. Jesus defends Mary.

Jesus rides into Jerusalem on a young ass, thus fulfilling scripture. He is greeted as king of Israel. The Pharisees agree that he is becoming too powerful.

At the Passover meal taken with his disciples Jesus knows that the end is approaching. Judas has already set his mind on betrayal. Jesus prepares his disciples for his death. He washes their feet and tells them to love one another. He predicts Simon Peter's triple denial. He tells them he is going to his father. He promises that he will return to them and that the Spirit of Truth will descend upon them. He prays that all who believe in him may be united.

With his disciples, he crosses the Kidron Valley. They enter a garden. Judas the betrayer also goes there with an entourage of soldiers, Pharisees and officials representing the chief priest. Jesus is arrested and taken to Annas, the father-in-law of Caiaphas the high priest. Simon Peter and one other apostle follow Jesus to the court of the high priest. While waiting outside, Simon Peter denies Jesus three times. A cock crows.

Jesus is taken to Pilate. Pilate finds him innocent. He offers to free Jesus or Barabbas the insurgent. The crows chooses Barabbas.

Pilate has Jesus flogged. The solders crown him with thorns and mock him. The chief priests and their officers insist that this is not enough: Jesus, the self-proclaimed son of God, must be crucified. Pilate becomes more nervous. He hands Jesus over for crucifixion.

Jesus is crucified on a hill called Golgotha. The soldiers cast lots for his clothing. Jesus dies. Joseph of Arimathea and Nicodemus bury Jesus' body in a new tomb.

Three days later Mary Magdalene goes to the tomb. She sees that the stone is rolled away. She runs and tells Simon Peter and the other disciple – the one whom Jesus loved – that someone has stolen Jesus' body. The two apostles run to the tomb. They find it empty. Mary stands weeping outside the tomb. She sees two angels, who ask her why she is crying. Through her tears she tells them it is because Jesus' body has been stolen. Someone else asks her why she is crying. She says that if he has stolen the body he must tell her where he has taken it. He calls her by her name. She realises it is Jesus. He tells her to let the others know that he has not yet ascended to the Father.

Mary returns and tells the disciples. That evening Jesus appears to them. Thomas is not there and remains sceptical. Eight days later Jesus appears to the disciples again and chides Thomas for his disbelief. He only believes because he has seen. Others will believe who have not seen.

Jesus appears again on the shores of the sea of Tiberias, gives them some fishing advice and makes them breakfast. Simon Peter has to confirm his faith three times. The stigma of the cock-crow is wiped away.

This is the testimony of John, the disciple whom Jesus loved.

Acts of the Apostles

A book of missionaries and martyrs. Jesus appears to his followers for forty days after his death. He promises them that they will be baptized with the Holy Spirit. They watch him ascending into heaven.

Jesus' followers return to Jerusalem. They choose Matthias to take Judas Iscariot's place among the apostles. On the day of Pentecost they are all in one room. They hear a sound like a rushing wind and see tongues of flame resting on each other's head. They are baptized with the Holy Spirit.

Peter goes out with the eleven other apostles and begins to preach with inspired eloquence. All who hear him, regardless of their mother tongue, understand him. Three thousand are baptized.

In Jesus' name, Peter heals a lame man and begins preaching in Solomon's portico. This annoys the Temple authorities. Five thousand are converted. The next day Peter is cross-examined by the scribes and elders. He preaches to them. They charge him and John not to teach or heal in Jesus' name. Peter and John refuse. They are released.

Jesus' new followers hold everything in common. Ananias and Sapphira sell some property and keep part of the proceeds back for themselves. They both drop down dead.

The apostles' reputation for healing and casting out unclean spirits increases. They are imprisoned. An angel frees them. They are arrested again and questioned. Gamaliel the Pharisee urges that no action be taken against them.

The first seven deacons are appointed, including Stephen, who is taken before the high priest and elders. He preaches eloquently about Jesus. The council is furious. He is thrown out of the city and stoned to death for his beliefs. A young man named Saul watches his death.

The young church in Jerusalem is persecuted. Jesus' followers scatter through Judea and Samaria. Saul hunts out and imprisons any Christians he can find.

Philip goes to Samaria, where he preaches and heals people sick in mind or body. Simon the Magician is baptized and is intrigued by the miracles he witnesses. He approaches Simon Peter and offers him money for the apostolic gifts of healing bodies and casting out demons. In fury, Simon Peter refuses.

Prompted by an angel, Philip turns south to the Jerusalem-Gaza road. There he sees an Ethiopian eunuch, a minister of queen Candace, sitting in a chariot reading the prophecies of Isaiah. Philip tells him about the fulfilment of these words in the life of Jesus. The eunuch is baptized.

Saul the persecutor turns his attention to Damascus. As he approaches the city he sees a great light and falls to the ground. He hears the voice of Jesus asking him why he is persecuting him. He is to continue to Damascus and await further instructions.

When Saul stands up he has been blinded. He is led to Damascus. For three days he cannot eat, drink or see. In a vision Jesus tells Ananias to seek out Saul and cure his blindness. Ananias obeys.

Saul stays in Damascus for several days and begins preaching that Jesus was and is the Christ. His new message makes him unpopular. A plot is hatched to kill him. He escapes by being lowered over the city wall in a basket.

He returns to Jerusalem and preaches there. His life is once again in danger. He goes to Caesarea and Tarsus.

Peter cures Aeneas at Lydda, and at Joppa brings Dorcas back to life. At the house of Cornelius Peter preaches and baptizes Gentiles.

The good news is spread among Jews and Greeks. Barnabas is sent to the believers in Antioch. He is joined by Saul. Together they work there for a year. In Antioch, Jesus' followers come to be known by a new name – they are called Christians.

Meanwhile king Herod Agrippa kills the apostle James. Peter is arrested and imprisoned. He is freed by an angel. King Herod dies.

Barnabas and Saul set off on their first major missionary journey to Cyprus. At Paphos they cross swords with the magician Elymas. Saul, who changes his name to Paul, preaches in Antioch of Pisidia. Many Gentiles are converted.

The two missionaries are less successful in Iconium. They barely escape a stoning. At Lystra Paul heals a cripple. The people decide that Barnabas is Zeus and Paul Hermes in disguise and prepare to offer sacrifice to them. Others from Iconium and Antioch are less enthusiastic. Paul is stoned and left for dead outside the city.

Paul and Barnabas continue through Pisidia and Pamphylia and return to Antioch.

In Jerusalem the issue of whether Gentile converts to Christianity need to be circumcised is debated. It is decided that circumcision for non-Jewish converts is not necessary. Judas and Silas are sent to Antioch. Paul and Silas set out on a missionary journey. Timothy joins them at Lystra. They travel through Phrygia, Galatia and Troas to Philippi in Macedonia. Lydia, a seller of purple goods, is baptized. Paul exorcises a slave girl soothsayer, much to the fury of her owners. Paul and Silas are imprisoned and their feet are put in stocks. There is an earthquake. The gaoler takes Paul and Silas to his own house where he and his family are baptized.

The three missionaries journey on to Thessalonica. Their preaching causes uproar. Paul and Silas slip away by night to Beroea. Paul moves on to Athens. He preaches on the Areopagus with mixed results.

Paul goes to Corinth to stay with his friends Aquila and Priscilla, fellow tent-makers. Paul meets up with Silas and Timothy. He stays there teaching for a year and a half and then sets off on his travels. He goes to Ephesus, Caesarea, Antioch and through Galatia and Phrygia.

Paul returns to Ephesus and teaches there for two years with great success. Demetrius the silversmith is concerned that trade in silver statues of Diana and Ephesus' commerical importance as a commercial and pilgrimage centre will be harmed if Paul is allowed to preach unchecked. Demetrius whips the city up into anti-Christian fury. There is a near riot.

Paul leaves Ephesus and goes to Macedonia, and then to Greece, where he stays for three months. He moves on to Troas. Paul preaches until midnight. Eutychus, sitting in a high window, falls asleep and drops out of his third-storey porch. He comes to no harm. Paul and his companions set sail for Jerusalem via Miletus, where he meets and says farewell to the Ephesus church elders.

The missionaries land at Tyre. Paul is warned not to go to Jerusalem. At Caesarea the prophet Agabus again warns Paul not to go to Jerusalem. Paul cannot be dissuaded. The missionaries are welcomed in Jerusalem. All is well for about a week. Then Paul is falsely accused of defiling the Temple by bringing Gentile Greeks into the inner precincts. The mob sets on him. He is saved by being arrested. He is allowed to address the people from the steps of the barracks. There is uproar. Paul is taken into barracks. He is about to be scourged when it is discovered that he is a Roman citizen. By law he cannot be beaten until a charge aginst him is proved.

Paul is taken before the Sanhedrin. His testimony causes dissension. He is brought back to the barracks for his own safety. Paul's nephew brings the tribune information about a plot against Paul's life. Paul is transferred to Caesarea. His accusers put their case to Felix, the governor. Paul defends himself. Felix is sympathetic to Paul. Paul is imprisoned but treated mildly.

Two years pass. Felix is succeeded by Festus. Paul's enemies ask for him to be transferred for trial to Jerusalem. Using his Roman citizenship, Paul exercises his right to appeal to the emperor. He is sent under escort to Rome.

Paul and some other prisoners sail on a coastal route for Rome. Trouble strikes off the south cost of Crete. The ship is driven by fierce winds for a fortnight. It is shipwrecked on the island of Malta. No one is drowned.

After three months the prison detail take ship again. They put in at Puteoli and travel to Rome by foot. Paul is welcomed by fellow Christians. He assures them that the charges against him are false. He is not put in prison but placed under house arrest, where for two years he is allowed to preach and teach quite freely.

Romans

A message of justification and salvation. Paul sends greetings to the Christians of Rome. God has revealed his righteousness. He knows no partiality. Through faith in Christ Jesus all believers can be redeemed: God has brought mankind to a new life through his son.

Christ was crucified for all mankind. His spirit frees people from sin and death.

God has not rejected the Israelites but through Christ Jesus he has reached out to both Jew and Gentile. The Christian church is a unity made up of individuals. Let it be bound by the laws of love. Be merciful, cheerful and hospitable. Do good to your enemies. Leave vengeance to God.

Paul expresses the hope that he will visit Rome on his way to Spain. He commends the deaconess Phoebe who is to work in the Roman church. He sends greetings to Prisca and Aquila and his friends and passes on good wishes from others and ends by giving glory to God.

1 Corinthians

A spiritual answer to a worldly city. Paul appeals for church unity. The wisdom of God is different from the wisdom of the world. Sometimes individuality can be destructive. Timothy will come to settle disputes and remind them of the teaching they first heard from Paul.

Meanwhile there have been alarming reports about immorality among the community – even a rumour that someone is incestuously living with his step-mother. This is not good enough. The corrupt must be thrown out of the church. Paul then answers specific questions from Corinth on marriage, food offered to idols and the conduct of the liturgy of the Lord's Supper. Whatever spiritual gifts people show they are only valuable when and if they come from the Holy Spirit. The most important are faith, hope and love – and the greatest of these is love.

Christ is risen and after death we too will live, transformed in the twinkling of an eye.

2 Corinthians

A personal message. Paul describes his trials and the joys of apostleship. Each Christian believes in a letter from Christ written not with ink but with the Spirit of the Lord. He can look beyond this world to his eternal home. In Christ are all new creatures.

The churches in Macedonia are generous but poor. Let some Corinthian wealth balance the material poverty of other churches. Happy generosity is repaid with divine blessings.

Paul concludes by promising to visit Corinth for a third time where he hopes to find faith not faithlessness.

Galatians

A message of freedom and independence. Paul reminds his readers of his credentials as a preacher of the true Gospel. Three years after his conversion he spent fifteen days at the feet of the apostle Peter, learning from him, but later in Antioch he opposed him on the Gentile issue. Now once more Paul insists that Gentile converts to Christianity do not need to submit to the laws of Judaism.

Legalism can blight religious life. It has been replaced by the freedom of faith in Christ Jesus. Live in a spirit of gentleness. Bear each other's burdens – that is the law of Christ. Circumcision is unimportant. All that matters is the new covenant of faith.

Ephesians

A message of unity and new life. God's purpose is for all believers to be united in Christ. Through Christ Jews and non-Jews have been brought into a new covenant.

Belief in Christianity must be mature belief based on daily practice of love and forgiveness. Revere one another for the sake of Christ. Put on the armour of God which is truth and righteousness – and at all times pray.

Philippians

A cheerful message of faith from prison. Paul explains all that has recently happened to him. He is in prison but is not downcast. He urges his readers to complete his joy by showing that they share fully in his Christ-centred faith. Timothy and Epaphroditus will soon be in Philippi.

Finally Paul urges the Philippians not to pay any attention to the circumcision lobby but to be steadfast in the faith they already hold and to rejoice in the love of Christ.

Colossians

A warning from prison against syncretism. Paul speaks warmly of the good reports he has heard about the Christian community at Colossae. He warns them to be on their guard against false teachers and tells them to pay no attention to anyone who insists on ancient legalism or new visions.

Let everyone give up old sins and older prejudices. In Christ there cannot be Greek or Jew, circumcised or uncircumcised, slave or free: all are one in Christ. Regardless of social status, all should live in loving harmony. Slaves and masters share one master in heaven.

Tychicus and Onesimus will bring further news when they arrive at Colossae.

1 Thessalonians

A message of praise for progress achieved. Paul offers insight into the days which are to come. The church in Thessalonia has done well. Paul urges them to shun immorality, to work hard and live quietly and thus gain the respect of the wider community.

Those who have already died will not miss the glory of the Second Coming. On the last day they will rise and will be lifted up in triumph. No one knows when the Second Coming will be. Therefore be prepared in faith at all times.

2 Thessalonians

A message of comfort. Paul encourages the Thessalonians. Their sufferings will make them all the more worthy of the kingdom of God. They must not be agitated by any letters purporting to come from Paul saying, the last day is imminent. First the son of perdition, the enemy of God, who claims to be God will identify himself. This has not happened yet.

Avoid idleness. Never tire of doing good.

1 Timothy

Pastoral advice for a young church. Christians must pray for those who lead the wider community. Among themselves they must have high standards. Christian men must lift their hands in prayer not anger. Christian women should adorn themselves not with silver and gold but with good deeds.

Bishops must be above reproach and deacons should be sober in thought and alcoholic practice. They should only have one wife. Respect the old and the young. Christian slaves must respect their slaves. Let wealth be a source of good deeds and generosity – a guarantee of everlasting riches.

2 Timothy

How to be an effective pastor. Be strong and hardworking. Avoid ungodly people – their conversation is like gangrene. The Lord's servants should be gentle, knowing that great strength will be required of them in the trials of the last days when false teachers will sway the weak. Preach the truth whether it is welcome or not.

Titus

Advice on church organisation. Take care over the appointment of bishops and elders. They must not have more than one wife and their children must be believers. They must be known for their moral rectitude. Sound teaching is all-important. Encourage the old and the young and be a model of Christian behaviour yourself. Do not encourage rebelliousness and avoid arguments within the community.

Philemon

A plea for a slave who is now a brother. Paul writes to Philemon of Colossae from prison, asking forgiveness for Onesimus a runaway slave who is now a Christian. Paul urges Philemon to welcome the runaway letter-bearer as a brother. If there is anything outstanding by way of debt or grievance, Paul will repay whatever is needed when he visits Colossae, as he hopes to.

Hebrews

A message for Jewish converts. Down the ages God has spoken to the children of Israel through the prophets. Now he has spoken through his son who is above the angels and supersedes Moses, Joshua and the high priests who descended from Aaron.

Christ Jesus is a high priest of the order of Melchizedek, the king of Salem who offered up bread and wine in the days of Abraham. There is no more need of daily animal sacrifices. Christ has offered himself as the eternal sacrifice.

Lessons in faith can be learned from Abel, Enoch, Noah, Abraham, Sarah, Jacob, Joseph, Moses, as well as the judges and prophets – they are a cloud of witnesses. Jesus is the mediator of the new covenant. He is the same yesterday, today and tomorrow.

James

A message about the living faith. Welcome trials in this life. They will strengthen your faith. Among Christians wealth should not procure status. The poorest man may be the richest in faith.

Let your beliefs be seen in your action. The cold are not warmed by good wishes alone. Faith must be brought alive by deeds. Revere wisdom and wait patiently for the coming of the Lord.

1 Peter

A message of hope for the fearful. Set your hope on the living cornerstone who is Christ Jesus. Your faith will be strengthened by the trials you are undergoing. Live upright lives in the community at large and in your homes.

It is better to suffer than to do wrong. Follow Christ in suffering and love one another. Church leaders must care for and not lord it over their flock. Be humble and remember that the suffering of the world is slight compared with the grace of eternity.

2 Peter

A warning against false teaching. Knowledge of Christ has brought the promise of salvation. The good news is not based on ancient myths but on eye-witness report. Beware false teachers and their temptations to immorality. Pay no attention to those who jeer or twist the teachings in Paul's letters. Keep the faith and do not be beguiled by error.

1 John

A command to love. Walk in the light of unity and of true active faith. In these last days there are many false teachers. Pay them no attention. Love one another, for love is of God. Keep away from idols, but remain strong in the promise of eternal life given to you through Christ Jesus, the son of God.

2 John

A reminder to love. Follow the commandment of love and be cautious of those false teachers who deny the humanity of Jesus.

3 John

A note about human nature. John thanks Gaius for the hospitality he has shown to travelling Christian teachers. Another letter has been written to the church, but there are problems there with Diotrephes, the local church leader.

Jude

A tract against heresy. Jude warns that there is a danger that the faith may be undermined by evil men who have secretly gained admission into the brotherhood. Remember that the ungodly have been punished in the past. Lead the misguided from error, avoid corruption and give glory to Christ.

Revelation

The book of the Apocalypse. On the island of Patmos John has a vision. A voice like a trumpet tells him to record what he sees and send it to Ephesus, Smyrna, Pergamum, Thyatira, Sardis, Philadelphia and Laodicea, the seven churches of Asia. John takes down a message for each of the seven churches – only Philadelphia escapes criticism.

John is then granted a vision of heaven where twenty elders surround the throne of God set in a crystal sea. All the creatures of heaven adore God. An angel brings forward a scroll sealed with seven seals. No one in heaven or earth is strong enough to break the seals. John weeps and is comforted by one of the elders. Suddenly John sees a Lamb, standing although it had been killed. The Lamb takes the scroll and begins opening its seals. Each of the first four seals brings a deadly rider – the four horsemen of the Apocalypse. The fifth seal reveals the souls of the dead who have died for their faith. The sixth seal brings forth a harrowing vision of the last days. At the opening of the seventh seal there is silence in heaven before the full horror of what is to come is revealed.

Seven angels blow in turn on trumpets. At the first trumpet there is hail and fire and a third of the earth is burnt up. At the second trumpet something like a burning mountain is thrown into the sea – a third of all sea creatures die. At the third trumpet a falling star turns a third of the water to wormwood. At the fourth trumpet sun, moon and stars lose a third of their light.

When the fifth angel blows his trumpet, creatures like locusts rise out of a smoke-filled pit and torture men so that they long for death. At the sixth trumpet a third of mankind is killed by a lethal army breathing fire, smoke and sulpur.

After the earth has been ravaged, the seventh trumpet is blown. Then the heavens open and the kingdom of the world is transformed into the kingdom of God.

John is then shown seven great portents. He sees a woman clothed with the sun, about to give birth. He sees a dragon waiting to devour the woman's child. He sees her child destined for kingship who is swept up to the throne of God.

The fourth portent is the archangel Michael fighting a war in heaven and defending the dragon who is Satan. The fifth portent is war on earth, with Satan fresh from his heavenly defeat attacking the children of the woman who have remained faithful to God.

Then John sees a beast coming out of the sea who rules as a servant of the devil. Finally the seventh portent is revealed. John sees a beast rising out of the earth. It makes all mankind worship the first beast and wear a number, 666, which is the mark of the beast.

But despite all these horrors on Mount Zion a new song will be sung by those who have kept faith with God and the Lamb. The power of the godless will crumble.

John then has a vision of the final seven plagues which will bring the suffering of the world to an end. Seven angels pour out the plagues from seven bowls. After the first bowl is poured out foul sores break out on those who worship the beast. After the second bowl the sea becomes like the blood of a dead man. After the third all fresh water is also turned to blood. With the fourth bowl the sun becomes scorchingly hot. With the fifth bowl the earth is covered in darkness and men gnaw their tongues. The sixth bowl sees the preparation for the final madness of war when Satan, the anti-Christ and the false prophet, will persuade men to gather at a place called Armageddon. The seventh bowl signals lightning, thunder and cataclysmic earthquake.

Babylon, the harlot, the symbol of godlessness is destroyed. A marriage is announced between the Lamb and the Bride, clothed in the righteous deeds of the saints.

John sees the heavens open. The Word of God rides out in triumph. The beast who is the anti-Christ and the false prophet are thrown into a lake of sulphur. Satan is bound for 1,000 years. When he is loosed he will urge the nations to war again. He will be defeated and thrown in the sulphur lake.

Then there will be a new heaven and a new earth and a holy city which is the new Jerusalem. There will be no more tears and no death. Everything will be alive with God.

In the middle of the city there will be a tree, not the tree of Eden or a Calvary but the tree of life. In its leaves will be healing for all the nations. Nothing will again be accursed. Everything will be lit with the brightness of God.

Chronology

Date	Bible	Elsewhere

Prehistory

Undated	Creation, Adam and Eve	Creation myths
	Noah and the Flood	Flood epics

Early Bronze Age

3,500 –	Terah migrates from	Old Kingdom in Egypt
2,000 BC	Ur to Haran	Early Sumeria

Middle Bronze Age

2,000 –	Abraham migrates to	Code of Hammurabi
1,500 BC	Canaan	Middle Kingdom in Egypt
	Joseph	Hyksos regime in Egypt
	Jacob migrates to Egypt	Hyskos driven out

Late Bronze Age

1,500 –	Israelites in Egypt	New Kingdom in Egypt
1,200 BC	The exodus	Rise of Assyria
	The conquest of Canaan	Akhnaton in Egypt

Iron Age I

1,200 –	The Judges	20th Dynasty in Egypt
1,000 BC	Ruth	Hittite Empire falls
	Capture of the Ark	Assyria weakens
	Samuel, Saul, David	21st Dynasty in Egypt

Iron Age II

1,000 –	David dies	22nd Dynasty in Egypt
587 BC	Solomon builds the	Assyrian expansion
	Temple	Rise of Babylon
	Israel and Judah divided	Battle of Carchemish (605)
	(931)	Fall of Assyria
	Kings of Israel and Judah	26th Dynasty in Egypt
	Samaria falls (721)	
	Jerusalem falls (587)	

Iron Age III

587 –	Exile in Babylonia	Fall of Babylon (539)
331 BC	Edict of Cyrus	Persian Empire expands
	and return (538)	Pythagoras, Buddha
	Second Temple built	Periclean Age
	Ezra and Nehemiah	Plato, Aristotle

Hellenistic Age

331 –	Ptolemies rule Judea	End of Persian Empire
63 BC	Seleucid rule	Alexander the Great
	Maccabean revolt	Punic Wars
	Temple rededicated (164)	Kingdom of Parthia
	Hasmonean dynasty	Roman expansion
	Pompey takes Jerusalem	Roman civil war
	(63)	

Roman Period

63 BC –	Herod the Great	Augustus (27 BC – AD 14)
150 AD	(37-4 BC)	Tiberius (14-37)
	Birth of Jesus (8-4 BC)	Caligula (37-42)
	Herod Antipas	Claudius (42-54)
	(4 BC-AD 39)	Rome invades Britain (43)
	Essenes flourish	Nero (54-68)
	John the Baptist	Fire of Rome (64)
	preaches	Christians persecuted
	Jesus crucified	
	(29/30 AD)	
	Paul converted (35)	
	Paul's journeys (45-58)	
	Council of Jerusalem (50)	
	Paul dies in Rome (64/65)	
	Fall of Jerusalem (70)	

Future

World destruction
Foundation of a new
    Jerusalem
Creation of a new order

Authorities

The authors wish to thank the following – each an authority in his or her field – for giving their time, sharing their knowledge and testifying to their faith.

Ackroyd, Rev. Dr P.R., DD, Professor Emeritus of Old Testament Studies, University of London

Anthony, Metropolitan, of Sourozh, Head of the Orthodox Patriarchal Church in Great Britain and Ireland

Askari, Dr H.S., Lecturer in Islamic Studies, Selly Oak College, Birmingham

Bahat, Dr Dan, Archaeologist with the Hebrew Education Service

Barker, Margaret, schoolteacher and member of the Society of Old Testament Studies

Barr, Rev. J., DD FBA, Regius Professor of Hebrew, Oxford

Bartlett, Rev. J.R., Associate Professor of Biblical Studies, Trinity College, Dublin

Bimson, Dr J.J., Lecturer in Old Testament and Hebrew, Trinity Theological College, Bristol

Blanch, Most Rev. and Rt. Hon. Stuart Garworth, Lord Blanch, PC, formerly Archbishop of York

Bruce, Dr F.F., DD FBA, Rylands Professor Emeritus of Biblical Criticism and Exegesis, University of Manchester

Calver, Rev. Clive, General Secretary, Evangelical Alliance

Carroll, Dr R.P., Senior Lecturer in Biblical Studies, University of Glasgow

Clements, Dr Ronald, DD, Samuel Davidson Professor of Old Testament Studies, King's College London (KQC)

Clines, Dr David, Reader in Biblical Studies, University of Sheffield

Cupitt, Rev. Don, Dean of Emmanuel College, Cambridge

Davidson, Rev. Dr R., DD, Professor of Old Testament Language and Literature, University of Glasgow

Drury, Rev. J.H., Dean of King's College, Cambridge

Dunn, Dr J.D.G., Professor of Theology, University of Durham

Eaton, J.H., Reader in Old Testament Studies, University of Birmingham

Evans, Mary, Lecturer in Old Testament, London Bible College

Falwell, Rev. Jerry, Baptist and TV evangelist

Flood, Dom Edmund, OSB

Friedlander, Rabbi Dr A.H., Dean of Leo Baeck College, London

Goldingay, Rev. J., Vice-Principal, St John's College, Nottingham

Gordon, Dr R.P., Lecturer in Divinity, Cambridge

Hooker, Dr Morna D., Lady Margaret's Professor of Divinity, Cambridge

Hume, His Eminence, Cardinal Basil, OSB, Archbishop of Westminster

Isserlin, Dr Ben, formerly Reader in Semitic Studies, University of Leeds

Jakobovitz, Sir Immanuel, Chief Rabbi of the United Hebrew Congregations of the British Commonwealth of Nations

Jesson, A.F., Assistant Library Officer, Cambridge

Jones, Rev. G.H., Reader in Biblical Studies, University College of North Wales, Bangor

Kendall, Rev. Dr R.T., Minister of Westminster Chapel, London

Küng, Dr Hans, Professor of Ecumenical Theology, University of Tübingen

Lambert, W.G., FBA, Professor of Assyriology, University of Birmingham

Laws, Dr Sophie, formerly Lecturer in Biblical Studies, King's College London (KQC)

Levi, Peter, Professor of Poetry, Oxford

McKeating, Rev. Dr H., Senior Lecturer in Theology, University of Nottingham

Magonet, Rabbi Dr Jonathan, Principal, Leo Baeck College, London

Mayes, Dr A.D.H., Lecturer in Biblical and Theological Studies, Trinity College, Dublin

Moltmann, Jürgen, Professor of Theology, University of Tübingen

Mowvley, Rev. Henry, Baptist minister, Bristol

Neuberger, Rabbi Julia, South London Liberal Synagogue

Nicholson, Rev. Dr E.W., DD, Oriel Professor of the Interpretation of Holy Scripture, Oxford

Oestreicher, Rev. Canon Paul, Assistant General Secretary, British Council of Churches

Orchard, Dom Bernard, OSB

Pettanuzzo, Sister Nilda, St Wilfred's Convent, London

Phillips, Rev. Canon Anthony, Headmaster, King's School Canterbury

Prag, Dr Kay, Near Eastern archaeologist, Stockport

Rogerson, Rev. Canon J.W., DD, Professor of Biblical Studies, University of Sheffield

Rowland, Rev. Dr C.C., Dean of Jesus College, Cambridge

Ruether, Dr Rosemary, Professor of Applied Theology, Garrett Evangelical Seminary, Evanston, Illinois

Sacks, Rabbi Dr Jonathan, Principal, Jews College, London

Sawyer, Rev. Dr J.F.A., Professor of Old Testament Language and Literature, University of Newcastle

Soper, Rev. Lord, formerly President of the Methodist Conference

Thiselton, Rev. Dr A.C., Principal, St. John's College, Nottingham

Tiongco, Romeo, Christian worker in the Philippines

Tutu, Most Rev. Desmond Mpilo, Archbishop of Johannesburg

Wansborough, Dom Henry, OSB, Revising Editor, New Jerusalem Bible

Werblowsky, Dr Zwi, Martin Buber Professor of Comparative Religion, Hebrew University of Jerusalem

Whybray, Dr Norman, Professor Emeritus of Hebrew and Old Testament Studies, University of Hull

Young, Dr Frances, Senior Lecturer in Theology, University of Birmingham

Yudkin, Mickey, Jewish adult educationalist

Index

Index